Dear Reader,

I trust that as you read this book it will be a blessing to you. To God be the glory.

Sincerely in Jesus,

Irene Maurer

Crossing Three Continents with Christ

The Missionary Life of Irene Maurer

Irene Maurer with Ronald and Anna Smith

ISBN 978-1-934447-20-8

Printed by
Country Pines Printing
Shoals, IN
USA

DEDICATION

This book is dedicated to all my dear friends and family, past and present, who have supported me with their prayers and finances for more than sixty years. Their faithfulness has made it possible for me to labor with Evangelistic Faith Missions in fulfilling the Great Commission in the countries of Egypt, Ethiopia, Bolivia, and the United States.

All who have been faithful with their support will share in the rewards when the Lord gives them on that great day.

CONTENT

FOREWORD

Evangelistic Faith Missions has been blessed to have Irene Maurer on its staff for more than six decades. God first called her to Egypt, and she has been a faithful handmaid of the Lord Jesus Christ over these many years. The book you hold in your hand will allow you to travel with this fine holiness missionary across three continents. Follow her ship across the choppy Atlantic Ocean to Egypt. Trek with her through the burning sands of the land of the pyramids. Marvel at the way she escaped Egypt during the Six-Day War of 1967. Walk with her over the sandy school campus in Decamere, Ethiopia, and sit in her classroom as she serves as a scholarly teacher.

Ride with her down the highways of the United States as she visits churches and raises support to fulfill her calling. Do not forget to buckle your seat belt because she has had some memorable accidents while traveling for the Lord.

Layer your clothing to endure the cold winds from the Andes Mountains of Bolivia and listen as Irene speaks to the children in Daily Vacation Bible Schools. She is good at shifting gears because she can teach children and then teach theology to pastors. What a full and rich ministry she had while serving in Bolivia.

Many years ago the United Auto Workers Union pushed for a contract that would allow their members to work thirty years for the company and then retire. The theme for that proposal was "Thirty years and out." It was adopted and many UAW members have benefited from that policy. Irene Maurer has not sought a place to stop serving the Lord Jesus Christ but rather has been a faithful part of Evangelistic Faith Missions for over sixty years.

Enjoy your trip as you travel with this veteran EFM missionary through the pages of her eventful life's journey.

President J. Stevan Manley, Evangelistic Faith Missions

ACKNOWLEDGMENTS

I thank God for His help that has enabled me to serve in His great harvest field in the heat of the day in northeast Africa and in the cold days and nights of the high altitudes of the Andes Mountains in South America. My heartfelt thanks go to the following individuals who contributed to the writing of my life story:

Doris Schmidt, my sister, put into scrapbooks my written accounts of special events in my life, copies of my articles printed in the *Missionary Herald*, and my personal letters to her. After her death in 2000, the scrapbooks became a treasure trove for me.

My sisters Eva and Helen also saved letters I wrote to them and, after my retirement from overseas ministry, they gave them to me. A few months ago Ronald Smith, one of the writers of my story, remarked to me that if there had been no letters, there would be no book. For the thoughtfulness of my sisters, I am grateful.

I owe a large debt to Ronald and Anna Smith who dedicated numberless hours in reading the scores of letters, many of them handwritten, and the articles and from them wrote my life's story. They wrote and rewrote as we communicated by telephone, e-mails, and visits from their home in Portage, Pennsylvania, to Bedford, Indiana, where I live.

J. Stevan Manley encouraged me to get my story into print, and he and his wife, Helen, gave useful suggestions that enhanced the writing. Helen and I spent many hours together as we edited the book chapter by chapter. She ably thought of additional adjectives and adverbs that enlivened the stories.

Ralph Woodworth and his wife, Erma, gave of their valuable time to edit the early document and do final proofing. In his communications with the Smiths, Ralph frequently offered insights from the viewpoint of a journalist.

Shirley Dye read the manuscript and shared her ideas with the Smiths.

Faith Hemmeter, my co-worker and friend, gave good advice from time to time, and during the last few months of my labors on the manuscript, freed me for the task by sacrificially taking my turn at kitchen duty.

Kevin Moser, my great-nephew, who is the art director and managing editor of *God's Revivalist*, volunteered to design the cover of the book and helped with choosing a title.

I deeply appreciate all who prayed for me as I re-read my letters and articles; spent much time on the phone interviewing members of my family, friends, and acquaintances to make my story as accurate as possible; and proofed the manuscript more than once.

Again to God I give thanks, honor, and glory for all that He has done.

Chapter 1

My First Twenty-Five Years
1924-1949

Early Family History

It was a happy day for Joseph and Mary Maurer and their four children—Doris, Earl, Charles, and Eva—when they welcomed me, Irene Betty, into their home on August 23, 1924. Three more children later joined our family—Leonard, Helen, and Gloria. We were saddened when Gloria died of pneumonia before age two.

Father's ancestors sailed from Germany in 1764 and

Earl, Eva, Doris holding me, and Charles on our front porch in Doutyville in 1924

Isaac and Malinda Schreffler, my mother's parents, circa 1880

eventually settled in the small village of Pitman near Shamokin, Pennsylvania. My father, Joseph Irvin, son of Lewis and Kathryn (Kutz) Maurer, was born in the Pitman area in 1886. He was the fourth of eleven children with three sisters and seven brothers.

The Schrefflers, Mother's ancestors, emigrated from Germany in 1749. Eventually part of the family moved to an area

The Lewis Maurer family in 1894 with my father, Joseph Irvin, on the left

My parents, Joseph Irvin and Mary Malinda (Schreffler) Maurer, on their wedding day in 1911

called Line Mountain, Pennsylvania, not far from Pitman. My mother, Mary Malinda, daughter of Isaac and Malinda (Daniel) Schreffler, was born in 1892 in Line Mountain and was next to the youngest in a family of twelve children consisting of four girls and eight boys.

My father was a mail carrier and met my mother on his mail route. They were married at the United Evangelical Church in Pitman on December 31, 1911, and first lived in Helfenstein. Then they lived near my mother's homestead in Line Mountain and finally moved to Doutyville where most of us children were born, including me. After our move to Doutyville, my father became a coal miner.

Grandma Maurer was my only grandparent living when I was born. At times my father drove over the mountain to Pitman to help her on the farm. One time I was with him when he stopped to see Grandma, and he left me in the car. My grandma came to the car and gave me a Mary Jane cookie. I was seven years old when she passed away.

Childhood Activities

When I was about four, my parents took us to an evening tent meeting service in the Pitman area. After service I got lost because I took hold of the hand of a lady who was not my mother. When the lady realized that I was not her daughter, she helped me to get reunited with my parents.

Doris, Eva, and I contracted scarlet fever when I was five. We were quarantined in one room until we recovered. Shortly after that time Father had a nervous breakdown. One of his brothers took him to a center for professional help, but he became homesick and wanted to return to his family. I well remember the day when Uncle Francis Maurer brought him home. We were in the living room, and my father's eyes were filled with tears—tears of joy to be home again. We were happy to have him home, too. The next two years were difficult ones because our father was unable to work, but God took care of us. Our garden and field produced well, and on at least one occasion, people from a nearby town brought us food.

The first eight years of my schooling were in a one-room school-house in Doutyville. Our school library included some of the literary classics for children such as the story of *Heidi*. The students learned well enough to compete in scholastic competition on a county level. We had fun during recess by playing games like hopscotch, marbles, drop the hankie, and red light. Not far from the schoolhouse was a wooded area where there was a large fallen tree. We imagined that it was a ship at sea, and we took turns being the captain, crew, and passengers.

I was in third grade when a doctor came to our school to check our tonsils. He placed us into three categories, namely, one, two, or three. Reports were sent home with recommendations that the children evaluated at two or three should have their tonsils removed. Mine received a one. I urged our father to give consent for some of my siblings and me to have ours removed. He finally consented. A truck came on a specified day to get the children from several of the villages in the township and

Doutyville students in 1933. Eva is on the left in the back row. I am on the right of the middle row. Leonard is in the middle in the front row.

took us to the Shamokin State Hospital for our operation. We were not to eat anything the night before and no breakfast on that day. In our home we did as instructed. Some of the other children went to an abandoned farm where they ate apples that were not ripe and got sick. On our way to the hospital, we were excited and noisy. We were well taken care of at the hospital where we stayed overnight. The next day on our way home, we were a quiet bunch with tender throats and could only whisper. At home we had VIP treatment. For a few days we drank milk and ate ice cream, which were special because it was during the Great Depression.

Each child in our family had a "school box" in which we kept papers and art work from our school activities. On cold winter evenings we sometimes played school. One of us played the role of teacher, which I often enjoyed doing.

In fairer weather we sometimes played in an abandoned car near an oxheart cherry tree at the edge of our field. It never entered our minds that snakes might be present. Thankfully none of us was ever bitten by one. At other times we played in an area near some wild huckleberry bushes. Occasionally we went to the east end of our village and played on an abandoned farm that had apple trees and was grown up with weeds. Those were **wonderful** days because we enjoyed our childhood to the fullest extent.

On the south side of our village was a black-sulfur creek that carried waste materials from the coal mines. Above the creek the electric company had placed two cables so that their workers could cross the creek to maintain the towers and wires. In our teens we sometimes climbed up to the cables, held onto the upper cable, put our feet on the lower one, and by slowly sliding our hands and feet, we could cross to the other side. What a challenge!

Our neighbor to the west was a bachelor who had a field that was separated from our property partly by a wire fence and partly by a stone wall. A number of his sour cherry trees grew near the stone wall, and we were permitted to pick the cherries from the branches that hung over the wall on our side. Just beyond the wire fence grew burdocks, a plant that produced burrs, which would stick to our clothes. Worse than the burdocks were the copperheads that sometimes were present. In my youth I was often scared to go down the path to our outhouse for fear of snakes.

Nearly every family had a vegetable garden. We were fortunate to have a half-acre field besides the garden area. Black raspberries, a few apple trees, and three kinds of cherries grew along the edges of our field. My mother dried apples and sweet corn and canned fruits and vegetables. We were **blessed indeed!**

Sometimes on payday our father bought a lot of unshelled peanuts. That evening he would stand at our kitchen table and divide them into equal piles so that each child had peanuts to enjoy. That was a special treat for us.

To help provide for our family during the Great Depression, Father picked huckleberries and sold some to our neighbors. He took a ten-quart bucket and some of us children with smaller buckets and climbed the mountain. Patiently, he picked huckleberries all day in order to get his bucket full by late afternoon. We children picked and frolicked, but sometimes we got our little buckets filled, too. The biggest dangers were hornets, yellow jackets, and snakes, especially copperheads and rattlesnakes. Once we saw a snake under a bush, and we scampered to get away. Another time while picking huckleberries with Earl, my oldest brother, I was stung by a hornet. It was so painful that we had to go home.

My father also sold dry goods and products for the E.C. Harley Company. He had various routes in the rural areas around Doutyville and would periodically visit the homes on each route. To help with family finances, for a time I sold a weekly newspaper called the *Grit,* which was published in Williamsport, Pennsylvania.

Frequently my mother would spend Saturdays making as many as twenty pies for our family. The pies included apple, green tomato, raisin, raspberry, huckleberry, peach, cherry, Montgomery, and one we called poor man's pie, which was a crust filled with flour, butter, sugar, and milk.

Life in Doutyville

Doutyville was a small village in East Cameron Township in Northumberland County, Pennsylvania, with nearly one hundred residents. It had a store, a community hall where Sunday school was conducted, and a small public school.

Most of the men in our village were miners who worked on the other side of the mountain that hemmed us in on the north. Early in the morning, even in the cold and darkness of winter and sometimes deep snow, the men climbed the mountain with their lunch boxes, metal water canteens, carbide lamps, and protective hats to which they later fastened the lamps. Down in the dark heart of the earth, they used dynamite to loosen the coal. Then with picks and shovels, they loaded the anthracite coal into little train-like cars and hauled it to the surface. It was dangerous, tiring, dirty work, but they were thankful for jobs to sustain their families. Most of the families lived in houses that were two-storied duplexes with two rooms to a floor plus a basement and an attic. Those houses were owned by the Reading Railroad Company, who also owned the mine.

The railroad company built a railroad that hauled large chunks of coal to the breaker they had built on the mountainside. After the chunks were broken, a shaker attached to the breaker sifted the coal into various sizes. The fine coal that was left by the shaker became a large

The company house in which my family lived in Doutyville. We lived on the right side of the duplex

coal bank, and for fun we sometimes climbed to that area of the mountain.

In his late teens Earl and another young man called Clippy mined coal in a coalhole on the mountainside. One day when they had set off dynamite to loosen coal from the vein, Earl returned to the mine too soon and was overcome by the gas produced from the explosion of the dynamite. When Clippy realized something had happened to Earl, he entered when he thought it was safe. He was able to get him out of the mine and bring him to our house. Earl was very sick, but God was merciful to him and Clippy.

A great step forward for our narrow valley nestled between two mountain ranges was the blacktopping of the dirt road that went through Doutyville. Another exciting event at that time was the purchasing of a family car shortly after I was born. We were the first family in the village to own a car.

During my early years a spring, enclosed in a shed-like structure at the end of the village, was our chief source of water. We children carried the water to our house in buckets. At least three of our neighbors had wells, and eventually one of them allowed our family to draw water from their well. After I finished high school and left Doutyville, most of the people had water piped to their houses and installed kitchen sinks and bathrooms.

Our father purchased a washing machine made of wood to replace the old scrub board. When we children pushed a stick up and down that was inserted into a metal tube, it turned the agitator attached to the underside of the lid. It was a big improvement over scrubbing everything by hand. For a short time we had a washing machine that was run by gasoline. It made an awful noise and managing it was difficult for my mother, who sometimes had seizures. Father sold it, and for a number of years, he paid women to do our family laundry in their homes. We did our ironing with a heavy iron that was heated on our coal stove.

Electricity was brought to our village when I was very young, but my parents did not have it connected to our house. We used kerosene lamps, which needed constant attention. After I left home, my family moved into another house in Doutyville that had electricity.

The west end of our village was hilly and made a lovely place for sledding during the winter. Sometimes three of us crowded onto one sled. It was safer to go sledding at night because we could see the lights of cars coming into the village from the west, and we would wait until the cars got to the center of the village before we took our ride down the hill. A delight of a fresh snowfall was eating snow ice cream. Our father would fill a large bowl with snow and add sugar, milk, and vanilla. Oh, what a treat! One year we had a two-foot snowfall. No vehicles could travel, and the bread supply in the village was getting low. The men of Doutyville cleared the road with shovels, and it was a happy day when the bread truck arrived.

Sometimes a junk collector came to our village. With a piece of metal, he clanged on some object on his truck, and then he would call, "Any rags, old iron, any rags." My siblings and I were always happy if we had something to sell. With the few cents that we received, we purchased a treat for ourselves.

The little village store did not have all the commodities that we needed. The valley at Doutyville was very narrow and there was no land for good farms. Farmers from another valley came with their trucks loaded with vegetables, apples, home-churned butter, and other foods. Another man brought eggs to sell. He would call out in Pennsylvania Dutch and English from his car window, "Frish oyer, fresh eggs." With his German accent, the word "eggs" sounded like the letter "x."

Occasionally, some of the farmers brought freshly butchered meat, liver pudding, and scrapple. Scrapple is cornmeal boiled with scraps of pork and allowed to set, then sliced and fried. A butcher who sold different kinds of meat eventually started a route that included our village. He had the back of his panel truck made into a refrigerated compartment. Leonard, my youngest brother, married Anna, a sister of the butcher.

Before a milkman started delivering milk to our village, Doris, my oldest sister, walked a mile to buy milk from another family. Later a milkman brought milk and blocks of ice in a truck. He deftly chiseled the size of block we wanted and carried it to our icebox, which had a compartment for the ice and a place to keep food.

Mr. Casey Orner had a store in Gowen City about three miles away and came to Doutyville to sell groceries. Later he acquired a bus and put steps at the back door. He arranged shelves on both sides in the bus, and his customers could shop from his "store on wheels." People bought on credit and paid their bill or part of their bill on payday. Unfortunately, many people did not meet their obligations, and after several years Mr.

Orner was forced to close his store on wheels. He then turned his debts over to Erb and Zaring Wholesale in Shamokin. Periodically my father would go to their office and pay on his bill. The office personnel told him that he was one of the few people who endeavored to pay his debt.

An ice-cream truck from Snyder's store in Ashland, about eleven miles from Doutyville, started coming when I was a teenager. As the driver entered our village, he drove slowly and rang a bell to announce his arrival. He sold hand-dipped ice cream from large cylindrical containers and Popsicles.

Spiritual Influences

Daniel Dubendorf, Charles Maurer, and
William Straub, circa 1920

Before I was born, William Straub and Daniel Dubendorf, two holiness preachers, came to Doutyville and conducted services in the community hall where Sunday school was held. They slept on wooden benches in the building until my father invited them to come to our house. My Uncle Charles Maurer came from Helfenstein to hear the preaching. Both he and Father gave their hearts to the Lord at that time. No church was established in our village, but some of the families traveled about three miles west of Doutyville to Gowen City where there was a Lutheran church and a Reformed church. Our family began attending the Pilgrim Holiness Church in Helfenstein. On at least one occasion my older siblings and I walked the two miles to church.

After attending the Pilgrim Holiness Church for several years, my father helped to start a home-mission church in Lavelle. Later that church was organized as an Evangelical Methodist church. Two of my uncles and aunts and their families attended that church for many years. For a short time when we did not have a car, Uncle Charles came from Helfenstein and took us to church.

Over the next few years, a number of Evangelical Methodist churches were organized. In 1938 Victor Glenn became pastor of the church in Pillow, Pennsylvania, and pastored there approximately two years. Shortly after the death of his father, Lewis, in 1941, he assumed the leadership of Faith Mission in Bedford, Indiana.

When I was four years old, the Lavelle church acquired land near Mowry from the Pennsylvania Railroad Company to establish a camp meeting. Each summer a big tent for holding services was pitched. The camp owners erected a building that had two rooms to accommodate camp workers and a pavilion for a dining area. A tent the size of a large room was pitched for each family that came for the camp meeting. The beds were springs put on low wooden horses or on the ground. Some of us used straw ticks for mattresses. Beside the beds a wooden platform held our boxes of clothing and food that each family brought for the ten days. When it rained, everything became damp. Wood-burning or coal-burning stoves were placed in the open area near the tents, and several families shared the same stove for cooking. The outhouses were a distance from the tents.

In spite of the inconveniences, God's presence was with us. The anointed singing and preaching brought down the glory. The saints shouted and praised the Lord; sinners were convicted of their sins, and some of them prayed and found forgiveness. The spiritual atmosphere drew some of the unsaved who often came and stood outside the tent to watch and sometimes to mock. They called us "holy rollers." Across the years many were saved and sanctified, one of whom was Mary Carrie Boyer, who was also healed and called to be a missionary to Africa.

Later several people built cabins on the campgrounds. After a few years a tabernacle was erected and later another building with a dining hall on the first floor and a dormitory on the second. Some of the buildings are still there but are no longer used for services.

One day when I was fourteen and attending a camp meeting, I went with a small group of ladies into the woods to pray, and God gloriously saved me. I felt as light as a bird with my burden of sin gone. It is sad to say that I lost out spiritually and followed the pleasures of the world for a time, but God in His mercy brought me back to Himself.

While I was backslidden, Eva and I sometimes attended a barn dance on Saturday evenings in a neighboring community. We kept it hidden from our parents by visiting Earl, who was married, and from there going to the dance. I went to the dances only a few times. In that kind of company, I tried smoking cigarettes, but after smoking a few of them, I promptly quit and never smoked again.

In addition to attending the camp meeting at Mowry, we attended the Evangelical Methodist Conference camp meeting at Berrysburg. Our family attended there until Father died in 1949. Sometimes we also attended a camp meeting at Sunbury. Those camps were a little more than twenty miles away, and that was the farthest I traveled in my childhood and early teens except for a trip to Lansford, which was forty miles from our house. Today neither of those camp meetings continues. A shopping mall is being built on the former campground at Sunbury, and the one at Berrysburg was sold in 2008 to a neighboring farmer.

God met with us in our church services at Lavelle and gave glorious times of revival. My father was a quiet man, but I have fond memories of seeing tears course down his cheeks as the Spirit ministered in a special way to his heart. At times my mother also responded to the moving of the Spirit. My parents were faithful in attending the services of our church and always took us children with them.

Evangelical Methodist Church in Lavelle, Pennsylvania

In early 1941 the church board discussed the possibility of calling an evangelist for special services. Some felt that the church did not have the funds to pay the expenses that would be involved. My Uncle Charles, a coal miner and member of the board, replied, "We will have revival if I have to pay for it." He meant the financial cost.

At that time one of Uncle Charles' young daughters offended someone in the church. When my uncle heard about it, he decided, in spite of the protests of some of his children, to go to the family and apologize for what his daughter had done. After he made the apology, he went to work in the mines, and that night, February 17, 1941, he was killed in an accident. The whole situation became known, and people were stirred. An evangelist was called, and God gave us a great revival. Some people who had never been saved before found the Lord and followed Him throughout their lives. Uncle Charles paid for that revival with his life.

On a Sunday evening in early summer of that same year, Eva and I stayed home from church. My main motive was to avoid the preaching that was usually evangelistic. A crippled neighbor came to visit, and our conversation turned to a discussion about things that would come to pass in the last days. God through His Holy Spirit used it to convict my sister and me of our sins. The neighbor did not seem to be spiritually moved, and after a while he went to his home. When our parents arrived after the service, we asked their forgiveness for our disobedience. We were both saved that summer not long before I entered my senior year in high school. God marvelously made us new creatures in Christ, and we lost our desire for things of the world. Eva and I have been serving God ever since.

High School Remembrances

East Cameron Township provided a high school in Gowen City for only freshmen and sophomores. At the end of the two years there was a graduation ceremony. In 1940 I was privileged to give the valedictory address.

The students of East Cameron Township who lived in Doutyville usually walked the three miles to the school. It was a pleasant walk in autumn and spring when we went as a group. Usually on rainy days a family member of one of the students took us by car. When we walked on very cold days in winter, our hands became so cold that they were stiff by the time we arrived at school. We warmed them by rubbing them in a basin of water. Few from my village attended high school because of the distance.

During my freshman year in Gowen City, some of the students participated in the annual county scholastic contests given in March. Three freshmen, Alva Fertig, Gerald Weikel, and I, were chosen to take the Algebra I test. Two sophomores, Mary Troxell and Clifford Artman, were chosen to take the spelling test. The day of the competition, our teacher took us to his home for a delicious meal before we left for Northumberland where the tests were given in a school. He said, "On the way home I'll take you to Martz's Ice Cream Parlor in Shamokin." That was a real treat in those days, and we were looking forward to it.

Before time to enter the room to take the tests, our teacher instructed us, "Don't sit near each other during the test, and save your work sheets." Only the answers to the algebra problems were turned in by each contestant. After we took the tests, everyone gathered in the auditorium. When it was time to give the prizes for the spelling test, it was announced that Mary and Clifford had won second place. The announcer gave the results of the Algebra I test and said there were three from the same school who had perfect scores—Alva, Gerald, and I. He requested that our teacher come forward and explain his method of teaching, but he declined and said, "I have no special method."

Because of all the tension, Alva was sick on the way home. One time our teacher made a quick stop for her. After we started again, Alva meant to open the window but mistakenly opened the door and fell out onto the road. She was not severely hurt, but gravel was embedded in her leg. Her concern was not her injury but her lost certificate, which one of the boys retrieved. The teacher drove to the hospital in Sunbury where Alva's injury was treated. Because of the trauma we did not get to the ice cream parlor. Alva was not able to return to school for some time, but with the help of her teacher and fellow students, she completed her school work that year.

My last two years of high school were completed in Shamokin where fewer students who lived in East Cameron Township attended because there was no transportation provided for them. When I was a junior, Elmer Artman, a senior from Doutyville, got his driver's license and used his father's car to take me and a few other girls from other communities to Shamokin. In my senior year our township grade schools were consolidated, the two-year high school in Gowen City was closed, and all high-school students were bused to the high school in Shamokin where I graduated in 1942 in a class of 226.

Shamokin High School senior
picture in 1942

Living in New Jersey

The summer following my high-school graduation, my cousin Ida Maurer with two of her classmates went to Bridgeton, New Jersey, to get summer jobs. Ida invited me to join them. We boarded with two of our Yoder cousins who were sisters, Eleanor Caine and Betty Shoop, who earlier had moved to Bridgeton from Pennsylvania. Ida and her two friends returned to Pennsylvania at the end of the summer to complete their last year of high school. I decided to remain in New Jersey.

My first job was in a canning factory where I stood along an assembly line and filled cans with beets. Soon I secured a job as a sales clerk at a W.T. Grant store. Providentially, on my first day of working at Grants, I met Elma Bump, another clerk, who appeared to have a holiness connection. A few months after we met, I moved into the Bump home in Bridgeton as a boarder and stayed with them for three years. All the family members were born-again Christians who enjoyed serving the Lord. They had a great influence on me, and during that time I grew spiritually.

I had been attending the Pilgrim Holiness Church in Bridgeton where A.A. Passmore was the pastor. After I met Elma, she and her family invited me to attend church with them at the Fellowship Church of Christ, an independent holiness church, in Vineland, New Jersey. The pastor of the church was John Bradway. On Sundays Elma and her family stayed at the church for the evening services because of the distance and gas rationing during World War II. Several other young ladies from Vineland also attended the same church. One of the highlights of the year for me was the annual camp meeting at Haleyville, New Jersey, which was sponsored by the church in Vineland.

After working at Grants for a short time, I got a job as an inspector at the M.C. Schrank sewing factory that made high quality women's nightgowns and pajamas. To help in the war effort, they also manufactured pajamas for wounded servicemen. Later I became a seamstress on a double-needle machine that made flat-fell seams. Elma and her oldest sister, Alice, also came to work at the Schrank sewing factory.

While I was working at the sewing factory, I began to break out in a rash, had bouts of nausea, and became weak. A Russian doctor found that I was suffering from nephritis, a chronic inflammation of the kidneys. I took off work for about a month to get rest and take medication. When the doctor was releasing me, he said, "You were seriously ill in spite of your religion." I thanked the Lord for His touch then and that I never had a recurrence.

One time I was shopping in Bridgeton and lost my wallet. From the identification in it, the man who found my wallet decided that it must belong to a working girl. He contacted me and returned it. Again God was showing His care for me.

The Bump family was very musical. Elma and her sister Marion played the piano. Lester, their only brother who later married my youngest sister, Helen, played the trumpet and taught me how to play. There was a small orchestra that played for our worship services, and as soon as I was able, I joined the group. I did not know then that some day I would play my trumpet in Egypt, Ethiopia, and Bolivia and teach a few people how to play one.

It is wonderful to look back and see how God had his hand on my life. One beautiful day Elma, Lester, two other young ladies, and I took a rowboat ride on a creek in the area of Haleyville, 17 miles south of Vineland. We were enjoying the day until the tide came in and began pushing our boat in the swift current. Lester was rowing frantically but was unable to get the boat to the riverbank. While we were being pushed along, we came to a low bridge over the creek and miraculously were able to grasp onto the undergirdings and pull ourselves and the boat to the riverbank. God helped us to safety, and we praised Him for it.

During the years I spent in New Jersey, I occasionally returned to Doutyville. I went by bus from Bridgeton to Philadelphia and then by train to Shamokin where Doris and her family lived. From there someone took me to Doutyville where I visited my family and friends and attended my home church.

Call to Missionary Work

In the fall of 1945, Mrs. Elkins, a missionary, was to speak in the Pilgrim Holiness Church in Bridgeton. I was invited to attend that special service. I do not remember what the missionary said, but God spoke to me a few days later while sitting at my sewing machine. "There are a lot of ladies who can do this work. But what about My work?"

After working for three years in New Jersey, I realized that it was time for me to return to Doutyville, and I went home in December. I got a job at Lark's Garment Factory in Shamokin where they made dresses to ship to New York. My first assignment was sewing buttons on finished garments. Later I became a sleeve setter on a pinking machine that made a zigzag edge as I set the sleeve. I worked there until I left for Bible school the following fall.

On a Friday evening in March 1946, I attended a youth service at the Friendly Holiness Church in Helfenstein. Again God spoke to me about being a missionary. At the close of the service, I went forward to pray, and God made it clear that He wanted me to be a missionary. I testified to my call. When I got home, I did not tell my parents about my call, and my pastor who lived thirty miles away knew nothing regarding that Friday evening service. The next day Satan whispered, "Oh, perhaps you've made a fool of yourself. You probably are not called." I asked the Lord to confirm His will for me.

Me in 1946

Sunday morning I went to church in Lavelle with my parents and Helen. In the afternoon we attended a revival in Frackville and returned to Lavelle for the evening service. During that worship hour Marlin Straub, our pastor who was sitting on the platform, began doing something unusual. As the congregation sang and testified, he would sit for a while and then get on his knees and pray. He did that several times.

While people were testifying, the Lord spoke to me, "Stand and testify about your missionary call." I hesitated because I had asked God to make the call very clear to me that weekend. Again He told me to stand and testify to my call. He dealt with me in such a way that I knew I must tell the congregation about the Friday evening service. As soon as I finished, Marlin Straub rose quickly to his feet.

Pastor Straub said, "**This is it. This is it.**" He explained that God had put an unusual message on his heart for that service. On his way to church, he told his wife that he felt God was calling someone into His service or that someone was receiving his last opportunity to get saved. He continued and said, "I'll give my text whether I get to preach the message or not. My text is John 11:28, 'The Master is come, and calleth for thee.'" Immediately God came in power and glory; while some shouted, others went to the altar. God confirmed to me that He wanted me to be a missionary.

Marlin and Hilda Straub with Marlin, Jr. Marlin pastored the Evangelical Methodist Church in Lavelle when I answered God's call to Egypt in 1946.

Shortly after those events God revealed to me that He wanted me to go to Egypt. I had heard Victor Glenn, director of Faith Mission, preach in camp meetings and revival services in our area. I contacted him and told him about my call to Egypt, and he suggested I go to Bible school at Intercession City, Florida.

I contacted Osie England, the school president who was one of the founders of that college. She also had a school and orphanage in Point Pleasant, West Virginia, and a school and orphanage in Beulah Heights, Kentucky. I was accepted at the college but had no savings, and my parents were unable to help me financially. However, I went as God had directed, and He supplied my needs. One of the couples God used was Ralph and Pauline Stuck, who attended the Evangelical Methodist Church near Richfield, Pennsylvania. After I went to the mission field, they continued to help on my support until Ralph died in 1996. Then Pauline continued sending her support until her death in 2003.

President England advised me to contact Lloyd and Elsie King, who lived farther west in Pennsylvania during the summer, to see if I could travel with them to Florida. They would be returning to Intercession City where they lived most of the year so that their foster daughter, Dorothy

Wallace, could attend the college. They eagerly agreed to take me with them. Marlin and Hilda Straub took me to the Kings' home, going part of the way on the newly finished Pennsylvania Turnpike. The Kings' vehicle for the one-thousand-sand-mile trip was a school bus fixed with sleeping accommodations. When we got to the cotton-growing fields in the South, Dorothy and I had our picture taken in a cotton field.

In a cotton field in the South on my way to Florida to attend Bible school

Intercession City Biblical College

When I enrolled in Intercession City Biblical College in the fall of 1946, the girls' dormitory was on the second floor of one of the buildings with classrooms on the first floor. That school year Elma Bump, Barbara Hall, Betty Cherry, and I shared a corner apartment that consisted of two bedrooms and a nice room where we could study. Elma later married

The front upstairs corner apartment where I roomed with three girls my first year in Intercession City Biblical College

Jacob Miller, whom she met at the college. Early in their marriage they served as missionaries in Jamaica and then spent many years in pastorates in the States until her death in 2003. Barbara went as a single missionary to New Guinea where she met and married Robert Scott, a missionary from Australia. Betty married Robin Haste and became a homemaker.

In my first year at the school, an eight-foot-long alligator caused a great deal of excitement. There was a pond along State Route 92 that went through our community, and one day some of us saw a group of people gathered by the pond. By the time we got there, the alligator had been killed by authorities because of its proximity to houses.

Each high-school and college student was required to work for the school an hour every day. Part of the time I worked in the president's home, helping with household chores. Another of my assignments was teaching a singing class to the third and fourth graders who were in one room. In that singing class I had two sets of identical twins, the Calhoun boys and the McQuait girls.

During that year several men renovated a building that was across the railroad tracks from the main campus and converted it into a dormitory. Elma and I returned for our second year and chose to be roommates in the new dorm.

One time a few of us girls saw a coral snake by the railroad tracks. We realized the bite of a coral snake is deadly and thanked the Lord for keeping us from getting bitten.

Another time a few boys in junior high school went to an area across the tracks to pray together. After a while, one of them said to the others, "Did any of you touch me?"

His friends replied, "No." Each of them felt that he had been touched by someone. When they looked around, they saw a poisonous water moccasin nearby. They realized God had touched them to keep them from being bitten by the snake. Those boys came back to the campus praising the Lord. We serve a loving, faithful, mighty God!

That October the residents of Intercession City began preparing for a hurricane by boarding up the windows of their homes. We students were instructed to go to a building on the campus we called the hotel, which was considered to be the safest place. Fervent prayer was made by the residents, faculty, and students. God answered prayer and the hurricane dissipated. Psalm 46:1 was certainly true for us: "God is our refuge and strength, a very present help in trouble."

While in my second year at Intercession City, a few of us students drove to Hobe Sound to attend the newly established camp meeting. H. Robb and Geraldine French and James and Ella Zuch were the leaders for the camp. The first buildings they used were Quonsets that they acquired from Camp Murphy, a military camp that was closing. The presence of God could be sensed in service after service.

Both years at Intercession City Biblical College, I was active in outreach. We ministered to migrant workers on a farm not far from Intercession City. Our primary team members were John and Mary Swentzel a middle-aged couple who were studying at the college, Elma Bump, and I. Mary, Elma, and I sang as a trio. Later Jacob Miller, another student, joined us as a bass singer. Jacob played a guitar, and I played the trumpet in those services. I also was part of another mixed quartet that was composed of Paul Light, Jacob Miller, Elma Bump, and me.

I enjoyed playing my trumpet in the school orchestra. Two other trumpet players in the group were Robert Wille, whom I taught to play, and Paul Light.

Ropeholders was a group of students who were interested in home and foreign missions. I profited by being a member of

Mary, me, Elma, Jacob, and John as an outreach group at ICBC

that fellowship. Six out of our group of twenty-two students gave a part of their life doing missionary work on foreign soil.

Each winter we had 100 days of services in the Morrison Memorial Chapel. Many Christians came to Intercession City for the winter months and occupied rooms in the hotel. Various evangelists preached during those days. We had the privilege of hearing some of the outstanding evangelists of the holiness movement.

While I lived in Intercession City, I enjoyed visiting the Singing Tower and Mountain Lake Sanctuary in Lake Wales where we heard one of the best carillons in the world. The Tower had 71 bells, and the largest weighed 11 tons. Another place I visited was Marineland where we saw their collection of sea creatures. On one occasion I went with some of my classmates to St. Augustine, the oldest city in the United States.

Marriage Plans

By the end of my first year in college, F, a ministerial student, began showing an interest in me. His mother was a teacher in the high-school department, and a younger sister was a college student. They lived in a house in Intercession City during the school year, and in the summer they lived in Michigan.

Victor Glenn wanted me to get some hands-on experience that summer, so after a brief visit with my family in Pennsylvania, I went to

Doris, Charles, Helen, Leonard, me, Earl, and Eva with our parents in 1948

Beulah Heights in Kentucky to work in the orphanage. I was in charge of ten boys, ages five to ten. We lived in a house that was a part of the orphanage. It was my responsibility to be with them day and night to be a "mother" to them. All the orphan boys and girls and the workers ate in a common dining room. A cook, Pearl Passmore, the sister to A.A. Passmore, and her helpers prepared the meals.

That summer F came to see me at the orphanage. During that visit he proposed marriage, and I accepted with the understanding that he would be able to evangelize in Egypt. At the close of the summer, I traveled to Michigan to visit his family and returned to Intercession City with them.

Victor Glenn, accompanied by his wife, came as an evangelist during the hundred-day revival. I introduced my fiancé to the Glenns. Brother Glenn's remark to me later was that if a person does not have a call to the mission field, he usually does not stay on the field very long.

F and I secured permission from Miss England to have our wedding at the college at the end of the school year. We selected our wedding party from among our friends at school and asked one of our beloved instructors, Fielding Howard, to perform the ceremony. F was a good preacher and respected by the people of the community, and for his sake a neighbor of their family who had many flowers in her garden offered to furnish the flowers for the wedding. Another dear lady offered to provide the wedding cake. We contacted a photographer in a nearby city to take photos on our wedding day. Everything seemed to be fitting into place.

Some days before the date set for our wedding, we wanted to be sure we were following the Lord's plan for our lives and therefore agreed to fast and pray. Because of scheduled events, our rehearsal took place several days before the wedding date. The day after our rehearsal, F went to Kissimmee to purchase some things we needed. When he returned, he sadly informed me that he could not go to Egypt. After much prayer we agreed to postpone our wedding plans.

In those days not everyone had a telephone, and we needed to notify several people of the change of plans. What was to be our wedding day was spent in going to the photographer to cancel the appointment, visiting a couple who were to have a part in the wedding and telling them not to come, and speaking to the minister who was to perform the ceremony. At the school the students and staff ate what was to be our wedding cake.

The following day I was walking with some of my friends to the local post office when F saw me and came to speak with me. He drew me aside and said, "Marry me, and I'll go," but I could not say "yes" to that proposal.

I now faced the need to find a way to my home in Pennsylvania because I would not be going to Michigan. Paul and Bertha Goss, a young couple from my area of Pennsylvania, and their baby found room in their car for me and took me with them.

Before F and I left the campus, we agreed to remain engaged and see whether the Lord would make it clear that he should go to Egypt where I knew that I was called. Victor and Jennie Glenn asked me to come to

Bedford, Indiana, to live with them and help in the home office. At that time the office was in a part of the Glenns' home.

I made the trip from Sunbury, Pennsylvania, to Indianapolis, Indiana, by train. Ruth Maurer, the wife of my cousin Raymond Maurer, was among those who took me to the train station. She gave me $5.00 and what a blessing that proved to be once I got to Indianapolis. Again God took care of me! I had two heavy suitcases with me and could not afford a taxi to take me to the bus station to go to Bedford. I found a lad who was willing to help me carry my bags for a small fee. While we were walking, he asked, "Lady, what do you have in this suitcase, bricks?" We stopped more than once to rest on our way. I worked in the office of Faith Mission from the summer of 1948 until the fall of 1949, when I sailed for Egypt.

That summer there was an indoor camp meeting at the Cadle Tabernacle in Indianapolis. The Glenns decided to go for a day and take me with them. At that camp Jennie Glenn introduced me to a young lady from Point Pleasant, West Virginia, who was preparing to go as a missionary to India. We were in line for one of the meals when my new friend, who had attended the college in Intercession City earlier, said to me, "Have you heard that B is about to land F?" I was surprised. While we sat at a table eating our dinner, she said excitedly, "Did you hear about the wedding that was to take place at Intercession City, and then the couple did not get married, and they had the cake and everything prepared?"

I replied, "Do you realize who I am?"

I wrote to my fiancé and told him what I had heard, and that if it was true, he was unfair to B and to me, and that I never wanted to hear from him again. After some time had passed, I received a letter from him saying that he was not marrying B, and he did not. However, that brought our engagement and any hopes for marriage to an end. I was **disappointed**, but it turned out to be **God's appointment** for me. The following poem expresses my sentiments.

Disappointment — His Appointment

"Disappointment — His Appointment"
Change one letter, then I see
That the thwarting of my purpose
Is God's better choice for me.

His appointment must be blessing,
Tho' it may come in disguise,
For the end from the beginning
Open to His wisdom lies.

"Disappointment — His Appointment"
Whose? The Lord, who loves me best,
Understands and knows me fully,
Who my faith and love would test;
For, like loving earthly parents,
He rejoices when He knows
That His child accepts, UNQUESTIONED,
All that from His wisdom flows.

"Disappointment — His Appointment"
"No good thing will He withhold,"
From denials oft we gather
Treasures of His love untold,
Well He knows each broken purpose
Leads to fuller, deeper trust,
And the end of all His dealings
Proves our God is wise and just.

"Disappointment — His Appointment"
Lord, I take it, then, as such.
Like the clay in hands of potter,
Yielding wholly to Thy touch.
All my life's plan in Thy moulding,
Not one single choice be mine;
Let me answer, unrepining —
"Father, not my will, but Thine."

—Edith Lillian Young

Chapter 2

Ocean Voyage to Egypt
November 1949

Setting Sail

My joy mounted as I made final plans to sail for Egypt, the land of my calling! Wednesday, November 9, I left Shamokin by bus to go to New York City. Because I grew up in a small village in Pennsylvania, the traffic in New York City was appalling to me. Taxis were buzzing everywhere, and people were running to and fro, dashing in and out of the traffic. At the bus station I hailed a taxi to take me to the Latham Hotel where I checked in. From there I went to the Marquis Travel Service and met Victor Glenn, director of Faith Mission, and Omar Lee, another new missionary. Omar and his wife, Geneva, and children, Anita and Daniel, were sailing to Egypt also. Victor purchased tickets for the Lee family

The Omar Lee family, me, and Harriette ready to sail for Egypt in November 1949

33

and me. Ryburn Ray, a Faith Mission board member, joined us for our evening meal.

When our group arrived at the hotel lobby after supper, Harriette Harp, a widow who was returning to Egypt for her second term with Faith Mission, had just arrived from New Jersey where she had been visiting friends. She had lost her husband, Charles, to Addison's disease in Egypt in 1944. Her brother, other family members, and a friend had already taken her baggage to the ship, the *Mohammed Ali el Kebir*, which was docked in Hoboken, New Jersey. The *Mohammed Ali* was a passenger vessel that also carried cargo, which meant that we would stop at various ports to unload and load cargo.

The beauty of New York City was the many buildings stretching skyward that gave a beautiful array of lights at night. Before going to bed, I called Leona Kerstetter, my cousin, who lived in that great metrop-

The *Mohammed Ali el Kebir*, an Egyptian passenger ship on which we sailed from Hoboken, New Jersey, to Egypt

olis. She was surprised to know that I was in the city on my way to Egypt. I called other family members to say a final farewell. The next morning the phone rang in my room. It was Leona calling from downstairs to let me know that she had come to visit with me for a few minutes on her way to work. We had a nice visit together.

After Leona left, our group did a little shopping, went to the office of the travel agency to get the title to the Chevrolet Carryall that the Mission was sending to Egypt, picked up Harriette's passport, and purchased a ticket for her. We then took the baggage for the Omar Lee family to the ship. My baggage and the Carryall had been shipped by truck to the dock the previous week. About noon we were allowed to check in our cabin luggage but were not permitted to board. Immediately after lunch Victor Glenn and Ryburn Ray left for Indiana. We returned to the ship and were permitted to board.

Wearing my yellow chrysanthemum
corsage from Harriette's brother
and his friend

Harriette's brother Kent Steele and his friend Tracy Killam gave her a corsage at Latham Hotel and gave me one before we left for the pier to board the *Mohammed Ali*. The corsages had a large, yellow chrysanthemum, autumn leaves, and a yellow ribbon. Later someone at the pier was looking for us, and one of the dock workers said, "Oh, you mean the two ladies with the big 'sunflowers'!"

We said our farewells to the few friends who were present, and our ship left the harbor at Hoboken that evening after dark. With mixed emotions we sailed down the Hudson River, past the Statue of Liberty, and out into the Atlantic Ocean.

Life on Board Ship

The cabin that Harriette, Anita, and I shared had two sets of bunk beds. At each upper berth was a porthole. Our other cabin furnishings included an arm chair, a large wardrobe, a chest of drawers, a full-length mirror, a washbowl, and a bed lamp beside each lower bed. The floor was covered with two woolen rugs made in Egypt.

In the dining room on the deck below us, we were more conscious of the swaying of the ship than in our cabin. There were lovely bouquets of roses on the tables. Our group sat together at one of the small tables. The children ate with their parents for breakfast and the noon meal. However, they were served first for the evening meal, and then the adults ate an hour later. Two stewardesses cared for the children while the adults ate.

Our first supper was typical of those throughout the voyage. The menu was in French, and we were not sure what we were ordering until the food was brought to our table. The meal consisted of five courses:

consommé containing julienned vegetables; fish filet with tartar sauce; chicken and native rice cooked with *semna*, Egyptian butter; roast beef, whole fried potatoes, tossed salad, and rolls; and last, coffee, an apple, and a jelly roll with nuts and creamy frosting. When each course was completed, our dishes were removed and clean ones brought.

After supper we went on deck and watched the lights of New York City as they receded. That night the noise of the motors, the rocking of the ship, and dreams about our ship plowing through narrow passages with trees on both sides kept me from sleeping well. In the morning all we could see was the vast ocean around us. For breakfast that morning we had fruit juice, eggs, toast, butter, jam, coffee, and apples.

To prevent seasickness I was taking Dramamine, which made me drowsy, and my missionary friends had to call a dozen times to arouse me for the noon meal. The luncheon was elaborate like the supper the previous evening. It consisted of *hors d'oeuvre* on a sectioned tray containing pickled carrots and turnips cut in small fancy pieces, potato salad, sardines, sliced tomatoes, olives, and sliced ham. That was followed by three additional courses: macaroni with cheese sauce; veal chops, fried potatoes, and cauliflower with *semna*; and crackers and cheese. At the end we had bananas and coffee.

A lifeboat drill added excitement to our evening. Previously, our steward had given us instructions about donning our life jackets and telling us where to go. The crew went through the normal procedure of lowering the lifeboats. When they were returned to their proper places, we were allowed to return to our cabins. What an interesting day it had been!

On board ship there was little scheduled activity that was profitable to occupy our time. However, one day our group explored the ship and found two comfortable lounges. The one near the front of the ship had a grand piano. Geneva played, and we sang while other passengers gambled. We took advantage of that piano on other days. At times our group met in one of our rooms for prayer; God drew near and ministered to us. We appreciated His tender loving care.

The days passed slowly, and I spent part of my time typing letters or sitting on deck enjoying the breeze, especially when the ship was not rocking. Harriette's friends had given her a bundle of letters, which proved to be a blessing to her as she read one or two a day. Periodically, we were instructed to advance the time on our watches when we entered a new time zone.

Most of the crew were Egyptians who spoke Arabic. Harriette had learned to speak Arabic during her first term in Egypt, and she was able to communicate with them and interpret for us. We had an obliging steward from Sudan who took care of our cabins. While we were in the dining room for breakfast, he changed the linens on our beds and brought clean towels and fresh water.

Thankfully, we had smooth sailing for the first few days, but then we encountered a storm that continued for several days. Because of the constant motion, I had difficulty eating.

Azores and the Strait of Gibraltar

By Wednesday morning we were anticipating our arrival at the Azores, a group of islands that belong to Portugal and stretch for nearly four hundred miles across the North Atlantic Ocean. Before breakfast we saw one of the nine islands on the horizon. During breakfast that morning we sang birthday wishes to Omar.

We passed other islands later in the day, and I thought how wonderful it is that they stand firm in the vast Atlantic Ocean. I could not help but think of the Christian's foundation in Jesus Christ our Redeemer, who is the Rock of Ages to our souls. While we watched the setting sun, we saw sailboats, men fishing from rowboats, and schools of porpoises jumping out of the water. Because we would not see land for a few days, Harriette and I enjoyed viewing the islands until it became too dark to see them.

On Friday, November 18, we saw the light from the lighthouse at St. Vincent, Portugal, and also lights on the west coast of Africa. When we approached the Strait of Gibraltar, more ships came into view. Saturday morning while we passed through the Strait, the clouds lifted, giving us a majestic view. I was surprised to see a number of buildings on the top and the slopes of the rock.

Most of Saturday afternoon Harriette and I rested, and then I joined Geneva and Anita in the lounge for tea. After a tasty supper our group went on deck and played shuffleboard while most of the other passengers attended a dance. While we played, the captain stopped and told us about a new stop we would be making at Leghorn, Italy.

Our group endeavored to observe Sunday as a day of worship. After the noon meal we went to the lounge and studied the Sunday school lesson together. Later in the day I finished reading Harriette's diary of her trip home from Egypt in 1944 during World War II. In the evening we joined the Lees in their room and played our musical instruments, and then we went on deck to enjoy some fresh air before retiring.

Genoa, Leghorn, and Naples

We arrived at Genoa, Italy, the next evening. From the deck we enjoyed watching a small boat come alongside the *Mohammed Ali*. From there the harbor pilot climbed the rope ladder and went to the bridge to guide our ship to the dock. The officials gave us cards that permitted us to disembark and walk through Genoa, much of it still damaged from the war. After having been on board ship for some time, we enjoyed walking on solid ground. We were hoping to find a place to celebrate Danny's birthday, but we were not successful because we were unable to communicate and get directions to the heart of the city. We returned to the ship and after supper went on deck and watched the men while they unloaded and loaded cargo. While we watched the men work, Harriette and I wrote a poem to celebrate Danny's second birthday.

Here we are in old Genoa,
The city of Columbus' birth.
We'll celebrate your second birthday,
And our hearts are filled with mirth.

We pray, God bless you, little Danny.
We hope that you will grow and grow.
May you also in the Spirit
More of your heavenly Father know.

Tuesday was a rainy day, discouraging us from going sightseeing and keeping the crew from unloading cargo. The next morning dawned bright and sunny, so the Lees, Harriette, and I made another effort to visit the city because we had obtained directions. We walked along the sea and made our way through some narrow streets to the heart of the city. Everywhere we observed the extreme poverty of the people and the destruction caused by the war.

In the city we found a guide, who, for a reasonable fee, took us to a nice restaurant. After we ate, he showed us some highlights of the city, including the house of Christopher Columbus. Finally he took us to the American Consulate where we dismissed him. We then spent several hours walking, using a guidebook that the consul gave us. From an elevated site we had a wonderful panoramic view of Genoa with its many narrow and winding streets.

The Lees wanted to buy some fruit, but because their children were getting tired, Harriette and I offered to look for a fruit market. They took our cameras and packages and returned to the ship. While we looked for fruit, we observed people entering an old church. Out of curiosity we followed and found ourselves in a Catholic Church where priests were chanting. It was interesting but sad! Then we found a fruit market and purchased eleven oranges for 20 cents, two dozen lemons for 25 cents, and a tomato-sized persimmon for 5 cents. After we returned to our ship, we estimated that we had walked at least fifteen miles that day. After supper I lay down to rest and immediately fell asleep.

During the night our ship left Genoa and sailed for Leghorn, Italy. At 4:45 the next morning, seven-year-old Anita, who was sleeping in an upper berth near a porthole, let out a cry indicating that she was wet. At that time the sea was the roughest we had encountered, and water came through the partially opened porthole. Harriette aroused, shut the port-hole, changed the sheets for Anita, and mopped up the water. I was trying to lie still, because I was getting nauseated. Soon both Harriette and I were sick.

Before sunrise our ship docked in Leghorn. A steward kindly brought food to our room because we got up too late to eat breakfast in the dining room. Later we learned that Omar and some of the other passengers also had experienced seasickness during the night.

Because Pisa was only a half-hour bus ride from our ship, we joined many of the other passengers to see the Leaning Tower. Some German engineers on our ship exchanged a couple dollars of our American money for Italian *lira*. From the bus terminal in Pisa, we walked a distance, winding our way through the streets. At last we found ourselves gazing at the Tower about which we had read in elementary school. Little had I dreamed that some day I would see it. Beside the Tower was a beautiful cathedral called St. Peter's Basilica. After an enjoyable visit in Pisa, we retraced our steps to the bus terminal and returned to our ship

A special supper was served at 8:00 that evening on the *Mohammed Ali* to observe the American Thanksgiving Day. The dining room was festively decorated with flags representing the countries of the people on board. It was a delicious meal and the dessert, called Bombe Vesuvius, caught our attention. It was a cake with ice cream and topped with creamy icing. In the center was a cylindrical object filled with alcohol that was lit and later exploded. The frosting was burning while they served it. About 9:30 we left the dining room.

Our ship then set sail for Naples, Italy. While we were leaving the harbor, Mr. Hines, a U.S. Naval officer en route to Turkey, pointed out the *U.S.S. Leyte*, an aircraft carrier on which he had served during World War II. The sailing was smooth, and we slept well that night.

The next afternoon we docked at the port of Naples, and that evening we took a short walk into the city. Naples was destroyed during the war and afterwards rebuilt into a beautiful city. However, the people were still suffering from the results of the war, and we were approached by children begging for money to buy food. Even though the weather was inclement the next morning, some of the passengers took a tour to see Pompeii, which had been destroyed by the eruption of Vesuvius in A.D 79. Our group did not go, and those who went said it was an unpleasant tour because of the unfavorable weather.

After supper that evening we watched the crew while they fastened a large Caterpillar truck to the deck of the ship. It was too large to go into the hold. While on deck we saw the captain and asked him when we would be leaving Naples. He indicated that we would not leave until the morning because of a storm at sea. I was glad we stayed in port because we were rocked by the rolling waves; it would have been much worse at sea.

Reaching Our Destination

When we left Naples the next morning, it was raining but it soon stopped, and we had a pleasant afternoon. Our ship passed the Isle of Capri, then the volcano of Stromboli, and finally the island of Sicily. All day we could see the shoreline of Italy and enjoyed seeing the lights after dark. From Naples, which marked our last stopping point, we had slightly over one thousand miles to go before reaching Alexandria. Our group was eager to arrive at our destination.

Sunday morning found us sailing southeast across the Mediterranean Sea. The name comes from the two Latin words *med* and *terra* which mean between lands. During the forenoon I read from Page Wilke's book *The Dynamic of Service*, a book full of admonition for young missionaries, and in the afternoon our group studied the Sunday school lesson together. After supper we went to the Lees' room and played a Bible game, thinking of characters in the Bible and what they did. The group guessed who they were.

The next morning, November 28, the captain returned our passports with entry forms for the Egyptian police. After a nourishing breakfast of ham and eggs, toast, jam, and grapefruit, we went on deck to breathe some refreshing salt air. We had been on the *Mohammed Ali* for two and a half weeks, and now we had fewer than sixteen hours until we would reach Alexandria.

That day the headwaiter took us on a tour of the ship. In the kitchen or galley, we marveled at the huge skillets they used. From the galley he took us to the lower part of the ship where we saw the powerful dynamos. I was amazed at all the mechanism that was below us. He also took us to the bridge where we saw the instruments used to plow the seas. It was interesting to see the radio room and the instruments used for navigation. Some of the children were allowed to steer the ship. We were privileged to step into the beautiful living quarters reserved exclusively for the owner of the ship.

About 6:00 on Tuesday, I awoke, peered out the porthole, and saw for the first time in daylight the African shore with the rosy-tinted sky above and the Mediterranean Sea in the foreground. There were palm trees and flat-roofed, mud-brick houses that were common in Egypt. We were early risers that morning and went on deck awhile before breakfast. It was to be an **exciting** day for six people on that ship. Our ship waited in the harbor until it was our turn to dock. The police came in small boats and climbed on board to examine our passports. They were dressed in black woolen uniforms trimmed with red and wore red hats called *fezzes*.

We were getting ready to go for breakfast when someone knocked on our door. Our steward was there with two Egyptian men who were asking for Harriette. They said they were sent by a man named Macowi to help her with her luggage. She could not remember the man who sent them but thought his name sounded familiar. Geneva, the children, and I went for breakfast while Harriette and Omar went to have their passports checked. After I ate, I had mine checked, and we were ready to leave the ship.

When our ship docked, we looked for people from the orphanage but did not see any of them. Soon Harriette saw John Peel, a Faith Mission missionary, and gave a shout. We kept asking, "Where? Where?" until we saw him. Eventually, we were allowed to disembark, and the two men who came to help Harriette also assisted the rest of us with our cabin luggage.

Our group was delighted to reach John and Ruth Peel and Hanem, one of the workers at the orphanage. Hanem welcomed Harriette with many kisses. While Omar and John stayed to take care of our baggage after it was unloaded, Ruth led us to a building to be sheltered from the hot sun.

Later Harriette and I were called to claim our baggage. From there we went to the customs house, and I marveled when I saw the young boys and men pick up our heavy trunks single-handed and carry them on their backs for a short distance. It would have taken several men in America to do the same job. The men in customs opened a few of our bags, and we paid only $20.00 (U.S.) for duties besides the duty on the Chevrolet Carryall.

We hired two horse-drawn carts to take our baggage the six miles to the orphanage, and Hanem rode on one of them. Ruth, Geneva and her two children, Harriette, and I went in a taxi while the men stayed to get the vehicle through customs.

Our hearts were joyful as we approached the orphanage; the girls came running with glee to welcome us to our new home. They began to sing a welcome song as we entered the large hallway where they usually had their devotions. It was hard to hold back our tears. Large letters were

Some of the orphans who welcomed us to the orphanage when we arrived in 1949

strung from wall to wall saying, "WELCOME HOME." There was an exchange of greetings with Carrie Craig, who was the matron of the orphanage, and the excited children.

In the evening everyone gathered in the living room for a time of fellowship. We played our instruments—guitar, accordion, piano, and trumpet—and sang before we retired after a strenuous but blessed day. We concluded our time together by singing:

> Praise God, from whom all blessings flow;
> Praise Him all creatures here below;
> Praise Him above, ye heavenly hosts;
> Praise Father, Son, and Holy Ghost.

What a **delight** to be in the place where God had called me four years previously!

Chapter 3

Ministering in the Land of the Pyramids
1949-1955

Initial Impressions and Duties

My first weeks in Alexandria were filled with numerous interesting sights. Many small markets on the sidewalks overflowed into the streets with people trying to make purchases. With awe I watched men carrying refrigerators and other heavy items on their backs.

Most of the men were wearing *fezzes*, red cylinder-shaped brimless hats with black tassels that swung while the men walked. Some of the men in Alexandria wore suits, but many of them wore the traditional loose garment called a *gallabia*. Many of the women, both Moslem and Christian, were wearing a *berda*, a black covering, which was draped over their heads and reached to their feet. Some of them had trouble managing their *berdas* when they carried small children or items purchased from the market.

The streets were lined with stately palm trees with their branches swaying in the sea breeze. All kinds of vehicles buzzed along the streets. Streetcars ran throughout the city. Large buses were so crowded that people stood on the steps and held onto the handrails. Orange and black taxis plus the privately owned cars of the wealthier people added to the traffic. Among those fast-moving vehicles, I saw carts and buggies pulled by donkeys or horses. The constant noise of horns blowing while drivers tried to make their way through the traffic often annoyed me.

Another common sound was the imams, or Moslem prayer leaders, who announced the call to prayer five times a day for all the faithful. On Fridays there were overflow crowds of worshipers at many of the mosques, Moslem places of worship. The men removed their shoes and prayed in the streets in front of the mosques. They knelt facing Mecca, the holy city of Islam, and touched their foreheads to the ground at intervals as they prayed.

During my first term of nearly six years in Egypt, my primary duty was working in the mission orphanage for girls. It was located in Rouchdi, a zone in Alexandria, and was on the corner of Rouchdi Pasha Street and El Corniche, the seaside drive that ran like a ribbon along the Mediterranean Sea. One could ride on the El Corniche for miles and see beautiful vistas of the sea, breathe the exhilarating fresh air, and feel the breeze, all of which were like a tonic. A bay reached inland almost to the orphanage. In the evenings I enjoyed gorgeous sunsets beyond the beautiful greenish-blue Mediterranean Sea.

The orphanage building located in Rouchdi, a zone in Alexandria, beside the Mediterranean Sea

Carrie Craig from St. Louis, Missouri, was the matron of the orphanage. She was a gracious black lady who was forty years my senior. I helped her with supervising the girls, administering discipline when necessary, and doing the bookkeeping for the orphanage.

Another major duty was teaching English to the girls in the upper grades in our school at the orphanage. We hired an Egyptian lady who taught the older girls the government curriculum. Bahgah and Alice, two of our older girls who remained as workers, taught the younger girls in the lower grades. The roof of the orphanage building was flat, and on it was a wooden cabin-like structure with two large classrooms. Strong rustic stairs in a large open stairway inside the building led to

Teaching English to the girls in the upper grades in our school at the orphanage

the roof from the main floor of the building. It was quite a climb up the wooden stairs, and in the winter, which is the rainy season in Egypt, we sometimes found it a little challenging to get from the top of the stairs to the classroom on the roof.

Stories Inside the Orphanage

Emma Haldeman, who had been working in Upper Egypt, came to Alexandria in March 1950. Because of her age and declining health, she was retiring from missionary work in Egypt, having spent almost 36 years there. She stayed at the orphanage for a month before sailing to America. One memorable event during her visit with us was a communion service that she conducted. She read some Scripture and then preached, using Alfie, a young man she had reared, as her interpreter. After that she administered the sacraments. We felt God's precious presence with us throughout the service.

Emma Haldeman in the 1950s. She was a missionary with EFM in Egypt for 36 years and had returned to the States to retire.

* * * * *

During Emma's visit three little girls came into the orphanage. Two of the girls were sisters whose mother was a widow and unable to care for them. The older one played the part of mother to the younger one and tried to comfort her when she cried for her mother. Amid all the activity at the orphanage, they slowly adapted to their new home and stopped grieving for their mother. We called them by the names their parents had given them—Widad and Zaghloula.

The third girl was a baby of eight months whose mother had died four months previously. Her sister, a child of ten, had been caring for the tiny child. The baby was hungry, thin, and a pitiful sight in her rags. Her name was Samiah, but we named her Elaine. One of the older girls, Ruby, took a great interest in her, and with plenty of food and loving care, she soon began to gain weight and get stronger. By June she was healthy and started to say a few words.

Ruby had come to the orphanage as a child at age four along with Julia, her sister, age one and a half. Their father had died and their grandfather, one of our pastors, brought the girls to the orphanage.

Not only did Ruby take care of Elaine but also took a keen interest in other young girls in the orphanage. When I returned to Egypt in 1958, I was assigned to teach in the Bible school in Girga, Upper Egypt. I wanted someone to help me in my apartment and to go calling with me. Ruby came to Girga and worked with me for several years.

With Ruby in 1963. She was my
helper for several years in Girga.

Ruby twenty years later in the States

Eventually Ruby returned to Alexandria where she worked as a nanny and then came to America where she married a Mexican-American policeman. At this writing, Ruby continues to serve the Lord and also gives on my missionary support.

★ ★ ★ ★ ★

When I arrived at the orphanage, Edna Mae and her sister Sophia were teenagers there. After Edna Mae completed her years at the orphanage, she taught English at the American Mission Girls' Private School (Presbyterian) at Tanta, Egypt. Then she entered their school of nursing, completed the course, took the government exams, and became a registered nurse.

In 1960 Edna Mae came to New York City and took postgraduate work in medical and surgical nursing. From there she moved to Canada, where she spent 45 years practicing and teaching nursing, advancing her education, and finally teaching at the University of Toronto. During those years she married Walter Hoey. At the time of

Edna with her husband, Walter Hoey, in 1981

this writing she lives as a widow in Orillia, Ontario, and serves as a volunteer providing transportation for people who need it.

* * * * *

Many exciting things happened while we were caring for the orphans. It was our practice to have evening devotions with members of the staff and the older girls leading. One evening in early April, after devotions I took the temperature of an eleven-year-old girl before she went to bed. It was 105 degrees! I recommended that she be given aspirin and lemon juice; then I went to my room to study for an Arabic lesson.

Soon a group of girls came running and told me that Joan, a four-teen-year-old girl, was sewing on the machine and ran the needle through her finger. She was very pale and cried when the girls tried to help her. Two of the girls and I took her to the homes of two doctors and then to two hospitals before finding someone who would help her. One of the nurses pulled the needle partly out by using her hand and then stooped over and removed it with her teeth. She urged us not to tell the doctor how or by whom it was removed. The doctor put alcohol on her finger, then Mercurochrome, and bandaged it. He wanted an Egyptian pound for his services, but we told him we thought it was too much for such a small procedure, especially because we were from a faith orphanage, so he finally accepted a half pound, or 50 *piasters*. We hurried home because we had not taken coats with us, and at 9:30 it was cold, and the wind was blowing dust and dirt into our faces.

The following Monday, Easter Monday, we had a hailstorm at 7:00 p.m. Lightning flashed, thunder rolled, rain poured, and hail fell until the streets were white as if covered with snow. We did not get all our windows closed in time, and every room except one on the second floor was flooded. Water also came in under the doors. On the ground floor the

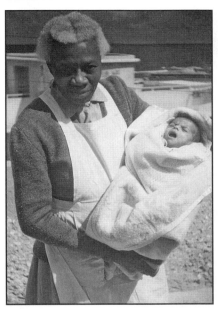

Carrie Craig, matron of the orphanage, with Mary Jane, an orphan, in 1954

drain was plugged, and the dining rooms, kitchen, and girls' bathroom were covered with water. Some of the girls waded through the water to open the drain. We had a hard time keeping the girls inside when it started to hail. They were not concerned about the house being full of water. As soon as the storm ended, they mopped the entire house. In the midst of all that excitement, the lights in our section of town went out. We had only one flashlight and no candles. Carrie sent two of the older girls to buy candles, and when they returned, they told us that the water in some places was ankle deep. Carrie and I were glad when all the girls were finally tucked into their beds.

* * * * *

Egyptian businesses started importing wringer washing machines from England about the time I arrived in Egypt. When one of Carrie's American friends heard about the washing machines, she sent money to buy one for the orphanage. The girls thought that it was the grandest thing that ever was. It certainly made it much easier to wash the clothes for the girls, especially the younger ones.

* * * * *

One of those girls was Jennie who came to the orphanage when she was 18 months. Soon she could recognize most of the girls and was learning to say their names. However, she could not say "Miss Maurer," so she called me "Money." Early in the morning she would come from her room to my door by the front porch, knock, and call, "Money! Money!" When I asked her what she wanted, she would reply, "Andy," meaning candy. I seldom gave it to her because Carrie and I did not think she should have it frequently. Sometimes when we knelt to pray in devotions, she would bow her head, too, and say, "Amen, Dod," because she

could not say God. During
nap time for the younger children, I often brought Jennie to
my room because it was
quieter.

Jennie and me in the spring of 1950

* * * * *

During that summer God
gave us some wonderful
times at the orphanage.
Several of the girls earnestly
sought God for salvation, and
four of them were sanctified.
We praised God for His special help! At the same time, we were having a
problem with ringworm on the scalps of the younger girls. A skin
specialist removed their hair with a series of X-ray treatments, and then
for several weeks we followed with a treatment of iodine and salve. The
doctor visited periodically until they were all cured.

* * * * *

Later that summer we accepted several new girls and each had a sad
story. Annette was one of them. She was fourteen months, of
Assyrian-Egyptian lineage, had no teeth, and could not stand on her feet.
She appeared to have rickets.

Another sad story involved two-year-old Anaam and her sister
Ferial, who was almost four. Their twenty-four-year-old mother had
been educated at the Presbyterian American Mission. Her husband was
seeing another woman and threatened to kill his wife. The husband's
mother said, "No, just burn her to death." One night he took his wife's
gold, which was her capital wealth. Her mother told her to bring the children to Alexandria to her. The father, who had kept the oldest daughter
who was five, threatened to become a Moslem and marry the other
woman. In all of that, the mother of the girls was expecting their fourth
child. We took the two girls temporarily and waited to see if the father
was willing for them to stay with us. We sent a contract to our pastor who
lived in the father's village, and the father signed it so that the girls could
stay permanently.

With the youngest orphans

* * * * *

A broom with this note given to me by the youngest girls for my birthday in August 1950

At 6:00 a.m. on August 23, 1950, the girls came to my door to sing "Happy Birthday." Throughout the morning they came and sang to me, and each time they brought me a gift. Two of the younger girls gave me two little rag dolls about three inches tall, which was all they had to give. The youngest ones came with their gift—a broom with a note saying, "I'm happy! Why? I'm gonna sweep for Sitt (lady) Maurer." Carrie had drawn a man with a happy face on the note. The missionaries who were visiting from Upper Egypt for the summer helped to prepare an enjoyable dinner, climaxing my first birthday in Egypt. It had been a pleasant day!

* * * * *

I wrote the following to my family on October 3:

You ought to see our lovely little ones. They are sweet. When we take two-year-old Jennie for a walk and she sees a horse or donkey, she says, "Horsey." She knows many of us just by our voices. The other day she was on the front porch, and we were looking at the sea. She said, "Want to go to the water." Elaine who was one year old in July is learning to walk and calls our names. She is healthy and fat. You would not believe that she is the same baby who came to us weak and dirty last March, seven months ago.

The fourteen-month-old Annette, who has been with us for about six weeks, is learning to stand alone. When she came, she was so weak she could hardly cry or lift her head.

Our older girls are learning to crochet. I could crochet a little, and this past summer Geneva Lee, one of our missionaries, taught me how to read crocheting instructions from a book. Now I am teaching the girls. We are making a set of doilies for the living room. Alice finished hers for the small table. Violet has finished hers for the top of one bookcase. Joan is making one for the phonograph, Hickma for the other bookcase, Stella for the table, and Una for the piano. They are doing quite well. We hope to finish the set soon. I wish you could see the lovely crocheting they do.

* * * * *

One day in November two of the girls were cleaning the pantry. The girl who was supervising the work was called to some other duty, and she sent a younger girl to watch them. One of the cleaning girls saw some small pies another girl had received from her brother. She took one and offered it to the second girl who ate it. Then she offered one to the girl who was sent to watch them, saying, "Taste it; it is nice."

"No, no, it will taste bitter in my mouth while I eat it. The devil is telling me to taste it, but I am not going to eat it. I know it is wrong because it is not ours; it is stealing. God is watching us, and He is writing down everything we do." When the owner of the pies came for them and found them gone, she was very disappointed. Later she learned what had happened from the girl who had the victory over the temptation.

* * * * *

Every three months we changed the work schedule for the girls. We had organized work teams, and the team that did the best work for those three months received an award. On one occasion some of the girls washed their floors three times that day to make sure they were kept clean.

* * * * *

In a letter dated December 9, 1950, I described our preparations for Christmas:

> We are busy getting things ready for Christmas besides keeping up with the regular schedule. I have all my gifts bought and wrapped for the children but not for Carrie and the little girl who is to arrive from America on Christmas Day with her father and mother. I had to spend some of my savings in order to buy for all the girls and missionaries, but I know it makes them happy to get things. I made a nightgown for each of the small ones and gave two pairs of nice cotton stockings to each of the older girls. I spent $.96 for each nightgown and about $1.08 for the stockings, so you see that adds up when buying for about forty-five individuals.
>
> We gave a little more to the three girls who have remained as workers after their twentieth birthday. One has been here for over thirty years, the others twenty and sixteen. I gave a pair of bedroom slippers to the oldest one. To the next girl I gave a pretty covered sewing box and the blouse that matched a skirt I had given her in the spring. Carrie Craig and I gave woolen yarn to the youngest one to make a sweater.

* * * * *

The contracts the parents signed when the girls entered the orphanage expired when the girls became twenty. The girls could then remain with the Mission or return to their families. One of our girls who became twenty in April chose to go to her family. She had been a big help to me when she started taking care of the little ones a few months previously. Sophia, who was twenty in January, chose to remain with the Mission. She completed eighth grade with us. After that she acquired her passport and went to Eritrea and helped in the orphanage for a while. She returned to Egypt where she lived the rest of her life.

* * * * *

Jennie had an infected ear when she was two and a half. After a couple shots of penicillin, she improved greatly. When I tried to give her the third shot in the series, she screamed, kicked, and stiffened herself. I gave up after making five attempts.

* * * * *

One of the babies that came to the orphanage I called "my baby." Her mother and a man owned some date palms. One day they were arguing, and the man kicked the woman. It caused the woman and her unborn infant to die. Someone then brought the woman's tiny daughter to Cairo, and I brought her to the orphanage.

The child's name was Labiba, but we often called her Hawawish

because she had come from the village of Hawawish. In one of my letters to my family, I wrote, "My baby has greatly improved. She has rosy cheeks, has gained weight, has a smaller stomach (a large belly signifies malnutrition), and little discharge comes from her ears. She has learned some English words and knows how to kneel for prayer."

* * * * *

While I was working at my desk in July 1951, Carrie and some girls came rushing to my room saying Nargis, one of the younger girls, drank "gas," meaning kerosene. She found the liquid and thought it was safe to drink.

With Labiba on the orphanage roof in 1955 with the Mediterranean Sea in the background

They turned Nargis upside down, and she vomited. Then Carrie and I held her while Isabelle LaRoche gave her some milk to make her vomit again. She seemed to be okay, and we decided not to take her to a hospital. Carrie took her to her room, but when I checked later, I saw she was getting sleepy, so we decided to take her to a doctor. She soon began to lose consciousness even while we talked to her and tried to keep her active. We quickly got a taxi and rushed her to the hospital. They gave her medicine, pumped her stomach, and sent her home. I told Carrie that I hoped her daddy would not come while she was sick. He had not been there since April but would be coming soon to visit her.

During the night Nargis was very sick, and her temperature rose to 104 degrees. The next morning we took her back to the hospital, and they told me to give her 400,000 units of penicillin. While we were at the hospital, the doorbell rang at the orphanage at 7:30, and it was Nargis' daddy to see her. Carrie told him about the incident. Thankfully the Lord undertook and the penicillin checked her fever. She was soon playing as if nothing had happened.

* * * * *

We were blessed and encouraged whenever we learned that some of the girls were strong enough in the Lord to withstand pressure to do wrong and bear a testimony for Christ when they went to spend time with their families. During one summer an older girl went home and was told to wear a piece of old fishing net around her abdomen to prevent an enemy of the family from putting the "evil eye" on her. She refused to wear it and tore up the piece of net, showing her family that such customs were to no avail.

* * * * *

Two of our babies learned words in English more quickly than in Arabic because they came to us before they could talk. They would come to my room and say, "Money, I love you. I love you very much." Another girl said in Arabic, "*Ahibic zay el bahr*," meaning "I love you like the sea," while another said, "*Ahibic zay iddinia*," or "I love you like the world."

* * * * *

During October the two Anglican Churches in Alexandria observed a Harvest Home Festival. In the morning one of the English women from the nearby church brought us baskets of food. About two hours later a taxi brought another English lady who was from the larger church in the heart of the city. She had an abundance of food. That evening a young man brought another basket of fruit that had been missed in the morning.

The orphanage staff and girls enjoyed apples, bananas, pomegranates, dates, and vegetables for several days.

During that same month four of the younger girls got whooping cough. We felt very sorry for them and did our best to give them plenty of nourishing food to prevent them from becoming weak and sickly. As soon as we realized that the girls had whooping cough, everyone received inoculations, which were effective in keeping the whooping cough from spreading. Praise the Lord!

* * * * *

The girls had daily devotions that were held in the largest hallway on the main floor of the orphanage building. The girls who were responsible for preparing the hall for devotions would bring benches and put them along the wall and also put straw mats on the floor. All the girls learned Scripture that they quoted. Then they would blend their voices in giving their praises and petitions to God.

* * * * *

One of the girls that came to the orphanage in the early 1950s was Amalia Rawi. She came from a village near Kafr el Dawar in the Delta. One day when she was nine, she was in the staff dining room where the devil suggested to her that she steal some food. Later she told one of the staff how the devil tempted her and how she gained victory over the temptation. She said, "I told the devil 'No' and ran out and shut the door."

Later Amalia returned to her village when the orphanage was closed in 1956. She continued her studies and eventually became a teacher in a private elementary school. She married, and God blessed their home with several fine children. I was thrilled to find her in her village in 1981 when I visited one of our churches in the Delta.

* * * * *

We were always glad for Christmas to come so

With Amalia and her two children in 1981

that we could celebrate our Savior's birth. Our Egyptian, English, Greek, American, Armenian, and Swiss friends gave us offerings and other gifts. It was a blessed time for the girls as well as for the missionaries.

The children came to my room early on Christmas morning in 1952 and wished me Merry Christmas and gave me their sacrificial gifts. Some of the girls had saved their pennies for months to be able to buy gifts. We gathered together in the living room and sang carols before going to the flat roof to sing for the neighbors. Then it was time to clean the house and have morning devotions. Following that we gave the girls their gifts. It was a joyous time for them. The entire day we were busy welcoming and entertaining visitors. When nighttime came, we were all ready to retire.

It was a delight that same week to have Samuel Doctorian, a young Armenian evangelist from Lebanon who was visiting Egypt, come and speak to us. He also spoke at another place in Alexandria, and we went and heard him. He returned to the orphanage and spoke again. My heart was touched while he preached Bible holiness, which rarely was preached in the Delta.

* * * * *

On November 3, 1953, Jennie had her fifth birthday. A few days later she came to my room and said, "Money, the devil's bad. Can we see the devil?" I told her we could not, and then she asked, "Money, when the earth opens, shall I spit on her (meaning the devil)?" Shortly after that event, Jennie's father, who was a medical doctor, came to take her home with him. Because he was breaking his contract with the orphanage, he was required to pay a sum of money before Jennie could leave. He had not visited her on a regular basis, and she did not know him. When he took her, she cried as if her heart would break. It was not only a difficult time for Jennie but also for the staff and the other girls in the orphanage. We were unable to maintain contact with her.

* * * * *

In December 1954 three missionaries arrived to help us at the orphanage. They were John and Marian Etzweiler and John's sister Betty. What a great help they were in caring for so many girls!

One of my responsibilities was to see that each girl had decent shoes to wear. It was especially important to have good shoes for Easter weekend and *Shem el Nessim*, a national holiday on Easter Monday.

Shem el Nessim means smell the fresh air. I began by checking the large box in the storeroom where we kept extra shoes that accumulated from donations or that the girls had outgrown. Some of the shoes could be repaired, and one year I found twenty-one usable pairs that needed to be taken to the repairman. However, every year we needed to buy some new ones.

Orphanage girls with missionaries John and Marian Etzweiler, Carrie Craig, Betty Etzweiler, and me

* * * * *

Wednesday was our evening for recreation. We took time to play games with the girls before bedtime. Then I would go to my room and spend some time in private devotions before retiring for a needed night of rest.

* * * * *

In April 1955 through the end of May, twenty-two of our girls had measles and sixteen had chicken pox. It required extra care with as many as twelve being sick at one time.

A few months later we accepted a three-month-old baby whose mother had died when she was born. They named her Hazina, which means sorrowful, but the staff changed her name to Mae.

A Typical Day for Zuzu

About 5:30 a.m. I hear echoes from a distant room and then the noise of feet running on the wooden stairs. This is the usual noise as the girls begin stirring every morning. Let us follow Zuzu, a nine-year-old girl, as she goes through her daily routine. Her Egyptian name is Isis Hanna.

Zuzu, or Isis Hanna, who was in the orphanage for several years

Zuzu begins her day by kneeling by her bed and asking God for His care and help. She then puts on her play clothes and runs downstairs in her bare feet to the bathroom for her morning cleanup. She returns to her bedroom, removes her comb from the pocket that has her name on the homemade muslin comb holder, and combs her black curly hair. If you look closely, you will notice that her hair and brown eyes are like most Egyptians. Zuzu knows we are watching her. She bows her head because she is bashful and then raises it, her eyes sparkling with life.

Because Zuzu is nine years old, she is a **big** girl, which means she is old enough to be assigned a daily chore. In size she is petite. For this month and the next two, every morning she will sweep and wash the floor of the bedroom where fourteen of the young girls sleep. The orphanage personnel cannot afford to buy a broom and scrub bucket for each cleaning girl, so this clever girl plays a trick and hides the broom and bucket in the yard by the woodpile. This assures that she will be first to use them. After Zuzu makes her bed, she darts to the yard to retrieve her working tools. She is really clever for her age.

In a short time Zuzu completes her chore, and she is ready for family prayers at 7:00. When the bell rings, she joins the other girls in a line. They enter the large hall and sit on grass mats with their legs crossed while the older girls sit on benches against the wall. We are reading the New Testament in Arabic, but only the older girls read while the younger ones sit quietly and listen. Prayers of thanksgiving and petitions for guidance are offered to the Lord. Because Zuzu's task is already completed, she now has a half hour of free time. Some days she decides to be a little helper and goes to Carrie's room to help care for our year-old baby.

Did you hear another bell? It is 8:00 and time for breakfast. With the other girls Zuzu files into the dining room and takes her place to enjoy a dish of *foul madamas* or cooked fava beans, one of Egypt's staple foods, with salad oil and a half loaf of *baladi* bread, which also serves as a spoon. This bread is more like a soft tortilla than a piece of bread. She is also happy for a cup of buffalo milk, the common kind of milk in Egypt.

At 8:30 the bell rings again, and Zuzu gets in line with fifteen other girls her age to go to the schoolroom. She is a little trickster like many of the other younger girls. This morning she tries to get by with putting her school dress over her play dress rather than changing. One of the workers makes her return to her room and change.

The furnishings in the classrooms consist of two large tables and four benches; some were made from the wooden crates in which the missionaries shipped their supplies from America. The blackboards are pieces of wood painted with special black paint and placed on large easels.

Miss Alice, one of the older girls who remained to help at the Mission, brings the girls to order and reads the Arabic Bible. Zuzu is in *Senna oula Roda*, which is similar to our first grade. She should be in second grade but did not learn well enough last year and is repeating first grade. She spends her morning learning to read and write in Arabic. She speaks some English but cannot read or write it. Zuzu writes her lessons and notes in small notebooks. At 10:30 she has a half-hour recess and then returns to school until 12:30.

After school Zuzu changes her clothes for playtime. She gets a group together in the yard, and they form two teams and play Lemonade. With excitement the game begins: "Here we come." "Where're you from?" "New York." "What's your trade?" "Lemonade." "Get to your work and show us something if you're not afraid."

One team imitates a certain type of work, and the other team guesses what they are doing. When the team guesses correctly, they chase the other team, and any tagged individual becomes part of their team. Team roles are then reversed and play continues until all are on one side. Some girls tire of that game and run to play tag, climb trees, or play ball until the dinner bell rings.

Today their dinner is *moulakhia*, the leaf of a plant cooked with buffalo meat and garlic and served over Egyptian-style cooked rice. This time Zuzu has a spoon to eat her meal and again receives a half loaf of *baladi* bread. She is delighted to have a special treat—a few fresh dates that are in season.

"All work and no play make Jack a dull boy," but all play and no work make Jack a lazy boy, so both must go together. Today Zuzu straightens the clothes on her closet shelf, and the girl who is supervising her makes sure that she folds her clothes neatly after mending any that are torn. Zuzu is quite young for this task, but she learns to take care of her own clothes this way.

Zuzu enjoys another play period and goes outside to play in the fresh air and sunshine. Sometimes she is mischievous and goes from room to room and gets into trouble. At 4:00 she returns to her classroom for a study period with Miss Alice.

When her studies are completed, Zuzu plays indoors because the breezes from the Mediterranean Sea make the evenings chilly. She likes to run and spin like a top. Carrie calls her "my little spider."

At 6:00 Zuzu skips to the dining room for her half loaf of *baladi* bread and white Egyptian cheese which she eats at a small low table with the other younger girls. At 7:00 the bell rings for devotions. Tonight they recite Psalm 1 and Psalm 46 in English. Some evenings they recite Scripture in Arabic. After devotions it is bedtime for Zuzu and all the other girls under fourteen.

Zuzu scampers to the corner of her bedroom where she finds the pink flannel nightgown that has her name on it. She likes to go without shoes after school even in the winter when it is cold, so it is necessary for her to wash her feet before going to bed. She sleeps with Emily in a twin bed, one at the head and the other at the foot. The two girls carefully remove their pretty spread, fold it to keep it nice, and settle down to sleep under their sheet and blanket in the large bedroom.

Isis Hanna, or Zuzu, enjoys a good place to call home, and she is thankful for the care and concern the missionaries show. Most of all she is glad to learn about Jesus and His love for her.

Experiences Beyond the Orphanage Walls

Two months after I arrived in Egypt, two of the orphanage girls accompanied me to Sohag, Upper Egypt. We first stopped for two days in Cairo, the largest city in Africa. There we visited the sphinx and the pyramids, the huge ancient monuments in the desert near Cairo. A guide took us to places recently excavated where we saw mummies and tombs.

Train travel was very amusing and sometimes frustrating in Egypt. There were first-, second-, and third-class compartments. First class was nice but expensive. The girls and I rode third class, which was the most economical. One of the native pastors helped us board the train at Cairo. He jumped onto the train, as many people did, while it was coming into the station and found seats for us. A young woman who had come to see us leave handed our luggage through the window to the pastor while we scrambled to get to our seats. She had been reared in the orphanage and had become a registered nurse.

As we traveled, men came through our car selling hot tea, peanuts, tangerines, candy, cheese, bread, and boiled eggs. Because proper sanitation was lacking, we ate or drank only what we took with us, along with tangerines we bought from the vendors. We traveled in the express train which went about three hundred miles in six and a half hours. Our coach had no glass windows but only shutters. It was my first trip, and I wanted to see the country; therefore, we opened our shutters. With the scenery we had to take the dust. When we reached Sohag, we were covered with dust and had to cleanup before eating supper.

Our Mission was conducting a three-day convention in a village, and it was attended by several hundred individuals from the surrounding villages. We were able to go to one evening service. God spoke to hearts during that service. Our pastors and orphanage girls worked with the seekers, and some found victory.

After our visit in Sohag, we returned to Alexandria by train. We soon learned that many times the trains were so crowded that people jumped from the windows to exit. Pushing, scampering, and running were part of the "game" when riding trains in Egypt.

* * * * *

Hanem, Harriette, Eskandra and I went to visit our new work in Abou el Matamir and nearby Asbit es Saieda on a Saturday in early 1950. One woman had prayed for three years for a holiness church to be established in Abou el Matamir.

At the time of our visit, the Mission was renting a house in Abou el Matamir for services and living quarters for Pastor Musod and his family. The pastor's family received us cordially and gave us something to eat after we had rested for a while. We then walked to Asbit es Saieda where we had a short service. They sang while I played the trumpet; someone led in prayer, and then we invited the people to the service in Abou el Matamir on Sunday.

When we returned to Abou el Matamir, we made a house visit and then held an unannounced service. Neighbors heard the music and came. Sunday morning the meeting place was almost filled with those eager to hear God's Word. In the afternoon we returned to Asbit es Saieda and visited in a number of homes. Our hearts were touched as we sensed the spiritual emptiness of their lives.

In one of the homes, Ageeb, a farmhand, told us that he believed he was possessed with an evil spirit. He said that he had to leave the worship services because he could not bear to hear the name of Jesus. In the middle of the night, he would awaken feeling as though someone were choking him. We told him to repeat the name of Jesus and plead His blood, but he would not do it. We explained to him that Satan must flee at the name of Jesus.

The evening service was conducted in one of the homes because it was cold for the people to go to the meetings in Abou el Matamir at night in winter. The women and children sat on the floor on straw mats, and the men sat on the seats, listening to the message as Harriette Harp brought the Bread of Life to them. It began to rain, and the road got too muddy for us to return to Abou el Matamir where we had our clothes and drinking water. We were very thankful for the oranges they gave us, which helped to quench our thirst. One of the girls of the home was engaged to be married to her cousin, and she had a lot of new dresses. She loaned one to each of us four visiting ladies for the night.

The people were very glad we had come and said, "It is as if He were here." When we left the next morning, some of them followed us to the edge of their village, begging us to return soon.

On a later visit Ageeb was in the service, and the demon caused him to injure his leg until it began to bleed. Musod prayed, and he became calm, and we were able to resume the meeting. The Scripture tells us that some demons do not come out of a person except by prayer and fasting. Musod decided to follow the Scripture and fasted and prayed for several days. Thank the Lord, Ageeb was delivered and was able to participate in the services and hear the name of Jesus without being tormented anymore. He sought God for salvation and became a believer. Our God is stronger than Satan and all the forces of evil.

During another visit to Abou el Matamir, the leader read from God's Word and exhorted in an evening service. Then he asked for testimonies, and a small boy rose from his seat, radiant with joy and testified, "I thank the Lord because He saved me. I was a naughty boy, but the Lord saved me and helps me."

A young man who had been saved recently testified. "I thank the Lord because He brought me back to the fold. I wandered in the wilderness so many years without rest or comfort. I used to be a very wicked boy and was lost in sin, but the Lord brought me back. I praise the Lord because I am saved. I am glad for our church here. I ask God's blessings to be on the church."

* * * * *

In March we again visited a village near Alexandria. During our previous visit a Coptic man died. Now we were visiting his widow who was mourning Egyptian style, which included not wearing shoes for forty days. The widow's son was trying to get her to break with some of those customs, but it was difficult for her to change. Later we shared the Bible story of Nicodemus with a group of people in one of the nearby homes. God met with us in a gracious way, and hearts were touched.

A different custom existed in Upper Egypt during times of mourning. There they believed they should not go to church for one year after the death of a family member for fear people would say they did not love that person.

By April the weather was getting quite warm in Alexandria. The cement tile floors in our rooms helped to keep the temperature a little cooler. However, the extreme heat in Upper Egypt forced all our missionaries from there to join us in Alexandria for five months. Some of them helped with the work at the orphanage while others were engaged in women's work and church activities.

* * * * *

Thomas and Edith Jackson came to Egypt in 1908 but were forced to return to the States during World War I. In February 1916 Thomas returned to Egypt, and his wife followed him nine months later. Thomas died on July 3, 1921, from a spinal affliction and was buried in Alexandria. Edith chose to remain in the land of her calling after her husband's death and was working in Upper Egypt when I arrived in 1949.

Edith labored in Egypt for thirty-four consecutive years without a furlough. Her family had sent her money on two occasions to come home, but she used it for the work in Egypt. In early 1950 she moved from Sohag to Alexandria with plans to retire and return to America. Isabelle LaRoche was leaving for furlough, and the two ladies were to sail together. In July Edith became ill with a liver and heart condition that left her heart very weak. A doctor was called, and he recommended that she go to a hospital for intravenous shots. She did not want to go, but on the eleventh of July, she consented. On Saturday, July 15, 1950, at the age of seventy-five, she passed away. During her illness she never complained but was resigned to the will of God. After her husband's death, Edith expressed a desire to be buried near him when she died. God granted her that desire.

The vice-consul came to seal Edith's few personal effects and saw that she had only one Egyptian pound, the equivalent of $2.88. He said, "She must have been a devoted person to leave just that much behind." It was my privilege to know Edith for a few months and to be challenged by her dedicated life.

* * * * *

Una, one of our teenage orphan girls, went with me to do some shopping in downtown Alexandria one fall day in 1950. She was my interpreter. I saw some apples priced 16 *piasters* for an *oka*, which is two and three-fourth pounds. Carrie was very fond of apples, so I considered buying some. We noticed that all the apples had bad spots on them. The vendor then showed us apples for 21 *piasters*. We told him we would buy them for 17 *piasters*. He was not willing, so we began to leave. He called to us and agreed. Una picked the apples we wanted, he weighed them, and we paid for them. When we got home, we had a bag of rotten apples. He was so sly that he exchanged the bags without us noticing. There was no need to return them because the vendor would make a big fuss and not give us good apples.

* * * * *

Carrie and I spent my first Thanksgiving Day in Egypt with the Presbyterian missionaries in Alexandria. We had a lovely time together and enjoyed the turkey dinner. I inquired about a good Arabic teacher, and they suggested one they knew. Miss Weed, a Presbyterian missionary, made the arrangements, and I met the teacher, Mounir Faragalla, in early December. He was a young man who worked in a bank in Alexandria and had two afternoons free each week to teach me.

When we began the first lesson, he said, *"Lazim ta calami Arabi a la toule,"* which means "It is necessary to speak Arabic immediately." He spoke to me in Arabic, and I was to answer him in Arabic if I knew how. If he said anything I did not understand, then I was to say, *"Ana mish fahma,"* which means "I do not understand" or *"Oul mara tania, minfudlak,"* which means "Say it again, please." Then he would tell me in English what he said. He gave me a textbook which did not contain one English word!

* * * * *

The next year I became seriously ill in August. The Swiss doctor we usually contacted was on vacation in Europe, and a nurse recommended Dr. Vasilaris, a Greek doctor. When he came and examined me, he thought that I had typhoid fever. Blood tests indicated that I did not, but I did have an intestinal infection. He prescribed medicine; I began to improve, and my temperature dropped. However, some days later on my birthday, I had a nervous collapse and felt that I would not survive.

The doctor came again and gave me a shot, but my condition stayed the same. I was unable to sleep that night, and the next morning I told Carrie that I did not think I would live through the day. I was so weak that they had to feed and care for me. The missionaries gathered in my room for prayer, and God definitely touched me. By Monday I felt well enough to receive visitors, and the children gave me my birthday gifts. That night I had a relapse, and the doctor was summoned. He prescribed a tonic and injections for me that I had to purchase. I went to his office by streetcar on the appointed days to receive the shots.

About a week later I had another relapse and asked Harriette to spend the night with me. She agreed to stay, and I regained some strength. A few days later after a strenuous day of activity, which included some bookkeeping, I retired for the night. Numbers rolled around in my head. I was weary yet sleep evaded me. It was then that the Lord said, "If you will get out of bed and kneel by your chair and pray, I will heal you." I knew it was the voice of my precious Savior, and I obeyed. I became aware of His touch. Although it was late that night and the girls were sleeping, I slipped from my room and went through the hall to Carrie's room and shared with her what God had done. We rejoiced together and thanked the Lord for His healing touch.

I was to have more injections at the doctor's office, and I had tonic left. The next day I asked Carrie, "What do you think I should do about my medications?"

"To strengthen your faith, I think it would be better if you quit taking them," Carrie wisely replied. I threw the tonic away and stopped going to the doctor's office for the injections.

A few months later we called the doctor to come to the orphanage to give the children inoculations. The doctor looked at me and commented,

"You still have some of your shots at my office."

Isabelle LaRoche, one of our missionaries from Upper Egypt who was visiting with us, replied, "The Great Physician healed her." He made no further comment, and I never returned to complete the treatment. **Praise the Lord!**

Isabelle LaRoche, Carrie Craig, and me on the balcony of the orphanage building

* * * * *

According to the custom in Egypt during my years there, especially in the villages, the mother found a husband for her daughter and a wife for her son. Often the mother did not look for a man with good qualities but rather for one who owned a house and some land. One of our orphan girls who was twenty chose to stay and help in the orphanage. She asked for a leave of absence to go to visit her family for a while. Her mother found a young man to whom she wanted to give her daughter in marriage. The young man and his family promised the girl that they would buy her much gold and treat her well.

The girl replied to the man and his family that she had been taught that it was wrong to wear gold. He told her she would only need to wear it the first year of their marriage. She was courageous and told him that she would not marry him under those conditions. He was a strict member of the Coptic Church, and she indicated to him that she would not return to the Coptic practices. Her family left the choice with her, and she held to her convictions. She was fortunate because many girls were compelled to marry whether or not they liked the man and his ways. She returned to Alexandria and continued helping at the orphanage.

★ ★ ★ ★ ★

Victor Glenn, director of Faith Mission, visited Egypt in January 1952. All our missionaries gathered at the orphanage for business meetings and special services. During one of our services, Harriette Harp and Isabelle LaRoche were ordained into the ministry. We certainly enjoyed the fellowship during those days even though it involved extra work.

★ ★ ★ ★ ★

One day in May, Hanem, my interpreter, and I were stranded about twenty miles from Alexandria. The bus had a flat tire and there was no spare. The driver continued on the flat tire to the nearest village where we waited an hour and a half for another bus. I read my Bible and talked with other stranded passengers. I thought of all the letters I needed to write, so I bought some paper for one and a half cents and started to write.

In one of my letters, I described a variety of interesting sights near me. To my left was a meat shop. It looked like a little old shanty. The meat hung on a rope in front of the shop and was wrapped with a cloth. Flies were everywhere. Buyers came and chose the piece of meat they wanted, and it was cut for them.

In front of me was a vegetable stand. The roof was made of burlap bags sewed together and supported by a pole. The vendor was a little boy, selling tomatoes and cucumbers.

I saw a man going from door to door selling kerosene. He had a horse pulling a wagon with a large drum filled with kerosene, called "gas" in Egypt, and gasoline is called benzene. Kerosene was the chief fuel used for cooking in the city. In the villages they used mostly dried chips made with animal dung and straw.

Small shops sold hot tea and Coca Cola, Pepsi Cola, and similar drinks, but there was no ice available. When one did not have clean drinking water, even warm drinks were refreshing. Men sat in front of the shops talking and drinking tea or a soft drink.

Beyond the meat shop and behind me, I saw fields with cotton stalks in the rich black soil. In that hot afternoon sun, it looked refreshing because the water was flowing into the irrigation ditches that were arranged systematically throughout the fields, and the ground was drinking the water of the Nile River, which is the life of Egypt. There were yellow fields of wheat ready to harvest. In the far distance grew stately date palms, and in the foreground I saw a few cows grazing and a boy hoeing in a cotton field.

At that point I was interrupted by the call, "The next bus is coming." We obtained second-class seats to the next town where we changed buses to go to Alexandria. The distance from Abou el Matamir where we started that morning to Alexandria is forty miles. With good connections it usually took about two hours, but because of difficulties it took us much longer. By 3:30 in the afternoon, I was getting hungry because I had not eaten since breakfast. I heard a boy calling the names of the foods he was selling—cheese, bread, and *tamia*, a little fried cake made of ground fava beans, parsley, seasonings, and eggs. Everything sounded good, but I feared they were not clean enough for me to eat.

Hanem and I made it home safely and thanked the Lord for His hand upon us. Many times our plans did not materialize, but we trusted in the wisdom of our heavenly Father.

Chapter 4

Visiting Eritrea and Furlough
1955-1958

My first furlough was near, and I was looking forward to seeing my family. Six years had passed quickly from the time I had arrived in Egypt.

Besides the work in Egypt, Faith Mission had a work in Eritrea, and I had a desire to visit that work before returning to the States. Isabelle LaRoche agreed to travel with me. Our traveling would be mostly overland by train, beginning at Alexandria and going to Shallal in southern Egypt; then by steamer on the Nile River to Wadi Halfa, Sudan; again by train to Khartoum, the capital of Sudan; and finally by plane to Asmara, Eritrea.

Traveling by Train in Egypt

Isabelle and I left Alexandria on Tuesday, August 30, 1955, and went to Cairo. We visited the home of Pastor Fawzy Ibrahim where we had a supper invitation. Shortly after the meal, we went to the train station to get the 8:00 train to Shallal. Oh, it was crowded! With an anticipated sixteen-hour ride, we endeavored to get a seat in one of the women's compartments of a second-class coach. In Egypt and Sudan the coaches were divided into compartments, some for men and some for women, with second-class compartments accommodating eight people. We rushed down the aisles searching for seats and discovered that the train was full. When we reached the last coach, we found that several men were in the women's compartment. I politely asked the men to move, but they would not. Isabelle arrived with her bags and said that she was going to get a train attendant to arrange our six pieces of luggage. When the men heard that, they quickly arranged our bags for fear of being moved.

One of the men, an employee in the telegraph office, was traveling to Minia with his wife and little girl. They were Christians and proved to be nice company during the three and a half hours that we rode together. Another man was the judge from Sohag. Before he departed, he gave me a fly swisher, which proved to be useful. After he got off the train at 4:00 a.m., we had enough room to relax and get a little sleep. Our other companions were an elderly man and his three young children going to Aswan.

Because it seldom rains in Egypt, traveling by train was always a dusty experience. In the morning we went to another coach to get water to wash our faces.

As we traveled through the southern part of Egypt, we saw the many graceful palm trees that dotted the area and learned that raising and drying dates was one of their main industries. We also noticed the extremely thin animals and the poor crops. Only at flood stage did the Nile River overflow its banks in that area in contrast to the well-irrigated lower delta areas. Consequently, crops were planted only once a year as compared to three times in the other areas. Near Aswan and Shallal there were long stretches of arid land with scarcely any vegetation.

At Aswan many passengers disembarked, including the elderly man with his three children. The trainmen filled the water tanks, and again we were able to wash and refresh ourselves. After the train left Aswan, our coach was empty except for us and a young Greek man who was born in Cairo. He was studying dentistry in the University of Athens, Greece, and was on his way to visit his brother, who was a dentist in Khartoum.

Sailing Up the Nile River

About noon we reached Shallal, which was the end of the rail line. A porter showed us his badge and asked if he could carry our luggage from the train to the customs office and later to our room on the steamer. We agreed on an amount for his services, and he was a great help. After we cleared customs, Isabelle watched our luggage while I went to the

floating ticket office to purchase our tickets. I was surprised to learn that the Sudan Agency in Cairo had failed to record our reservations, but thankfully, there was a room on the auxiliary boat, which was a small barge fastened to one side of the steamer.

A steamer on the Nile River

Our neighbors in the room on one side of us were two Egyptian servant girls whose employers were on the steamer going to Sudan. The *farash*, the man who kept the barge clean, occupied the room on the other side of us. He made our trip more pleasant by accommodating us at various times. Next door to him was the young Greek man whom we had met on the train.

We were disappointed with our room because it was hot and without water, and there was no way to lock the door. I returned to the ticket office and spoke to the station master, and he assured me that all rooms were without locks. Isabelle and I were able to get some fairly clean water from the water jar at the end of the barge and managed to washup and felt much better.

The Greek man came and asked if we would like to have some "cocoa." We followed him and were amused when he stopped at the shower room and showed us the cocoa. What we saw was the Nile River water at flood stage coming from the faucets. Although that water was not used for drinking, some of the passengers did not mind using it for showers, but we knew we should not take the risk because it had harmful microbes.

For our trip to Wadi Halfa, we took some nonperishable food and supplemented it with cooked meals that we purchased on the steamer. Traveling on the barge seemed almost like camping—narrow quarters, bunk beds, and camp-style eating. One of our biggest problems was getting good drinking water. First class on the steamer had it, but we were in second class. We were thankful that the *farash* was able to get good water for us from the steamer. We wished we had brought a gallon thermos instead of a pint-size one because of the constant desire for water as we sailed farther south into the tropics.

Although the sailing was smooth, I could not sleep the first night. As I was leaving my upper berth, I accidentally stepped on Isabelle in the lower one. She moaned but continued sleeping. After awhile I went back to bed and slept.

To help pass the hours, I did some crocheting. I also enjoyed watching the settlements along the scantily cultivated section of land beside the river beyond Shallal and wondered why people lived there. The *farash* told me that before the Aswan Dam (not the Aswan High Dam) was built in the late nineteenth century, a large section along the Nile was cultivated. When the Dam was built, the people were paid for their land, but they chose to build their houses higher on the banks of the river and remain, even though their living conditions worsened. Many of the men left their families to go to Lower Egypt or Sudan to work, but a few men always remained to protect the women and children.

The only means of travel for those people was on the Nile River. It was likely that most of them never saw an automobile or train. The *farash* told us that they obtained their sugar and cooking oil as rations from the government. The rations were deposited in each village for distribution to the local residents. The people could buy food from a sailing grocery store. They received medical help from a doctor who traveled from village to village. One time we saw his boat anchored by the riverbank at one of the villages.

Later that day as I was reading a handbook on Eritrea, the Greek student, who was studying for his final exams, brought his dentistry books to Isabelle and me and shared some interesting illustrations about teeth. He was very friendly and helped us greatly by occasionally jumping from the barge to the steamer to get us drinking water in our thermos.

While we were on deck in the early evening of the second day, we noticed something different about the sun. It was to our left, and we were supposed to be going south toward Sudan. We concluded that there was a lengthy northern bend in the Nile River, and for hours we sailed north. What a lovely sunset we beheld! It nestled among the barren western hills and left behind it a golden glow accenting the lovely green islands of corn where some large birds were resting. In the evening the moon shone with its glittering rays across the gently rippling water. It was a pleasant day.

We enjoyed conversing with some dark-skinned Christians who were on board. One young man from Sudan told of his conversion from hoodlumism. Now he was returning from a visit to Egypt and told us of his desire to live for the Lord back home.

When we awoke on Friday morning, the steamer was anchored along the western bank, and we learned that we had been there since 2:00 a.m. At that location we had a close look at Egypt's frontier people. How thin and dark they were! As we watched them, I wondered if they ever had heard the name of Jesus. They brought melons and dates and sold them extremely cheap to the passengers. After the long stop for repairs, already the third one on the trip, we started southward again. I knew it was southward because the sun was to our left in the morning. We did not travel far until the steamer was forced to stop again for several hours for more repairs.

Earlier Isabelle saw a woman on the barge who she thought was one of our former orphan girls. The next time we saw her, we asked her if she was Moneera, and she was. She was traveling with her half brother and his family. He was a teacher at Atbara, Sudan. We were happy to see someone we knew and to get acquainted with Moneera's relatives.

That afternoon the *farash* told Isabelle and me that we were in the area where crocodiles inhabited the Nile. We watched for a while, and then he decided that there were none that day and walked away. We lingered a little longer and were rewarded by seeing one on the bank bathing in the sun.

Early in the evening we stopped at Abu Simbel, 175 miles south of Aswan. We were allowed to leave the steamer to visit a gigantic temple carved out of a limestone rock mountain and dedicated to Amon, the sun god of ancient Egypt, and Ramses II who reigned from about 1304 B.C. to 1237 B.C. The front of that imposing temple had four 67-foot-high carved statues of Ramses in a seated position with wives and children at his feet.

The building of the Aswan High Dam began in 1960 and threatened to completely and permanently cover the renowned temple at Abu Simbel. Ninety countries cooperated with the Egyptian government to disassemble the monument and move it to a higher location. It took 2,000 workers about eight years at a cost of $36 million to cut the temple into more than 1,000 numbered and labeled pieces, transport them, and reassemble them where they overlook Lake Nasser, which was created by the High Dam project.

From Abu Simbel the steamer proceeded to Balana. There it stopped, and the passengers could buy fruit.

Experiences in Sudan

Saturday morning before sunrise our steamer reached Wadi Halfa, Sudan. The passengers had to wait to clear customs because people on a train from Khartoum en route to Egypt were going through customs. When it was our turn, we were given a landing card that gave us permission to go into the small town. Our top priority was to buy something to quench our thirst and some bread for the next part of our journey. After we returned to the barge, the Greek man asked if we had checked our reservations for the train to Khartoum. Hurriedly we went to check and found that we had none. Seeing our predicament, the headman of the Sudan Railways was successful in getting accommodations for us.

After dinner we went through customs again and were soon in our assigned compartment on the train where we waited for our 5:30 departure. Our traveling companions were two Sudanese women with their young nephew, two Egyptian girls, and a Sudanese-Egyptian teacher from Khartoum. We had a nice time together while we traveled the 18 hours to Atbara.

The train stopped at ten stations through the desert between Wadi Halfa and Abu Hamed, a ride of about twelve hours. We saturated our wash cloths with water and put them on our faces trying to get relief from the heat and dust. Sleeping was difficult that night because our compartment was crowded. When the train stopped at the stations, many passengers disembarked and stretched for about twenty minutes. When the whistle blew for departure, the passengers slowly came on board because they knew the train started gradually.

People had their wares for sale at the stations. They called, "Tea with milk, plain tea," as they brought the tea pots and small glasses. Others were selling hand-woven baskets, mats, fruit, toothbrushes that were made from small branches of a special tree, head scarves, and men's little caps called *tobagas*. Because it was Sunday, we did not buy anything.

About noon we reached Atbara where many of the passengers disembarked, including the two Sudanese women and their nephew, who changed trains for Port Sudan. We bade farewell to those with whom we had made acquaintance. During the twelve-hour ride to Khartoum, we were thankful to have more space to stretch and get some rest.

Near midnight we arrived in Khartoum, and Melad Girgis, a cousin of one of our orphan girls, met us and took us to a hotel. We wanted a room that was not too expensive, so we had to be content with a lack of amenities. Our door could not be locked from the outside, but we learned that in Sudan things were safe, which was not true in Egypt where we had to keep everything locked.

Monday morning we went to check our plane reservations to Asmara, Eritrea, for the morning of the 7th. We also made reservations for our return trip to Egypt by train a week later, and we were able to obtain half-fare rates. We then sent a telegram to the missionaries in Keren, Eritrea, notifying them of our arrival time. After a lovely chicken dinner at our hotel, we went to our room to rest. In the evening we went downtown again so Isabelle could get her sunglasses fixed. We found a Jewish shop of some renown where she left her glasses and returned later for them.

On Tuesday evening Melad's friend took us to the airlines office to check in our luggage for our morning flight. After that he took us to see the governor's palace and the place where the Blue Nile and White Nile rivers join to flow north into Egypt. We stopped at a local shop and bought postcards and souvenirs. For our return trip we purchased some groceries, which we left with Melad. That evening we spoke with Melad and his friend about spiritual things; they both showed interest and wanted prayer.

Enjoying Eritrea

The Ethiopian Airlines bus came to our hotel at 6:30 on Wednesday morning. It also stopped at two other hotels for passengers and the crew. At the airport we quickly went through immigration and then had breakfast at the airline's expense. We waited in the lounge until the call came to board the Douglas DC-3 twin-engine prop plane. It was the first time for Isabelle and me to fly, and we were excited. After an uneventful two-hour flight, we landed on the dirt runway at Tessenie, Eritrea, for a brief stop. A short flight took us to the airport near the capital city of Asmara.

As our plane taxied to the terminal, we could see our missionaries—Carrie Boyer and the Lewis Jones family. After we cleared customs and exchanged greetings, we went to the home of Lewis and Donna Jones and their children, David, Edith, James, and Thomas, where we had an enjoyable time and a delicious meal. After we had finished eating, the Theodore Meckes family and Zettie Finch stopped to greet us and visited briefly before they returned to the orphanage in Decamere where they worked.

Most of the afternoon we spent taking care of travel business. Lewis took us to the immigration office to register, then to the Sudan Agency to apply for transit visas for our return trip, and to the airlines office to make reservations for our return flight on the thirteenth. Later we returned to the immigration office to get exit visas from Eritrea. That evening Harry and Blanche Atkins from our high school in Keren showed slides of Ethiopia and their trip to the Holy Land in 1952.

The next morning the Lewis Jones family, Carrie, Isabelle, and I left for Keren about fifty miles from Asmara. There we met missionaries Fred and Marilyn Cromer, Joe and Martha Moutz, and Marilyn Van Kuiken. Because they were in a staff meeting, we visited briefly and continued our journey to the lowland station of Agordat. The weather was definitely warmer in that area. Summertime temperatures can reach 120 degrees.

While an Eritrean woman prepared supper, Carrie showed Isabelle and me the orphanage and the outside clay ovens used for baking native bread. In the evening Lewis took us to see the property the Mission wanted to buy in order to move from their rented quarters. He then drove up a knoll where we could see the town of Agordat. That night we slept well after an exhausting day.

The next morning we visited the home of one of our first Christian Eritrean couples; both were teachers in the mission school. In the afternoon we visited an Arab family who gave us a hearty welcome. They were Moslems who, like many other Moslems, believed in the virgin birth of Jesus. The father was happy because I could speak Arabic, and during our conversation I spoke to them about Christ.

On Saturday morning we left Agordat to go to the mission station in Ducumbia where Rosella Hughes was working. She was the only missionary there because Carrie, who had been on that station, was preparing for furlough. It was quite an adventure to travel to Ducumbia. The first part of the road was blacktopped, but then it became gravel. At Barentu we left the main road and turned onto a trail that crossed several riverbeds and wound through wooded areas. We saw a few gazelles and many guinea fowl. The missionaries living in Ducumbia went to Barentu to get their mail, and sometimes during the rainy season, it was two weeks before they were able to go.

Our group reached the primitive village of Ducumbia after a two-hour drive. Because recent rains had damaged some of the buildings the Mission was renting, we found Rosella living in a house with mud walls, a dirt roof with grass growing on it, and consisting of only one room. Her door and window curtains were made from cheesecloth to keep out the insects. She told us that recently she had killed a snake by her door.

While Rosella prepared dinner, some of us went to the marketplace where I bought a souvenir. Close to the mission station, a woman let me take a picture of her *tukul*. We were shocked when Lewis called to us and said, "Maybe you ladies do not know where you are, but you are at the Ducumbia saloon." That woman sold home-brewed beer.

A typical *tukul* in the lowlands of Eritrea

Lewis, Carrie, and Amare, the Eritrean who served as interpreter for the Ducumbia station, took Isabelle and me to see the nearby Gash River. We had heard about the snakes in that area, and were afraid and alert while we walked past the tall grass. Lewis and Carrie went ahead, and we stayed with Amare who was asking us questions about Egypt. Suddenly I heard a noise in the grass. I jumped and let out a fearful sound, only to learn that Lewis had thrown something into the grass to play a trick on us.

After dinner we drove to see the land purchased by the Mission where a house was being built for the missionaries. Later they added a clinic and a schoolhouse on that property. Carrie wanted to visit some of the pagan families, and Isabelle and I accompanied her. We walked on another path through tall, thick grass, and again I was fearful of snakes being present, but my fears slowly subsided. The families that Carrie wanted to visit were working in their fields. However, we saw a small arbor where they some-times had services.

On our return to Rosella's one-room house, we saw a woman who had her hair fixed into two twists. Each twist was filled with white grease. We tried to take her picture, but she would not

Me, Isabelle LaRoche, Carrie Boyer, Rosella Hughes, and Donna Jones in Ducumbia

permit us because she said that we were trying to take her spirit. When we offered her money, she readily consented. After we took some pictures, we asked her to go with us to the mission house to get the money. On the way I spoke to her about God through the interpreter. The woman indicated she knew something about Jesus because she attended the services held by the missionaries. I gave her 30 cents in Ethiopian money, which was a day's wage, and she was happy.

Later we visited the chief of police who was an Arab from Sudan. I conversed with him in Arabic, and we had a good visit. That evening our group returned to Agordat. Rosella went with us to attend a special meeting that Leonard Hinds was to have with the missionaries. When we arrived, the children were in their evening service. I attended even though I did not understand the language. It was a joy to know that the gospel seed was being sown in that lowland area.

Near midnight we heard the beating of drums and cautiously went to investigate. From a distance we could see men dancing in a circle to the beat of the drums. Some women joined the men while other women were preparing food. All the activity was preparation for a wedding and the feast that would follow.

Our group returned to Keren the next day. We visited with the missionaries and some of the students. After dinner we drove to a hilltop where we had a better view of the town. Soon it began to rain, and we returned to the mission compound. It rained so hard that we had to wait in the vehicle before we could go into the house.

After the rain stopped, Carrie took us to visit an Arab family. I spoke in Arabic and told them about the Lord. They were pleased when I sang a song in Arabic. Before we left, the family served us tea, and we had prayer with them. That evening we attended the service in the chapel.

Monday morning our group returned to Asmara. Isabelle, Carrie who was planning to go overland with us, and I went directly to the Sudan Agency to get our transit visas. We were surprised to find the Agency closed until we realized that day was the Coptic New Year. The Joneses helped us make arrangements to meet the secretary at her home at 4:00 p.m. to get our visas. Because we had several hours before we could meet her, we went to the home of Mr. Drowdy, an American engineer who was working for the American government in Asmara. His wife kindly prepared a noon meal for us, and we visited until time to return to the home of the secretary.

When Isabelle, Carrie, and I arrived at the secretary's house, she informed us that no telegram had come from Sudan granting Carrie a transit visa. Isabelle and I were told we could not get our transit visas until 9:00 the next morning, so we had to change our flight time.

In the evening the Jones family took us three ladies to Decamere to visit with the Meckes family and Zettie. We enjoyed a delicious supper and then took a tour of the compound and saw the 150 orphans living there. Later that evening the Drowdys joined us. Our group and the Drowdys returned to Asmara after dark and saw two hyenas along the highway, something that was unusual.

Returning to Egypt

The next morning Carrie, Isabelle, and I arose early, packed our suitcases, and went to a small Italian restaurant for breakfast. We were at the Sudan Agency by 9:00. The clerk prepared transit visas for Isabelle and me. Regretfully, no approval for a transit visa for Carrie had come from Sudan. Disappointed, we returned to the airline office and changed Carrie's ticket so she could continue her flight to Cairo. The three of us flew from the Asmara airport at 10:30, and two hours later we landed in the tropical heat of Khartoum.

Isabelle and I deplaned, but Carrie remained to continue her flight to Cairo. We went to claim our luggage and discovered that Carrie's luggage had been unloaded also. We contacted personnel who returned it to the plane. After we got our luggage, the airline's bus took us to our hotel. Later Melad brought us the things we had left with him. Then he and a colleague took us on a ride around Khartoum. His colleague had communist leanings, but we spoke with him about salvation.

Wednesday morning at 6:00 we went to the train station, purchased our tickets, and found our reserved seats. The man in charge at the station asked if we objected to having with us the male friend of the French woman teacher who was also assigned to our compartment. Regulations in Sudan were that men did not share compartments with women, but with us being foreigners, he thought that we might not object. We knew this was a thirty-hour trip, so we told him that we did not mind if he sat with us during the day but not at night. The teacher's friend kept his reserved seat in another compartment in the coach, though he spent most of the day in ours. We found them quite congenial companions for the long ride.

We reached Wadi Halfa about noon the next day and had to wait before going through customs. The Egyptian customs official remembered us from our trip south and invited us into his office for tea. He told us of his wife's recent death, and that now he was working in Wadi Halfa because he received a higher salary than in Egypt. He wanted his children educated and asked us to visit them because they lived with relatives near our orphanage in Alexandria. Before we left for our steamer, he asked for some religious literature that we gladly provided.

There were two steamers ready to leave. We were assigned to one, and our French friends were assigned to the other. On our steamer we got acquainted with a Sudanese marine officer who had studied in England and knew English well. We had an opportunity to witness to him about Christ; he courteously received what we shared with him. Even though we were traveling second class, he got permission for us to sit on the upper deck, which was first class. When the steamer docked in Shallal on Saturday morning, September 17, and we had finished going through customs, he arranged for a taxi to take us to the train station in Shallal. The marine officer, an Egyptian customs official, and another man went with us. When we arrived, the customs official would not permit us to pay our portion of the fare. It was wonderful how the Lord took care of us.

We bought some alabaster souvenirs from vendors at the train station, ate dinner, and settled in our compartment for the last long stretch of the trip. When night came, our coach and the adjoining one had no lights because the train's electrical system was faulty. Isabelle and I were alone in our compartment and were able to lie on the seats and rest. Five hours after we left Shallal, an Indian lady and an Egyptian lady joined us. Later an Egyptian mother with her daughter and baby came, and we rode together to Cairo, arriving about 9:30 on Sunday morning.

Isabelle and I were glad to be back in Cairo. After refreshing ourselves in the train station, we ate some food from our suitcase. We were unable to eat supper the previous night because of the darkness, and we were very hungry.

On my way to Alexandria on Monday, I stopped at the American Mission hospital in Tanta, Egypt, for a complete physical checkup. I then returned to Alexandria and eagerly finished packing for my return to the States.

Furlough and College

A few days after I returned to Alexandria, I sailed to America. Carrie Boyer, who flew to Cairo and went to Alexandria by train, and Bahgah, one of our orphans who had remained at the orphanage as a worker and was immigrating to America, sailed with me. After an uneventful trip, our ship docked at Wilmington, North Carolina, on October 14, 1955. My sister Helen and her husband, Lester Bump, met us at the dock and took Carrie and me to their home in Vineland, New Jersey, where we stayed for a few days. Later in Shamokin we had a family photo taken of our mother, her children and their spouses, and her grandchildren. Bahgah went to Chicago where she later married an American.

My mother, Mary Maurer, with her children, their spouses, and her grandchildren

Carrie and I were members of the Evangelical Methodist Church in Lavelle, Pennsylvania, not far from our respective homes in Ashland and Shamokin. Our conference president, Marlin Straub, and his wife, Hilda, came to New Jersey and took us to our homes.

The mission leaders arranged for Carrie and me to travel together in deputation throughout the year of 1956. Our travels took us to several states for services. While we were traveling in Pennsylvania, I became acquainted with T. Emerald and Dorothy Smith. Several times Carrie and I stayed in their home for the night and were thankful for their hospitality.

Carrie and me visiting the Smiths in November 1956 during furlough

Their teenage son, Ronald, began to sense God's call upon his life. A few years later, Ronald with his wife, Anna, went as missionaries under EFM to Ethiopia. I never imagined that one day they would work diligently with me to write my life's story.

One significant experience for me during that year was that I learned to drive a car. I was thirty-one and never had had an opportunity to learn. My nephew Frank Schmidt and Carrie were my teachers. One time I was driving and Carrie, my nine-year-old nephew Bill Schmidt, and I stopped at the home of my brother Leonard in Doutyville. While we visited, Bill said to me, "Aunt Irene, there is just one more thing you need."

I replied, "What?" thinking he was referring to a driver's license.

Bill surprised me with his reply when he said, "You need a man."

There was one embarrassing incident that took place during the time Carrie and I traveled for deputation. We had been invited for supper before the evening missionary service to the home of the Rev. and Mrs. Tallman, who were pastoring one of our Evangelical Methodist churches in Pennsylvania. We forgot about the invitation and did not arrive in time to eat before the service. They were a gracious couple and served the meal after the service.

That fall the Mission arranged a deputation service for Carrie and me at the Church of God church in Auburn, Pennsylvania. We invited Jane Maurer (Heisler), my cousin, to go with us. When we reached the church, a thunderstorm was brewing. The only local people present then were Elmer and Irene Fahl, a brother and sister. At first we were not aware that Irene was blind, and Elmer had limited eyesight. While we were carrying our display items into the church, lightning struck a transformer on a post nearby, causing the lights to go out in the area. We wanted to leave the church but were afraid to exit through the door because the transformer was on fire.

Elmer, who was familiar with the church layout, took his sister and went to the basement, and they left the building through a door on the ground floor. Carrie found a window, opened it, grasped hold of the windowsill and dropped to the ground. I did the same. Jane did not grasp the windowsill but jumped instead and felt the jar of the five-foot jump. In the dark with the storm threatening, Elmer led us through a field to a house on the street below the church. It was traumatic, but God protected us. We had a service in a neighbor's home by using kerosene lamps.

Before I went to Egypt in 1949, I had studied for two years at Intercession City Biblical College in Intercession City, Florida. In January 1957 I enrolled in God's Bible School (GBS) in Cincinnati, Ohio, to complete a Bachelor of Theology degree. In addition to attending classes, I traveled sometimes on weekends for deputation services for EFM.

Shortly after the start of my first semester at GBS, the school had its annual winter revival with Millard Downing as the evangelist. It was my first time to hear him preach, and I greatly appreciated the depth of his messages. His wife was present for the last half of the revival and sang a number of special songs under the anointing of the Holy Spirit. Many victories were won throughout the revival.

John Dorsey and Harold Schmul served as evangelists for the camp meeting held the next June. I was one of the speakers on mission's day and spoke once in the young people's services. I was responsible for the two children's services each day with the attendance reaching more than 80 on Sundays. On the last Sunday morning, the children presented a program of memory verses and choruses to the congregation gathered in the large sanctuary. One of the choruses they sang was "Jesus Loves Me" in the Arabic language.

The following summer I worked in the mission office in Bedford, Indiana, and lived in a second floor apartment of the mission office building at 8th and J Streets. I also took a social studies course from GBS by correspondence under Dorothy Walter. That fall I returned to classes at GBS.

During the two semesters I spent at GBS, I was privileged to study under godly teachers such as Leslie Wilcox and Nettie Peabody. My extracurricular activities included involvement in personal evangelism and a small orchestra. Part of our personal evangelism activity was visiting residents in nursing homes and doing house-to-house visitation in Cincinnati. The orchestra was directed by Esther Elliott, a young member of the faculty, who later went to Africa as a missionary. Janet Ferguson, a high-school student, was also a member of the orchestra. She later married Leonard Sankey, and for several years they served under EFM in Central America.

The big event of the fall semester at GBS was the special dinner served for the poor children of the Greater Cincinnati area on Thanksgiving Day. For several weeks prior to Thanksgiving week, the GBS students stood on the sidewalks in downtown Cincinnati and made appeals for money. The students would cry out, "Give for the Thanksgiving dinner at God's Bible School for needy children of Cincinnati."

There were no classes the week of Thanksgiving because everyone was occupied with preparing for the special dinner. Some cleaned; others cut pickles or made snack bags. Wednesday evening we cleaned several hundred turkeys, and early Thursday morning we prepared the potatoes. For the dinner that day, we had between six and seven thousand children present. Those children came on chartered buses from Cincinnati and the northern part of Kentucky. Policemen came to the school to help keep order.

I was assigned to a bus that gathered children from northern Kentucky. Even though I had helpers, it was a challenge trying to corral that large group of children. It was my duty to be sure they were fed and that they got on the right bus to go home.

The GBS students did not eat until all the children were fed, received their snack bags, and left for home. Our vacation started after cleanup was finished. I did not go anywhere for Thanksgiving vacation because I was trying to finish the semester's work, except for Greek, before Christmas.

Chapter 5

Returning to the Land of My Call
1958-1965

Second Voyage to Egypt

The *Concordia Fonn* sailed from Brooklyn, New York, on January 24, 1958. My cabin mate was a young American lady going to Eritrea to

Concordia Fonn on which I left Brooklyn, New York, for Egypt in January 1958

join her husband who was stationed there in the U.S. Army. I was thankful that she did not smoke. That was an answer to prayer. As far as I was concerned, she was the pick of the passengers.

As our ship entered the Atlantic Ocean, we encountered a storm with wind velocity reaching 70 miles an hour and 60- to 70-foot waves. Some of the passengers who had traveled for years told us that they

In my cabin on the *Fonn* with Helen and a friend who came to bid me farewell never had seen such a storm. I spent much of my time in bed trying to prevent seasickness; I suffered with it only one time. For the first few days, most of our motion was pitching with the front of the ship rising and then falling as each wave passed. Then our 475-foot ship began a side-to-side rolling motion, causing the luggage in our room to keep sliding across the floor. Several times I put it back under my bed only to have it slide out again. Finally I gave up.

Mealtime was difficult. In the dining room the tables were fastened to the floor, and they had a wooden guard called a fiddle along the edges to help keep the dishes in place. Whenever a bad roll came, even with the guards, some of the dishes slid off the tables and went sliding across the floor. One time the captain went "sailing" along with some of the chairs and a portable sewing machine, but amazingly he was not hurt. After such a meal the dining room was in shambles.

Another time one of the stewardesses was injured when she fell against a chair in the hall outside the dining room. A passenger who was a doctor examined her and did not think she had any broken bones.

During a couple nights I could hardly stay in bed because of the rolling. Once I was aroused by a bad roll and wondered if our ship ever would right itself. Everyone was looking forward to reaching the Mediterranean Sea with hope that the waters would be calmer. Later the captain told us that in all his years at sea, he never had seen the barometer in that latitude as low as it was during that storm.

The ocean calmed enough so that our ship was able to stop at the Azores one week after we left Brooklyn. The harbor was not built for large vessels, necessitating the captain to anchor out a distance. For three days the ocean was still too rough for the barges to reach the ship. Eventually they could unload the cargo, which was mostly food for the American Army stationed there.

February 5 we left the Azores. When we reached the Mediterranean Sea, we enjoyed lovely sailing, some of the smoothest I had ever experienced. One evening we ate dinner partly by candlelight to celebrate the captain's 53rd birthday.

We reached Casablanca, Morocco, three days after leaving the Azores. Several of us left the ship to sightsee, and I mailed some letters. From Casablanca we had only five sailing days to reach Alexandria. Once during that time our ship stopped in the middle of the Mediterranean for about five hours. We learned later that we had stopped because of a leak in an oil line.

When I arrived at Alexandria on February 14, the Guy Troyer family met me at the port and helped me after I cleared customs. While I had been on furlough, two significant developments took place concerning our work in Egypt. First, the Mission closed the orphanage in Alexandria because the government made demands that we could not meet, including the requirement that we teach the Koran, the Moslem holy book.

Second, fighting had erupted between Egypt and Israel in October 1956, and all our missionaries in Egypt had gone to Eritrea. During that time the Bible school in Girga was closed. Guy and Dana Troyer and their sons, Charles and Stephen, were able to return to Egypt in December 1957.

Working in Upper Egypt

Because the Mission no longer had an orphanage, I moved to Girga in Upper Egypt, which is nearly five hundred miles south of Alexandria. There I helped to reopen the Bible school, officially known as the Theological Institute of Faith Church, and worked with the area churches.

Soon after I arrived in Girga, the Troyers, our interpreter, and I were visiting in a village. News spread quickly that we were present and that one of us would preach in the evening. A man in the village who was despairing of life was making plans to hang himself that day. He heard about the service and came. God faithfully dealt with him. The following night he went to our Egyptian pastor and told him that Jesus had not only saved him but also healed him of the illness that doctors said could not be cured. Our God is truly wonderful!

Bible school building on far left in Girga, Upper Egypt

When the hot months came in Upper Egypt, the Troyers and I went to Alexandria for the summer. It was encouraging to see how God was giving special help in the church there. The attendance was increasing, and people were receiving spiritual help. A newly converted couple was walking in the light God was giving to them and were growing in the Lord. The wife was saved first, and then her husband quit smoking, sought God, and received forgiveness.

I visited some friends I had made during my first term and learned that they were hungry for holiness. We met in their homes several times for prayer. We also had special prayer meetings in the Troyers' apartment with some of our former orphanage girls who desired heart purity.

At the end of the summer, the Troyers and I made plans to return to Girga. On our way we stopped in Cairo and visited our church. I spoke twice in the Sunday services where four people claimed salvation. The next day we went by bus to Suez. I spoke in our church that evening and was thankful for the Lord's presence and help. We were glad for the opportunity to visit that church although we slept on beds without springs that night. The next day we continued our trip to Girga.

Classes for the Bible school started the first week in October. My subjects were English, music, and Theology of Holiness. We taught mostly in English because we wanted our students to learn English well enough to be able to use English Bible study books. At that time there were few Arabic reference books on the Scriptures. Because the students did not know English well, sometimes I helped them by teaching in Arabic. We used an English/Arabic dictionary to refer to words that were not clear to the students.

The Nile River overflowed its banks during the late summer and early fall resulting in rich soil and good crops, but it also brought many mosquitoes. We had to spray almost every night before going to bed so that we could sleep. That fall a group of us went by train to Lahaiwa to hold a service. On our return to the station after the service, we were surrounded by the mosquitoes. It was almost like being in a rain shower except it was mosquitoes.

The train station at Lahaiwa was very interesting. There was no platform and we had to jump from the train when it stopped

Waiting with some of the mission workers at the train station in Sohag

briefly. It was challenging to get back on the train. We had to grab the handrails and quickly pull ourselves up the steep steps.

I longed to hear from my family and friends in the States, so several weeks before Christmas, I wrote to them suggesting that it would be nice to hear from them. I listed the cost of mail—boat mail was 8 cents for 1 ounce, air mail was 15 cents for ½ ounce, and an aerogramme was 10 cents. I appreciated the response, including the cards I received.

God began to give special help in our churches in Upper Egypt in December. Many of our pastors witnessed outstanding revivals with one pastor reporting that fifteen people were saved.

In another place our pastor visited a man in the community and invited him to come to church. The man did not accept the invitation nor did he give serious consideration to the pastor's reminder that life is short. In a few days he was near death, and whenever the pastor visited him again, he begged for forgiveness from the pastor and from God. Later the pastor and I went to see him, and although he remained seriously ill, he was rejoicing in the Lord. Several days later God took him home.

On Christmas Eve the Troyers came to my apartment where we sang carols, exchanged gifts, and had refreshments. Christmas Day we met in the Troyers' apartment and feasted on a delicious turkey dinner with all the trimmings. In Egypt Christmas is celebrated by the Christians on January 7. That day Dana Troyer and I spent eight hours in house visitation, which is customary among both the Evangelicals and the Orthodox people. At each home we were served tea and homemade cookies.

The weather in Upper Egypt in January is cold compared to the rest of the year with the temperature sometimes in the upper 40s. Our classrooms were on the ground floor of our Bible school building, and by the time I returned to my apartment above the classrooms, my feet were ice cold. My problem was temporary because the cold weather lasted only a few weeks. Most houses in Egypt have flat roofs, and in the cold season our students often spent their afternoons on the roof enjoying the warm sun while they studied.

The second semester was filled with more busy days. In addition to my Bible school duties and secretarial work, the Troyers, Paul Harp, and I visited the village churches almost every Sunday. Paul served as our interpreter. I enjoyed the village work and the direct contact with the people.

On one occasion Paul and I went to our church in Bindar about two miles from Girga. We took the bus as far as we could and then walked the rest of the way. After we visited in two homes, we attended the Saturday evening service where Paul preached. Sunday I spoke in both services. Several people testified. The

Paul Harp, his wife Angail, and their children Charles, Timothy, and Violet in 1963

next Sunday we went to another church that was off the main road and required a 45-minute walk. The church folks loaned us donkeys for our return trip to the main road.

Graduated from GBS in absentia on May 28, 1959

As the 1958-1959 school year came to an end, I worked diligently to finish my Greek studies so I could graduate from GBS with a Bachelor of Theology. Although I did not get it completed on time, GBS allowed me to graduate summa cum laude in absentia on May 28, 1959, and I completed my Greek later.

In June I went to Eritrea again, but that time I flew rather than going overland. There was a shortage of missionaries when I arrived. Consequently, I was asked to fill in as director of the orphanage until Leroy and Myrtle Adams came later that summer. Although I had worked in our girls orphanage in Egypt, supervising all the work involved for 150 boys and girls was different. The Lord gave me sufficient strength and wisdom for the task. I was so busy that for 14 weeks I did not get a letter written to my sister Doris. She became quite concerned but was relieved after she got word that I was all right.

I had several interesting experiences that summer. On July 4 one of the older boys fell on the concrete of the play area and received a slight concussion. He had complications and remained in bed for several weeks, but he eventually recovered completely.

Another boy had a leg infection that had not healed after several months although he had been taken to the hospital for treatment. We then took him to an Italian doctor who operated and removed the infected portion. We applied streptomycin powder on the wound and gave him streptomycin injections. When I left Eritrea at the end of the summer, his leg was healed almost completely. We thanked the Lord for His healing touch.

A boy named Gebreab developed a problem with his eyes. I delegated one of the workers to take him to a doctor in Asmara. The medication the doctor prescribed cleared up the problem. I later saw him at a camp meeting in Orleans, Indiana, in 2001, and with gratitude he reminded me of that childhood experience.

The climate during my stay was invigorating, and because it was the rainy season, it rained nearly every day, which kept the weather pleasantly cool. I was glad to be of help during that summer in Eritrea.

I returned to Egypt, and during the new school year, I taught English I, English II, Minor Prophets, Theology II, and music. It was a challenge to get everything done—teaching my classes at the Bible school, visiting our nearby churches, and completing my Greek studies.

That fall we had an ordination service for Girgis Eskander in the church he pastored in East Zuouk while he completed his four years of Bible school. The Troyers and I drove the 16 miles to his church where revival services were in progress with an Egyptian evangelist. Arrangements were made for the ordination so that the revival services would not be hindered. People came from several surrounding villages to attend that service.

After we sang, the evangelist brought an appropriate message with an evangelistic appeal. Then Fahim, the secretary of the conference and brother of Girgis, led in the

Dressed in Egyptian garb

ordination ceremony. Following prayer and scripture reading, the Bible school students sang several special songs. Guy Troyer gave a brief address before the preachers laid their hands on Girgis and one of them led in prayer.

Girgis made a few remarks including the experience that led to his conversion. When he was a student in public school, he and a schoolmate were walking in the middle of a street when they heard a car coming behind them at full speed. Girgis ran to one side, and his friend hurried to the opposite side. He was shocked when he realized that his friend was struck by the car and killed instantly. That tragedy became the turning point in Girgis' life. He gave his heart to God and later began teaching in one of our church schools.

While Girgis was teaching, God called him to proclaim His Word. He became a pastor with EFM, was an exemplary Christian, and pastored for a number of years. He eventually joined his brother Fahim in Australia and died there in 2005.

Revival efforts in our churches that winter were fruitful with definite victories. Benjamin, a young man from one of the villages, was saved. During the months that followed, his family testified that his life was changed. In another village a young married couple experienced a work of grace in their hearts and made changes in their lives to please God. Our hearts thrilled as we saw lives transformed.

In February 1960 I had an interesting visit in the home of a Catholic family where the mother was suffering from bronchitis and a heart attack. Among their visiting friends was a couple, the man a Coptic and his wife a Presbyterian. We made an interesting group of people—Catholic, Coptic, Presbyterian, and holiness. Our conversation turned to the coming of Christ, then to the question of whether or not Jesus had brothers and sisters, and finally to the ability of Mary to intercede for us. The Catholic family and the Coptic man were unable to give any biblical support for what they had been taught on those subjects. When I finished reading to them various passages of Scripture to support what I was saying, the Catholic man expressed an interest in hearing more of what the Bible taught.

Paul Finch, accompanied by his daughter Angeline, came to Egypt from Eritrea for special services in June. After those services I was privileged to visit the Holy Land with them for a week. It was a blessed experience to see some of the places mentioned in the Bible and to walk where my Savior had walked.

In the old walled section of Jerusalem, we visited Mount Moriah, the Wailing Wall, the pool of Bethesda, the place where Peter denied Christ, Pilate's judgment hall, and the Via Dolorosa. Outside the wall we visited Gethsemane, Calvary, the Garden Tomb, the Mount of Olives, and the Kidron valley. We also visited Bethlehem, Jericho, the Jordan River, the Dead Sea, ancient Shechem where we drank from Jacob's well, and ancient Samaria where we saw the ruins of Omri's palace on an eminence that provided a wonderful view of the surrounding countryside.

In August a new EFM missionary family joined us in Girga—Eugene and Fern Tierney and their daughter, Ruth. They came to take the place of the Troyers who were going on furlough the following summer.

The first evangelical wedding conducted in the village of East Zuouk was in early 1961. Esther, the bride, was a daughter of one of our pastors. When the Troyers, Tierneys, and I arrived, we were taken to the pastor's house, and from there we proceeded to a neighboring village where Esther was staying with her grandparents.

After two hours several vehicles took Esther, her family, and guests to the groom's home where many people enjoyed the wedding supper. Following the meal she was brought out of her hiding place and was received by the groom. The custom was for the bride to be carried to her seat beside the groom. A slender fellow began to do the honors, but he lacked the strength to finish the task. Soon Esther's husky uncle intervened and carried her to the seat reserved for her. I was delighted to accompany the proceedings with music on my accordion.

During the ceremony our Bible school students provided special singing and read Scripture. The school principal made a few remarks, and then the preacher had the young couple join hands while he united them in marriage. During the ceremony Esther's maternal grandmother sat next to her and made sure that her veil and covering concealed her face. Whenever her white veil showed, the grandmother would tuck it under the dark outer covering.

Immediately after the ceremony Esther's uncle carried her into her room where some women joined her. The groom remained in the courtyard with the guests and hired musicians who entertained them throughout the night. The villagers were impressed with the orderly fashion in which the wedding was conducted in contrast to their traditional weddings.

I went to Alexandria during the early part of June. Right before I went, the country suffered a heat wave with the temperature reaching 119 degrees one day in Cairo. Although I enjoyed teaching, it was refreshing to be free from the classroom for a few months and to focus my efforts on other facets of our work. In September the Tierneys and I returned to Girga to prepare for the new school year.

The week before Christmas Eugene was scheduled to preach for revival services in one of our village churches. He became ill, and I was asked to replace him. Paul went with me to interpret. On our return to Girga, a small boy in the village of Birba, not far from Girga, suddenly decided to cross the road. He ran into the right front side of the mission vehicle. Because a bus was coming the other direction, I was not able to swerve. Thankfully, I was driving slowly and was able to stop immediately.

Paul quickly got out of our car, but I urged him to get back in, having heard that one should not stop if involved in that type of accident but should leave immediately to prevent being harmed or killed by the local residents. A number of men sitting at a shop saw that something had happened and quickly came with clubs, probably intending to harm us or at least block our way. Some of them beat on the hood of our car with their clubs, but providentially no vehicle was coming in the opposite direction, and I was able to get away.

After Paul and I reached Girga, we went to the police station to report the accident. They dispatched an emergency vehicle to go to Birba to bring the boy to the hospital in Girga and to bring his mother and uncle to the police station. We learned later that the boy suffered a fractured skull, and his left leg was broken below the knee. While we waited, the officer in charge courteously provided soft drinks for us. The uncle testified that I had stopped immediately. The police questioned the mother to see if she knew me or had seen me previously. Her reply in the negative proved to the police that there was no enmity between the family and me. The police then took me with them to investigate the scene of the accident and saw neither skid marks nor any sign that I was driving too fast.

When we returned to the police station, the officer in charge informed me that I was placed under arrest. With great respect he said, "We will not put you in custody. You may go to your house, and if we notify you to come to the station, do so." I was surprised that I was arrested, but grateful to the Lord and to the police that I was allowed to return to my home where I stayed until the day appointed for the court hearing.

In spite of the evidence in my favor, the family took me to court. The hearing took place in the Girga courtroom where the accused was customarily placed in a cage-like booth during his trial. When the officials decided not to put me in the booth, the family members and friends of the boy became quite angry. I was thankful that Paul and the Bible school students were with me. I realized that the authorities of the court were showing the same type of respect that the police department had given me the day of the accident. I was acquitted at that trial, but the prosecutor appealed it.

The second trial was held in March 1962 in Sohag, the provincial capital. I was again acquitted by a panel of three judges. One of the judges said that he could not picture me being a criminal. I was very thankful for God's intervention, both at the trials and with the boy's complete recovery.

The boy's family had sold a cow to have money for medical bills and court costs. After I was acquitted, the Troyers and Tierneys gave me money to give to the family to help them.

On Easter Eugene, Paul, and I attended the morning service at our church in Hawawish. Eugene gave the message and then extended an invitation to those who wanted to pray. Several women went to the back of the women's side, and a man went to the altar. Eugene, Paul, and Pastor Saied went to pray with the man, and I went to pray with the women.

We had just started to pray when I sensed disturbance near me. A woman began making a strange noise and shaking her body. I soon realized that she was demon possessed, and I summoned the pastor. Several of the believers immediately gathered for prayer. While we prayed in Jesus' name and the pastor dealt with the demon, it struggled to stay, and a devilish look showed in the woman's eyes. After the demon departed, the woman became calm and her countenance was once again normal. We praised the Lord for another manifestation of His resurrection power.

While I was in Alexandria for the summer, I invited Pastor Melad Barsoom, his wife, their five children, and his sister and her son for dinner. In the afternoon I took them to the zoo, and later we ate a lunch in a nearby municipal garden. When we were ready to leave, Melad's eight-year-old boy said, "The nicest vacation day has come to an end." They enjoyed the day, and I was glad that I could give them a special treat.

Sometimes our Christians used the names of missionaries for their babies. Fozia, the daughter of Pastor Melad in Cairo, and her husband Alphie, named their daughter Irene. Three other ministers named one of their daughters Irene. A couple from our Ard el Shirka church later named their daughter Maurer. In Egypt the surname of a child is the first name of the father. Since I was called Miss Maurer, the family did not know my first name and thought it was Maurer. A family in Upper Egypt also named their baby Maurer. I gave a small gift to each baby, which was expected when parents used one's name for their child.

We had a beneficial Sunday school conference that summer in the Delta, and nearly all the pastors and teachers who attended returned to their churches with renewed interest and zeal for the Sunday school work. We held a similar conference in October for our churches in Upper Egypt.

Sunday school convention in Girga with missionaries Eugene Tierney and Guy Troyer on the right

I visited all our Delta churches during my stay in Alexandria, but as summer came to an end, I was eager to return to Upper Egypt. I wanted to prepare for the coming school year and to visit our churches again in that part of Egypt.

As Christmas approached, we were busy making nearly 500 plaster-of-Paris plaques. We used pictures from old Christmas cards. It was a huge task, but the plaques were greatly enjoyed by the children.

Transformed Lives

Rifka was one of our two Bible women. Our Bible women taught children's Sunday school classes, visited with the women in their homes, helped in the women's meetings, and interpreted for the missionary ladies. Rifka had an interesting conversion story. When she was thirteen years old, she went to a church in her village where she heard the message of salvation and earnestly began seeking God. One day while she was praying, God said to her, "Arise, thy sins are forgiven thee." She arose with great joy and a song in her heart.

When Rifka's older brother at home saw her newfound joy, which kept her praying and singing, he began praying and going to church with her. He would pray and say, "Oh, Lord, save me and show me the sweetness of salvation, for I want to get saved like my sister." He sought the Lord until he obtained forgiveness.

Rikfa, one of our Bible women

After Rifka married Bishay, they pastored in Mangoug. To reach Mangoug one had to cross a footbridge without a railing, and I was always fearful when I had to cross. When Bishay died, Rifka continued to pastor the church. Yacoub, an elder in the church, helped her.

Women and children from the Mangoug congregation

I wanted to do something special for Rifka because of her faithful labors. She was thrilled when I gave her a pair of dark blue Mary Jane shoes that she especially liked.

* * * * *

In the late 1940s Mary, one of our Sunday school children in Girga, came to know Jesus. During her teen years she became one of our Sunday school teachers and helped a Bible woman with the children.

Sunday school children in Girga

Without Mary's approval her family arranged for her to marry a Coptic deacon who played cymbals when the priest chanted the mass. The day came for the wedding, and relatives and friends were present to prepare the bride for the occasion. She objected to worldly adornment, but her friends tried to force the issue. An unsaved aunt came and defended Mary's stand because she knew that her niece had vowed that she would not use worldly adornment even on her wedding day. God honored her determination to please Him.

A typical village bride and groom in Hawawish

Because Mary's husband, Talaat, was still studying in the Coptic Church, they lived for a short time with her family. Consequently, her father controlled her and often would not allow her to go to church. A few months after their wedding, Mary's husband went to church, got saved, and quit his studying in the Coptic Church. Soon they moved into their own dwelling in Girga where both became faithful members of our congregation. God blessed their home with two precious children.

* * * * *

During the fall of 1960, a young woman was touched with the gospel in a revival meeting in one of the villages. She had been to church but never had given her life to the Lord. That time she got under conviction, prayed through to victory, and had a sweet smile because Jesus Christ had come into her life.

Later the woman married. When a son marries in the villages of Egypt, the custom is that he brings his bride home, and they occupy a room in his father's house. The father was angry with his son because he did not beat his wife, as most men did. She did nothing to deserve punishment, and because he loved her, he refused to hurt her. Many times the father-in-law forbade her to go to church.

Whenever the pastor visited the home, the young wife devoured every word that he said. She was so hungry to hear the Word and receive encouragement. In spite of the persecution, she remained a victorious Christian. Later we saw her in a service in that village, and she had the same smile and glow upon her face.

* * * * *

We witnessed another remarkable victory in the spring of 1961. Near one of our village churches, a man lived whose life had been one of dissipation, drunkenness, and dope addiction. He was so enslaved by alcohol that before he had emptied one bottle, he sent for another. He gradually was selling his property to satisfy those abnormal appetites.

The man became very ill, and the doctors had little hope of him living much longer. In his state of weakness and illness, he called almost every day for the pastor to come and visit him. The pastor spent many hours dealing with the man and urging him to seek Jesus, but he always answered, "Next week I will get saved."

The pastor warned, "You have no guarantee of another day. How can you say next week?" God heard the prayers of His people in behalf of the man, and he marvelously recovered. He stopped his drink and dope habits and started attending our church. He became an earnest seeker after God, found forgiveness, and had a transformed life.

* * * * *

When we held a revival in another village church, an elderly man prayed through to salvation. Previously, he had seldom darkened the church door. He was invited to the revival and became interested enough to attend. His interest increased, and soon he sought the Lord and was saved. A later report indicated that he was attending church on the weeknights and was sitting on the front seat. A week before the revival began, his case seemed very difficult, but God answered prayer.

* * * * *

In the fall of 1961 Ray Chamberlain came to Egypt to minister in our churches. He spent ten days with us in Upper Egypt, ministering to our Bible school students during the day and preaching in nearby village churches each evening. He also preached in our churches in the Delta. His ministry was Spirit-anointed, and God used him to reach many individuals.

* * * * *

In our visitation work I spent many hours ministering to women in the village of Kombadar during revival meetings, women's services, and special times of prayer. Oum Edwar, a widow in that group, sought God on several occasions but did not find the Lord until she was willing to correct a situation in her life.

Later I was back in Kombadar. I met the woman and asked her about her spiritual welfare. She replied, "You know I am a widow and used to mourn and chant sad songs, but from the time of that revival, I stopped singing sad songs and am happy in Jesus." What a delightful change God made in the life of that village woman.

* * * * *

I visited our church in Suez the last Sunday of July 1962, and the pastor asked me to teach the Sunday school children in the afternoon. In Egypt Sunday school was only for the children and usually was taught on Sunday afternoons. We sometimes had "Sunday" school on other days of the week because it was more convenient for the children. That Sunday I used flannelgraph, which was something new we were introducing in our Sunday school work.

When I gave the lesson, the children listened attentively and were responsive. The next evening as I visited in the pastor's home, two girls from the Sunday school class came and said they wanted to get saved.

The pastor and I instructed the girls how to pray and give their hearts to God. We all knelt and prayed, and soon the girls found forgiveness and testified to what God had done for them. Their Sunday school teacher, who arrived before we finished praying, later said the girls had been under conviction for several weeks. It was a joy to see those girls with a shine on their faces.

* * * * *

In March of 1963 Victor and Jennie Glenn and Juddie and Eunice Peyton with their daughter, Betty, came to Egypt for special services. Ray and Mary Ann Chamberlain arrived about the same time for six months of evangelism.

Jennie and Victor Glenn; Juddie, Betty, and Eunice Peyton; me; Mary Ann Chamberlain; Fern, Ruth, and Darrell Tierney; Guy Troyer; and Eugene Tierney in Girga

Ray and Mary Ann Chamberlain

That summer while the Chamberlains were in Kombadar for services, I went with them to visit Shahatta. He was a man about 25 years old but extremely crippled because of a childhood illness or accident. His legs were limp, underdeveloped, and bent beneath his hunchbacked body. He spent his time sitting beside the doorway of his little abode where a loving grandmother took care of him. I interpreted as Ray spoke to Shahatta about his soul. He wanted to pray, and God came and met his need. I visited Shahatta on later occasions, and although still crippled and unable to get to church, with Jesus living in his heart, he experienced comfort and cheer.

God blessed the ministry of the Chamberlains who spent several months in Upper Egypt. He ministered in the Bible school chapel services during the day and held revival services in the nearby village churches in the evenings, which he had done on his previous visit.

Bible school students, missionary teachers, preachers, and
Mary Ann Chamberlain in 1963 in Girga

Second Furlough Events

The world changed rapidly while I served my second term in Egypt. My previous mode of transportation to and from the mission field had been by ship, which took about two weeks. Now as I prepared for furlough, I made plans to go by plane. It was hard to believe that I could be in New York City in less than 24 hours.

From Cairo, Egypt, I took a Comet jet to New York City in April 1963. Before time to land, the plane encountered much turbulence. The passengers became somewhat apprehensive; and some of us prayed that we would have a safe landing. When our plane touched down, the passengers clapped, applauding the captain.

I went to the airlines desk and was told that the flight to my final destination at Philadelphia, Pennsylvania, was canceled. With dismay I replied, "I am stranded."

The clerk responded, "You can get a hotel in the city."

"I have no money to do that and, furthermore my family is waiting for me in Philadelphia. If they knew that I am stranded here, they could come and get me," I explained.

The clerk realized my predicament and said, "We can page your family for you."

It was good to hear Doris' voice on the telephone. I really was relieved when she said, "You stay at the airport, and we will come and get you." Family members at the airport discussed who would make the trip. Lester and Helen, Eva, and Leonard came to the airport in New York to get me.

Night had come, and only a few people remained in the airport. I was watching my baggage, but I was hungry and decided to get some peanuts from a vending machine. I tried once unsuccessfully; then I went to another machine that accepted my dime but did not release any peanuts. I notified a person in charge of the machine, and he helped me get the peanuts, but I had to sign a form that I had put a dime in the slot and not received any peanuts.

What a relief when I saw Leonard coming through the doorway two hours later. We joined the other family members, and I told them I was hungry. Leonard hurriedly went and brought me something to eat. We all went to Eva's home in Allentown, Pennsylvania, and from there Lester and Helen went to their home in New Jersey. The following day Eva took me to Doris' home in Shamokin, Pennsylvania. She was waiting anxiously for my arrival. It was good to be home again!

After a short visit with some of my family, I began traveling for EFM, helping in spring conventions. During the summer I spoke in missionary services in various churches and camp meetings. While I traveled in New York, one special blessing that I had was visiting Harriette Harp with whom I had sailed to Egypt in 1949 and who also worked with me at the orphanage during the summer months. She had returned to the States nine years previously to care for her aging parents.

An enjoyable part of my deputation work that year was touring some of the Pilgrim Holiness churches in New York. When I was at one of their camp meetings to represent the Mission, someone chose the song "I've Pitched My Tent in Beulah." The chorus is:

> You need not look for me, down in Egypt's sand,
> For I have pitched my tent far up in Beulah land;
> You need not look for me, down in Egypt's sand,
> For I have pitched my tent far up in Beulah land.

It was amusing because I already had served two terms in Egypt and planned to return.

Another amusing incident took place in a parsonage before time for us to go to the church for the evening service. The pastor's small daughter asked, "Who is going to speak tonight?"

I replied, "I am if the Lord helps me."

She surprised me with her reaction, "And if He doesn't?"

Leave it to innocent children! They react in ways that sometimes amuse us.

* * * * *

One day a man and his wife who were my friends talked to me about a special concern they had. Several years earlier the woman was the dean of women in a Bible school, and a retired minister gave her a gold dollar piece. At that time he told her, "I want you to keep this. I am supporting a missionary, and that missionary is you. I want you to take this and keep it."

Years later after the minister had gone to his eternal reward, my friends began talking about the gift she had received. It was a keepsake, but the couple wanted that treasure to work for God. They first thought about selling the gold piece and inquired about its value. They were offered twice its face value but were not satisfied with the meager amount. Then they went to a man who dealt with old coins, and he appraised it at 20 times its face value and said that it would have been worth more, but it had a dent.

After the couple discussed the matter further, they decided that they would give the coin to a missionary, thinking that a missionary might know better how to use it. I was highly honored when they entrusted that special gift to me. The Mission recently had started a campaign in Egypt to collect good books, translate them into Arabic, and print them to help our pastors in their ministry. I told my friends that I would invest the worth of the gold coin in that project.

* * * * *

While on furlough the Mission granted me permission to continue my education. I desired to specialize in history because ancient history includes Bible history. I agreed to do deputation work on weekends. The Mission graciously provided a Volkswagen "Bug" for me to use for deputation and to attend my classes.

I began classes in January 1964 at the University of Cincinnati (UC) in Ohio. The school accepted some of my credits from Intercession City Biblical College in Intercession City, Florida, and God's Bible School in Cincinnati, Ohio. That made it possible for me to be classified as a junior. The University was on the quarter system and I took five successive quarters, ending in the spring of 1965. At that time I lacked one subject to graduate. On my next furlough I attended summer school, successfully completed my work, and graduated in August 1971 with a Bachelor of Arts in history.

On May 25, 1964, I left class at the University and was returning to the campus of GBS where I was boarding. I turned onto Young Street and stopped and offered three GBS students a ride to the Laundromat. They declined, so I continued on my way. As I entered the intersection of Young Street and Carmalt Street, a car entered on my right. A bush on the corner obstructed my view, and I hit the car on the left side. I knew immediately that my right leg was broken. A man behind me stopped and called the police.

Two police cars soon came. One of the policemen asked the driver of the other car if he had been drinking, and he said he had one or two drinks. Then an officer came to my car and asked if I wanted to go to the General Hospital. I told him I wanted to go to Christ Hospital, which is not far from GBS. Two policemen helped to get me out of my car and took me in a police cruiser to the hospital. Thelma Witherup, who was also attending UC, notified the University of my accident.

At the hospital I learned that my left ankle was crushed and that I had two broken ribs on my left side. I wanted to lie down to ease the pain of my broken leg and crushed ankle, but my broken ribs were too painful. To make myself comfortable, I spent most of my time sitting, propped against pillows. My injuries kept me in the hospital for sixteen days, and during that time camp meeting was in progress at GBS. My days were brightened by many people coming to visit me. I had a very caring orthopedic surgeon, and after I was discharged from the hospital, I continued under his care at his private practice.

In Christ Hospital in Cincinnati, Ohio, after my
accident in 1964

The morning of my discharge, a policeman came to my hospital room with a notice for me to sign. It stated that I was to appear in court on a certain date for a hearing. To my astonishment I learned that I was accused of reckless driving. I was granted a postponement until I was able to appear in court.

Two men from GBS came in a van and took me to Newport, Kentucky, to stay for a few weeks with my nephew Ronald Moser and his family. His son, Kevin, was a baby, and when his mother went on an errand, she would put Kevin in his car seat and place him on my bed with me to keep him safe while she was gone. Later Lester and Helen and their two sons, who were attending a camp meeting in Kentucky, took me to Doris' home in Shamokin. She was a blessing to me as I convalesced.

During the month of August, I was with my sister Eva and her husband, Harry Moser, in Coopersburg, Pennsylvania. While at their home the Ebenezer New Reformed Church where they attended in the Coopersburg area gave me a "sunshine box." Each day I looked forward to opening a gift from it.

When my cousin Raymond Maurer and his wife took me back to Cincinnati to attend the court hearing in September, I was still using a wheelchair. After my accident a yield sign was put on Carmalt Street because Young Street was traveled more than Carmalt Street. A policeman was at the hearing and showed a photo of that yield sign. The judge asked him if the sign was there the day of the accident, and he replied, "No, but it is there now." The judge made remarks about too many people not having liability insurance and dismissed the case. Evidently the other driver did not have liability insurance, but EFM carried it on the Volkswagen that I was driving, which was damaged beyond repair.

After the court hearing my cast was removed from my right leg. I returned to my studies at UC and continued boarding at GBS. The students were not allowed to use the university elevators, but because of my injuries, I was given a key to the elevators so I could get to my class-rooms. I hired various GBS students to take me there and assist me in getting to the floor where my classes were held. I could get from class to class by using my wheelchair. Whenever my classes were finished for the day, a GBS student came and took me to my room on campus.

Later I began using a walker, and then the day arrived for me to begin using crutches. Beverly Fay, a student at GBS, and at present a missionary in Canada, came to my room to help me get started. I lost my courage because I was afraid I would fall and break my leg or ankle again. Bev left my room stating that she would come another day to help me. After she left, I thought to myself, *If I don't learn to use crutches and learn to walk again, I will never get back to the mission field.* With the Lord's help, the next time Bev came, I was able to start using them. Even-tually I could walk by using only one crutch, and finally after five months I discarded that one. I certainly praised the Lord for all the assistance He gave me throughout that ordeal.

* * * * *

The following spring the GBS students and their spouses decided to raise money for missions. I joined them in the project because I was living in the dormitory. We were divided into teams of two, and my team-mate was a young married woman whose husband attended GBS. Our instructions were for each team to invest a dollar, find a way to make profit, and reinvest the money until the project ended. My teammate and I decided to make house slippers from washcloths. She made all sizes, and I sold them. Our initial investment was $1.69, and over a period of several months, we made $70.00. It was a thrill to invest that much money in missions.

Chapter 6

Continued Egyptian Ministry and Evacuation
1965-1967

Going to Egypt Again

In early October 1965 Doris took me to Pierrepont Manor, New York, to again visit my friend Harriette Harp. I was on my way to Montreal, Canada, to sail to Egypt for my third term. Mark Kolva from Berrysburg, Pennsylvania, previously had trucked my baggage to Pierrepont Manor. I was returning by ship rather than by plane because I could take my baggage free on the ship.

Ronald, Margaret, Timothy, and Dennis
Robbins

Ronald and Margaret Robbins with their young sons, Timothy and Dennis, were already in Montreal. They were new missionaries to Egypt under EFM and would be sailing with me. They were driving a Rambler that was being shipped with us to Egypt.

Leonard and Lillian Lum in Brushton, New York, asked Harriette and me to have a missionary service in their church on Sunday. With permission from the Lums, I contacted the Robbins family and invited them to spend Sunday with us. Harriette and I drove to Brushton on Saturday evening and met the Robbins, who had arrived that afternoon.

During Sunday school Harriette and Margaret told about some of their missionary experiences, and Ronald and I spoke in the morning service. After a delicious meal with the Lums, the Robbins, Harriette, and I drove to Pierrepont Manor for an evening service where Levi and Lydia Troyer pastored. I talked to the young people, and Ronald and Margaret

109

spoke in the main service. At the close of the service, Harriette and I returned to her home, and the Robbins family stayed with the Troyers.

Monday was a day of pleasant surprises. In the morning we had a short visit from our mission director Victor Glenn and Juddie Peyton who were on their way to Harrisburg, Pennsylvania, after having a week of meetings in Canada. Later, while we were eating dinner, we had another unexpected visitor, Eugene Tierney, who was in the area for missionary services for EFM. That evening he showed slides of Egypt at the Troyers' home and spent the night with them.

The Troyers and Eugene bade the Robbins and me farewell when we left for Montreal Tuesday morning at 4:00. William and Ruth Ann Caster, Harriette, and two other ladies traveled with us. William rented a small trailer to take my baggage from Pierrepont Manor to Montreal. After the Casters unloaded my baggage at the dock, our group ate dinner and then went to our hotel. I was happy to see Harry and Eva, who had just arrived at the hotel.

After breakfast the next morning, our group went to the dock because we had been told that the Dutch *Bengkalis,* the ship on which we were to sail, would arrive about 8:00. We had plenty of time because it did not dock until 11:30. Harry and Eva wanted to see my cabin, but they had to leave for home before we were allowed to board.

Because our ship would not leave until the next day, we had time to go sightseeing. In the afternoon most of our group went to see the magnificent architecture, sculpture, and paintings at the Notre-Dame-De-Don-Secours Church in Montreal. Ronald did not join us because we learned that the Robbins' baggage, which had been shipped six weeks earlier, had not arrived. He finally located it in a warehouse in Detroit, Michigan! After several telephone calls it was arranged to have their baggage flown to Montreal. However, our ship would leave before the baggage arrived, so Ronald planned to get a rental truck and take the baggage to Quebec City, which was the next stop for the *Bengkalis.*

Wednesday afternoon the Leonard Lums and another lady came from Brushton to bid us farewell. They spent several hours on board ship with us and our friends from Pierrepont Manor. Some of the ladies from Pierrepont Manor returned with the Lums, and that made it possible for the Casters to stay and help Ronald with his baggage problem. They used the trailer they had rented to bring my things to Montreal and hauled the Robbins' baggage to Quebec City.

Before the *Bengkalis* left Montreal, a florist delivered a beautiful pot of sixteen yellow chrysanthemums to the ship for me. It was a gift from Lester and Helen. Our ship left shortly after midnight on the 15th and docked at Quebec City at 11:30 a.m. It was a relief to see Ronald and the Casters arrive with the missing baggage at 3:30. We were grateful that William was willing to miss another day of work to help with that difficult situation.

The *Bengkalis* left Quebec City at midnight on Friday. Soon after we left, our captain received news of hurricane Elena in the North Atlantic. He veered south to miss the worst part of the storm, but we lost ten hours in doing so. Although we avoided the actual hurricane, we were affected by rough seas. We experienced twenty-foot swells, which were only about one-third of the height I had faced while crossing the Atlantic in 1958.

Early on the trip the Lord gave me Psalm 118:17 as a promise: "I shall not die, but live, and declare the works of the LORD." That promise was precious to me when the ship was tossing in those ocean swells. I closed a letter to my family with the words: "God has been so good to me, better than I deserve. Oh, how I love Him, my precious Redeemer. I want to give Him the best service I can render to help needy souls find their way to Him."

We reached the Azores by Wednesday evening and then enjoyed smooth sailing. Amazingly, no one had become seriously seasick during the previous stormy days. As we sailed past the islands, the captain allowed us on the bridge to see one of the beacon lights. He explained the instruments and told us that we had averaged about four hundred miles a day while crossing the Atlantic in spite of the hurricane.

One day the captain and chief steward showed us the pantry and the kitchen. The cook appeared to be about twenty-five years old, and the baker looked somewhat younger. However, he was a good baker, and we looked forward to fresh homemade bread for every meal—wheat, white, raisin, Italian-style, hard rolls, and pastries. Our meals were always served in courses with the evening meal being the largest. I felt sorry for the dishwashers because we were given clean dishes for every course.

It was a delight to have the Robbins family on board. We enjoyed Christian fellowship and sometimes shared our evening devotions. Timothy and Dennis attempted to call me Miss Maurer but usually said, "Mee Mau." There were three other passengers on board, Mr. and Mrs. Eagan and Mary, a sister-in-law.

While we sailed through the Strait of Gibraltar late Saturday night, we faced forty-mile-an-hour headwinds, which reduced our speed to fifteen knots. The captain sailed a few miles off the coast of Algiers, endeavoring to find a current flowing east that would save fuel. He was successful. After we reached the Mediterranean Sea, we had smooth sailing again and began seeing more ships.

Earlier in the week Ronald received permission to have a service on Sunday. I typed copies of a few songs from memory for the service. On Sunday, the 24th, the Lord helped Ronald preach on the subject "Show Me Thy Way." Four officers and the captain with the other three passengers attended the service.

In the afternoon we arrived at Malta, an island off the southern tip of Italy, and anchored in the harbor for a few hours. No one went on shore because he would have needed to take a rowboat. A new captain and also the wife of the first mate, the man next to the captain, came on board. Soon after we left Malta, we passed the island of Crete. Later I realized that the ship on which the Apostle Paul sailed docked at the Fair Havens in Crete, and that Malta is the island where they suffered shipwreck and spent three months before continuing to Rome to testify before Caesar.

All the stewards were Chinese except the chief steward. One was named Tan, one was named Wee, and another one we called Smiley because he was very sober. Later we learned that his name was Lee. The captain told us that when Lee got his mind set on doing something a certain way, he persisted in doing it that way. For instance, if he started at one end to clean the officers' rooms and came to a room that was occupied, he waited until the officer left so that he could clean it before going to the next room.

We arrived in Beirut, Lebanon, early Friday morning and were permitted to go ashore. The Eagans, Robbins, and I took a tour of the ancient cities of Byblos and Baalbek. Later that day we viewed the lofty mountains of the Lebanon and Anti-Lebanon ranges, the broad valley of Bekaa between the ranges, and Mount Hermon in the distance. We enjoyed traveling through colorful valleys, arriving back at our ship at 6:30 that evening.

The next day when a launch was taking the Robbins and me to shore for another sightseeing tour, Ronald noticed an American ship, the *Steel Voyager*, docked nearby. We knew that the families of Maurice Hobart and Leroy Adams, EFM missionaries on their way to Eritrea, Ethiopia, were sailing on a Steel ship. We inquired and learned that they were passengers on the *Voyager*. We visited with the Hobarts and the Adams children, but Leroy and Myrtle were ashore. It was exciting to see EFM missionaries at the port in Beirut.

After the crew finished loading the cargo and making some engine repairs, we sailed for Port Said, Egypt. On Saturday evening we gave the stewards their tips, which was customary and expected when traveling by ship. The next morning, October 31, we landed at Port Said.

Before we left the ship that morning, I gave my beautiful chrysanthemums to the Eagans because it would be impossible to take them through customs. They planned to give the flowers to the captain when they disembarked. We had sailed approximately five thousand five hundred miles. I was thankful to God for a safe journey back to the land of my calling.

The Guy Troyer family and Ruth Franklin were at the dock to meet us and help with our luggage after we cleared customs. Ruth and I were to have sailed together in September 1964, but because of my accident, she sailed alone. She was living with the Troyers in Alexandria until my arrival.

Guy and Ronald had no problem getting the Rambler or the Robbins' baggage out of customs, but my baggage was a different story. It was the middle of December before my things were released from customs.

Ministering During a Third Term

Ruth Franklin, my co-worker in Egypt and Ethiopia from 1965 to 1969

The Robbins family, Ruth, and I went to Girga in Upper Egypt soon after we arrived. The Robbins moved into a large apartment above our church, while Ruth and I lived in an apartment above the Bible school classrooms. Ronald, Ruth, and I taught Bible school classes. It was a joy to be back in Girga, teaching and visiting our village churches. The Rambler was a big help in visiting those churches.

Our classes were held Tuesday through Friday, leaving Monday free for the students who were pastoring some of those churches to return to Girga. Besides teaching I spoke once a week in chapel and at least one time every weekend in our churches.

For Christmas that year the Robbins family, Ruth, and I went to Alexandria to be with the Troyers. We enjoyed helping to make various Christmas candies—teaberry- and chocolate-flavored fondant, sea foam, peanut clusters, peanut brittle, and taffy.

Following Christmas break we returned to Girga and continued our teaching and village visitation. Our second semester closed with a graduation ceremony on May 24, 1966. Ruth and I stayed in Girga for a couple weeks to prepare materials for Sunday school lessons; then we went to Alexandria for two months. It was always refreshing to leave the dry, dust-filled air of Girga and enjoy the wonderful sea breezes from the Mediterranean Sea.

In July we attended our fourth annual Sunday school convention being held at that time in Aboukir. It was the second year that we joined the convention with the young men's conference and also the second time to have delegates from the northern and southern districts. We set aside the first two and a half days for the Sunday school convention, and the rest of the week for the young men's conference.

Sunday school convention in Aboukir in 1966

Our topic for the convention was personal evangelism. Each day we had two preaching services, one teaching session, a discussion period, a time for learning new choruses, and sessions of prayer. Several of our missionaries gave the lectures, and Ronald Robbins and Tewfik Mishriky, an Egyptian minister, served as our evangelists.

God met with us in a special way in the second evening service. A spirit of prayer was prevalent the entire time. Two workers prayed through to entire sanctification, and the Spirit moved on hearts with rejoicing and shouting. When the neighbors heard the shouting, they came, thinking someone was being harmed or killed. Some of our younger men had never seen such a manifestation of the Holy Spirit.

Our time during the young men's conference was filled with classes and group discussions. We focused on issues relevant to our young men in an Egyptian society.

On the last Saturday in July, Ruth and I rode a second-class, air-conditioned train to Cairo, but from there we experienced a dusty train ride through the desert to Suez. I preached Sunday morning, and Ruth preached in the evening service. That afternoon we both attended Sunday school and taught new choruses to the children.

Monday morning we met with the Sunday school teachers and workers for about two hours, giving them suggestions for evangelizing children. Then we worked on preparing Sunday school lessons, and I prepared a message for the evening service. We were served a tasty noon meal. The menu included goose, spaghetti, cracked wheat, and *moulokhia*, which is a soup made from leaves of a plant and seasoned with garlic. Mangoes were served for our dessert. That evening we attended a young women's meeting before going to the revival service. After we prayed with seekers at the altar, we went to a believer's home for tea and cake at 10:00. We were not hungry when we went to the pastor's house later for supper.

On Tuesday we returned by express bus to Cairo, did some mission business, and then took the noon train to Alexandria. We thanked God for a profitable trip to Suez.

Ruth and I returned to Girga on August 11 to get ready for school. Painters whitewashed and painted our apartment, some of the Bible school rooms, the stairwell, and Robbins' apartment across the street. It took them about two weeks to complete everything. The Robbins family returned to Girga later that summer.

Our Girga pastor decided to leave the church, so we covered his responsibilities until another pastor came. Ronald preached for the Sunday services. Ruth and a Bible school student took the women's meeting and "Sunday" school on Thursdays at our smaller meeting place in another part of town. I took the women's meeting in our main church on Tuesdays.

I never knew whether an ordinary day would end with joy or sadness. One evening I took some garbage to the neighbors because they wanted to dry it and use it as fuel for baking bread. When I arrived, I found their baby boy had been sick for a few days and was seri- ously ill. They had taken

Speaking in a women's meeting in Ameeria, Cairo

him to a doctor, but I offered to take the mother and baby to a young Presbyterian doctor in town, and she consented. Upon examination the doctor found the baby had a high temperature, pneumonia, and was very near death. He told me in English that the infant would be dead by morning and asked me to tell the mother after we arrived back at their home. There was nothing he could do for the baby at that stage. We heard wailing at 11:30 p.m. and learned the next morning the infant had died. He was buried that day without embalming, which is the custom in Egypt.

During 1966 Ruth and I did not have a cook. We spent much time preparing our meals and making food items that we could not buy such as ketchup, crackers, and peanut butter. For example, to make peanut butter we shelled peanuts and put them through the food grinder ten times before they reached the proper consistency. We soaked our vegetables and fruits in a solution to kill bacteria and parasites, sifted our flour to remove worms and bugs, and ground meat to make hamburger.

A few weeks before Christmas, a woman came to visit me and brought her ten-year-old son who frequently had been sick for the past seven years. He was stunted in size and was unable to stand straight. The family was extremely poor because the husband was not able to get work on a regular basis, and when he did work, he earned only 20 cents a day. It was evident that the boy needed help. I contacted a doctor who examined the lad without cost. He wrote a prescription for treating worms, but when the mother went to the pharmacy to get the medication, she did not have enough money. With disappointment she returned to my house, and I went with her and helped pay for the medicine.

Because the Egyptian people did not celebrate Christmas as we Americans did, there was nothing in our town to remind us that Christmas was approaching. However, Christmas cards and letters received from the States served as a reminder. It was special to have the Troyers come from Alexandria to spend Christmas vacation with us. On Christmas Day the Troyers, the Robbins, Ruth, and I went to Sohag to spend the day with the Tierneys, who had returned from the States in August.

Egyptian missionaries at Christmas time 1966. Back row: Eugene Tierney, Stephen Troyer, Timothy Robbins, Fern Tierney, me, Ruth Franklin, Margaret Robbins, Dana and Guy Troyer. Front row: Darrell and Marie Tierney, Dennis Robbins, Deborah and Naomi Troyer, and Ruth Tierney.
(Picture taken by Ronald Robbins)

Prior to the Egyptian Christmas on January 7, 1967, the Robbins family, Ruth, and I made small calendars for our Sunday school children by using the pictures from religious greeting cards. We made 1,000 calendars, and that was not enough.

Immediately after the Egyptian Christmas, Ruth and I went to visit a poor widow who attended our Girga church. Her husband had been killed tragically about a year and a half prior to our visit, and since then she had been sad and sick. I asked her about her spiritual condition, and she acknowledged she was backslidden but said that she wanted to be restored. We knelt in her dingy little room, and God met her need.

Our praying attracted the widow's in-laws who lived next door. Her sister-in-law came and sat on the steps outside the door to hear what we were saying. That gave us an opportunity to talk with her, and soon she invited us into her home. There we met her eighty-year-old husband, who suffered from poor eyesight, and their married daughter. All three wanted to pray for salvation, but the elderly husband did not know how to pray. I asked him if he ever had been saved, and he answered, "No." I prayed a prayer of repentance and asked him to repeat it after me. We were thankful for the privilege of ministering to that family.

Later I spoke with our widow friend in church. She indicated that things were much better since she prayed.

In February Victor Glenn, Glenn Griffith, and Ray Chamberlain visited the work in Egypt. They held special meetings in our churches in the Girga area. As they ministered, God used them to give help and encouragement to our workers and the believers. A father in our main Girga church was sanctified.

Our annual conference was held in Girga in May. The Troyers and Robbins came from Alexandria. The Robbins family was staying with Troyers because Ronald was recuperating from hepatitis. They returned to Alexandria after conference ended.

The speakers in our February convention in 1967:Ray Chamberlain, Glenn Griffith, and Victor Glenn

* * * * *

One of my major concerns during that term was the work in Bindar. By the fall of 1965, our work there looked bleak because attendance was low and there was no pastor. I became convinced that God would be pleased for a group of us to visit Bindar. We made plans to go on a Wednesday afternoon. After we had prayer at the Bible school, Ruth, some of the students, and I went. Many children quickly gathered around us, so one of the students took them inside the church for a service and the rest of our group went calling in homes.

We were encouraged by the good response, so a group of us started going to Bindar every Wednesday afternoon. We continued having children's services for several months, and the number ranged from 100 to

150. Soon we started evening services that were also encouraging, and the number kept growing until we averaged 80 or more. Two Bible school students continued the weekly visits during the summer while Ruth and I went to Alexandria for two months.

When Ruth and I returned to Girga that fall, we continued going to Bindar. In November Ibrahim Farah accepted an assignment as pastor of the church. He attended Bible school while he pastored. In January the public schools were on midterm vacation, and he chose to spend part of his vacation in revival services in Bindar. The services went well, and the people asked for another week of meetings. Ibrahim arranged for speakers, and crowds came nightly. God blessed and people claimed victory. In some services the people asked for a second message. One night the church was crowded with more than 200 people. Then they asked for a third week of services, and finally they asked for nightly services to continue. In the months that followed, God mightily blessed the work in Bindar.

Six-Day War and Evacuation

Guy Troyer, who was the missionary field director, was living in Alexandria. He called us during the third week of May and asked us to change the date of the Bible school graduation from June 7 to May 31 because political tension was mounting between Egypt and Israel. He had received notice from the American Consulate advising us to evacuate. We were to prepare to leave Egypt on short notice.

Busy days followed. We gave final exams, packed things that would remain in Egypt, sold some things, packed others to take with us, and visited with friends who came to bid us farewell. We had graduation on the 31st. The Tierney family, Ruth Franklin, and I left Upper Egypt on Saturday, June 3, and went to Alexandria. I never went to bed the previous night because I was busy turning over financial accounts to our national workers.

Politically the situation was tense, but there was no violence or rioting. We missionaries met in the Troyers' home to discuss what we should do. After we sought God's direction, we decided that at least the women and children should leave Egypt. However, hostilities broke out on Monday morning before we could carry out those plans. Israeli aircraft bombed the airport in Cairo and fighting began in the Sinai Peninsula.

We then decided that all EFM missionaries should leave, but Guy insisted on remaining for a while. We spent the next day getting our exit and reentry visas and going to the bank. Each person in our group was allowed to take only $11.00 (U.S.).

That same day the American Consulate in Alexandria was burned. Two Americans locked themselves inside the fire-proof safe for three and a half hours. When the police and trusted friends came, the Americans opened the safe and were taken to the police station for protection. Later they were released. At night we experienced blackouts and could hear the firing of the antiaircraft guns.

After diplomatic relations were severed between the United States and Egypt, several young men gathered outside the Troyers' house. One of them looked at us with a sneer, and we began to fear trouble. We contacted Rubeel, a retired police officer of high rank, and asked him to stay at the Troyers' home to provide protection for us.

Guy, Eugene, Ronald, Ruth, and I went downtown on Wednesday with our passports to look for passage from Egypt. Hundreds of foreigners wanted to leave. Our names were placed on a list for passage on an Italian ship or on a Yugoslavian ship.

Shortly before 3:30 p.m. the shipping agent called and said we could go on the Yugoslavian ship. Guy and Eugene hurriedly went to purchase our tickets. After they returned, Eugene told us that some of the people in the travel office, when asked where they wanted to go, said, "Anywhere. It doesn't matter, just so we get out of Egypt."

Guy took his wife and children, Ruth, and me to the harbor in the mission vehicle. The Tierneys and the Robbins came to the harbor in two taxis. As they were putting their suitcases into the cabs, about fifteen young people with clubs gathered on a corner a short distance away. Rubeel went and showed them his badge. When they saw it, they refrained from any action. He was used of God to protect our missionaries.

The travel agents told us the ship would wait for us even though it was past the scheduled departure time. We hurried to the harbor but got there in time to see it leaving. We learned later that the government ordered it to leave at 5:30, and we got there about 5:45. God was working in our behalf because that ship would have taken us to Yugoslavia, and from there we would have needed to get flights to Greece and then flights to either America or Ethiopia.

The agents then assured us that they would get passage for us on one of the two Italian ships that were in the harbor. We spent the night in a hotel near the travel agency. Thursday morning Guy and Eugene were called to the agents' office. Eugene returned and hailed two taxis to take us to the office. Because much time was spent in preparing the tickets, it became necessary for us to return to the hotel. We stayed in the taxis to avoid any unnecessary delay. Finally, Guy and Eugene came with one of the agents to hurry us to the harbor.

In customs the Americans were thoroughly searched and had many items confiscated. I lost all the slides of America and Egypt that I had with me, plus the diary of my trip to Egypt in 1965. I also lost my graded thesis for my degree from the University of Cincinnati and my recent income-tax papers. Ruth's sermon notes and Ronald's tapes and slides were taken. Officials searched Ruth's and Margaret's shoes and Margaret's hair that was in a bun. The lining of my handbag was ripped to make sure nothing was hidden there. They also took our films. After we cleared customs, we proceeded to immigration. By 12:30 p.m. our group was on board the *La Esperia*. **What a relief!** Then we noticed there was a commotion in the harbor a short distance away and were told that an Israeli frogman had been captured. Our ship finally left Alexandria at 5:30 that afternoon, and we were able to relax.

The passenger capacity of our ship was 250, but there were more than 1200 on board and over 200 of them without beds. Some had only chairs on the decks for their quarters. Baggage was stacked in the wider hall areas. The food and service were excellent in spite of the large number of passengers.

The *La Esperia* docked at Naples, Italy, on Sunday morning. American embassy personnel came on board, helped us through customs, and took us in a U.S. Navy bus to a hotel. Dana Troyer and her children soon left by plane for Paris where they stayed overnight before flying to the States. The Tierneys went by train to Rome on Monday and then flew to the States. Guy eventually left Egypt on the 24th and joined his family.

The Robbins, Ruth, and I were planning to go to Eritrea, the northern province of Ethiopia. We had not purchased air tickets in Egypt because our first report indicated that it was not safe for us to go there. The next report indicated otherwise. After we arrived in Naples, we purchased tickets to Rome, the capital of Italy, and to Asmara, Ethiopia. We also obtained tourist visas. Later that day we flew to Rome and went directly to the Ethiopian airlines counter. The clerk refused us flight to Ethiopia because we had neither resident visas for that country nor tickets to a destination beyond Ethiopia, which was required when entering on a tourist visa. However, our luggage had been put on the plane to Ethiopia, so we had to file a claim to have it returned.

After midnight on Sunday we went by bus to the bus terminal in Rome, our first time there. Providentially, an agent of the Pensione Werder, a small hotel, was there and offered to help us secure rooms for a reasonable rate. A few days later the same agent found cheaper rooms at Pensione Olivieri. At the first place we paid $34.00 a day for room and board for the six of us, whereas we paid only $28.00 at the second place. On Tuesday our luggage was returned to Rome. What a relief to have clean clothes again. We stayed in Rome for three weeks, and during that time we visited the Vatican City where St. Peter's basilica is located. We also saw some of the sights of Rome—the Roman Forum, the Colosseum, the Old Appian Way, the two main catacombs, and the Flaminian Way.

Victor Glenn contacted Mark Budensiek in Ethiopia and asked him to work on obtaining resident visas for us. Eventually he obtained visitor visas for us for Ethiopia. Our flight from Rome to Athens, where we had to change planes, left several hours late. We had planned to spend the afternoon touring parts of Athens, but we did not clear customs until 9:00 p.m. A clerk at the Ethiopian Airlines desk arranged for a taxi driver to take us on a quick tour of the city. Unfortunately, he could not speak English, but we did see the Parthenon, King Constantine's palace, and some other sites of interest. After an hour he took us back to the airport.

On our TWA flight to Athens, half of our group had a full-course meal and the others received only snacks. We did not know which half received the wrong menu, but those who received snacks were hungry after taking a tour of Athens. We went to eat before our 1:00 a.m. departure for Cairo and Asmara on July 4.

We joyfully greeted our fellow Americans—Mark and Nancy Budensiek, Arlene Troyer, and Faith Hemmeter—who welcomed us at the airport in Asmara. After we cleared customs, we visited with the Wayne Sanders family who was living in the city, did a little shopping, and then our group went to the U.S. Army base for breakfast. From there we traveled to Decamere and enjoyed a special native meal with the Budensieks. We ended our American Independence Day celebration by eating homemade ice cream with the missionaries in Decamere.

Chapter 7

First Years in Ethiopia
1967-1971

Early Happenings

Living in Decamere was quite different from living in Alexandria. I had become accustomed to the large city and the constant noise in the streets of Alexandria. Decamere, on the other hand, was a quaint little town with a small population and little noise. In fact, sometimes I felt lonesome in the quietness when the other missionaries were occupied.

Shortly after the Robbins family, Ruth, and I arrived in Ethiopia, the mission leaders sent Ruth and me to the lowland town of Agordat to work with Zettie Finch who had been transferred from the orphanage in Decamere. On our way there we visited with EFM missionaries Meredith and Marteena Armour in Keren. I first met them when I was a student at GBS in the early 1960s. Meredith had been working at Christ Hospital in Cincinnati in 1964 when I had my accident, and he helped to take me to my room after surgery.

When we arrived in Agordat, we noticed that it was much warmer than Decamere and similar to the hot summers in Girga, Upper Egypt. Although it was the rainy season, the rains were spasmodic. The town had many Arabic-speaking Moslems, and because Ruth and I spoke

Faith Mission church in the capital city of Asmara, Eritrea

Arabic, we spent some of our time in house-to-house visitation among them.

During the first two weeks of August, Tekie Mebrahtu, one of our national pastors, conducted revival services at our church in Asmara, the capital of the Eritrean province of Ethiopia. There was much

123

interest, and attendance increased to over 400 some evenings. Several sought the Lord.

I was asked to come the following week and continue the revival services over the next two Sundays. Every evening except one the altar was lined with young people seeking God and some finding peace in their souls.

Fucadu was one of the young ladies who found the Lord. She had attended services in other churches but found no satisfaction. One day while she was walking by our church, she decided to attend the services. From the very beginning she was interested in salvation and began to seek God. She also went to the home of Pastor Mesgun Tedla and his wife, Zewdie, several days during the meetings and had Bible studies with them. The fifth night of the services, she found the peace that she had been seeking.

Another of the converts was Yefter, a young man who spent a few of his childhood years in the mission orphanage in Decamere. His friend Yemane also gave his heart to the Lord in that revival. Both of those young men were about eighteen. Today each of them is married and still serving the Lord. Yefter is a taxi driver in Indianapolis, Indiana, and Yemane has an upholstery business in Asmara, Eritrea.

During one of the services, Fessehaye, a young naval officer assigned to the flagship of the Ethiopian

With Yemane and Maoza on their wedding day

navy, stood outside the church listening. The Lord dealt with him about his spiritual condition, and before the revival ended, he gave his heart to the Lord.

The last night of the revival a young man came to mock, and a demon took control of him. While the Christians prayed, the young man confessed his sins, found deliverance, and was saved. It became evident from his confession that he had gone to the depths of sin, but our God forgave every transgression. There were other wonderful victories for which we praised God!

For two years after Fessehaye's conversion, he faced much persecution. He stood the test and gained the respect of the other sailors. Eventually he was allowed to preach on his ship. At first, attendance was optional, but later it became mandatory. God helped him, and he had the joy of seeing many of the sailors saved. The Holy Spirit began dealing with the new converts about correcting their past. When the ship stopped at various ports where it had docked previously, several disembarked and made their restitutions.

Some of the sailors, including Fessehaye, came to a later convention as their leaves of absence permitted. The only one of them who had not been baptized was baptized the last day of the convention. It was a thrill to see their zeal for the Lord. Those sailors were stationed at various places in Ethiopia, and at each location they held services or Bible studies for their fellow servicemen.

Later when a new captain was assigned to the ship, the former captain advised him to allow Fessehaye to continue holding services on board. He informed the new captain that the sailors had stopped fighting with each other because of Fessehaye's preaching. With emphasis he said, "If you want peace on this ship, I advise you to let these services continue."

One day the crown prince, the son of King Haile Selassie, came on board. He saw Fessehaye and asked, "Are you the Fessehaye Asgodom that holds services on this ship?" He answered that he was. The prince admonished him, "Stick to the Coptic Church."

At first Fessehaye did not know what to say. He bowed his head and breathed a prayer asking God how he should reply. Then looking at the crown prince, he humbly said, "I'll mind God."

The crown prince answered, "You do that." To that comment he added, "Tell me where you want to go to Bible college, and I will pay your way. It does not matter if you want to go to England or to the United States; I will pay your way."

Fessehaye answered that he wanted to attend Faith Mission Bible College in Decamere. The prince paid his way to attend our school to become a navy chaplain.

Victor Glenn and Glenn Griffith came for our fall convention. The Eritrean field usually had two annual conventions, one in February and the other in September, and both were held in Decamere because of adequate facilities to accommodate 400-500 people. It was my first time to attend such a convention in Eritrea. The missionaries, most of the national workers, and many believers attended those conventions. They were the highlights of the year, were times of spiritual refreshing, and were like holiness camp meetings in America—prayers ascending day and night and times of fasting.

During that convention there was shouting in some of the services, but others had a more serious tone. Oh, it was wonderful! Twice the Holy Spirit came with such conviction that individuals sought God before there was any preaching. Many received spiritual help. One of our teachers was sanctified and two young men from our church in Massawa followed Christ in the sacrament of water baptism, which has more significance in Ethiopia than in the United States. It is a testimony that they have broken from a formal religion or a pagan culture to follow Christ.

After the convention Ruth returned to Agordat to help Zettie in the elementary school, and I was assigned to teach in the high school in Decamere. My classes included social studies for grades nine through twelve and Bible for grade twelve.

I moved in with Arlene Troyer who was living on the first floor of the apartment building on our high-school compound. Elsabet, an Eritrean teacher and wife of Tekie Mebrahtu who was studying in the States, lived in the apartment across the hall from us. Faith Hemmeter and the Robbins family lived in the two apartments above us. We four ladies—Elsabet, Faith, Arlene, and I—ate our noon meals together on Monday through

With my ninth-grade social studies class in 1967

Thursday; on Friday we attended the noon prayer and fasting time in the chapel. Each of us prepared one noon meal a week. We three missionary ladies also took turns preparing our breakfasts and suppers.

By October the evenings were getting chilly and damp from the fog that resulted from the cold mountain air. One of the rooms in our apartment had a fireplace, and I enjoyed sitting near the fire to keep warm while I worked on school material or wrote letters to my family and friends. Later I purchased a bottled-gas heater for my room, and it did an excellent job of dispelling the chill and dampness of the winter nights.

The Budensiek family invited Arlene, Faith, and me to join them for a delicious ham dinner on Thanksgiving Day. They also invited three of our national high-school teachers for the meal. Even though it was not an Ethiopian holiday, we missionaries were excused from teaching our classes that day.

The missionaries and national preachers went to Agordat the following day to attend a holiness convention. There were no dormitories or special guest rooms available for the weekend, and our places of lodging varied. The Eritrean men slept in classrooms, the single ladies stayed with Zettie in the mission house, and the missionary families slept in tents or make-shift abodes using tarpaulins and their vehicles. We had services on Friday evening and three times each day on Saturday and Sunday. Missionaries and nationals challenged us with their messages, and we shared some precious times of prayer. God met with us in a special way and encouraged our hearts in Him.

Christmas Vacation

As the Christmas season approached, the missionaries planned activities that represented our cultural background. On Christmas Eve Leroy Adams, several high-school students, Faith, Arlene, and I went caroling. We left the high-school compound at 10:00 p.m. and walked down the main street of Decamere and sang until 12:30. At each place where we stopped, Leroy and two students played their trumpets before we sang. Even though we had permission from the police captain to carol, we had some misunderstanding with a few Ethiopian soldiers near their barracks because they did not know about our school and the permission we had. It was a misty night, and we were damp when we arrived back at the compound.

Faith, Arlene, and I enjoyed two Christmas meals that year. The three of us and Elsabet had a candlelight supper on Christmas Eve. Then on Christmas Day the missionaries in Decamere and the Sanders family from Asmara met together for a traditional American Christmas dinner.

Ruth and I flew from Asmara to Addis Ababa, the capital of Ethiopia, two days after Christmas. We had entered the country with visitor visas but needed resident visas to remain in Ethiopia. The Ethiopian government required us to leave the country, obtain resident visas, and then reenter. We chose to go to nearby French Somaliland. Menghistab Ghebrechristos, one of our believers in Addis Ababa, was excused from his work at the Ethiopian Airlines and went with us to the French Embassy to help us apply for our visas to French Somaliland. Menghistab spoke to our taxi driver in Amharic, the language used in many parts of Ethiopia, who then spoke to the clerk in Italian because no one at the embassy could understand English or Amharic.

While we waited a few days for our visas to French Somaliland, we toured parts of Addis Ababa. We also worshipped with the believers on Sunday and attended their first service in a newly rented place. The compound had living quarters for the Robbins family, a large room for worship services, and a place for the national pastor to live. We stayed

Menghistab and Nigisty Ghebrechristos with their children, Lydia and Eritrea, in Addis Ababa, Ethiopia

in the apartment where the Robbins would be living.

When our French Somaliland visas were granted, we flew to Djibouti, the capital of that country. We went directly to the Ethiopian embassy and without any difficulty obtained our resident visas. Because of our flight schedule, we spent the night in Djibouti and returned to Addis Ababa the next day. During the flight we were pleased that the pilot invited us to see the cockpit.

The Wednesday evening before we returned to Asmara, the Robbins family reached Addis Ababa. For three days they had driven over unpaved mountain roads.

After we returned to Asmara on January 4, 1968, Ruth and I started the process of obtaining work permits. Later that month Arlene, Faith, and Elsabet went to Agordat to visit Zettie. Ruth could not return to Agordat at that time because she was ill and needed to stay in Asmara under doctor's observation. I could not go until the next day after the work permits for Ruth and me were completed, so I went by bus with the Agordat pastor, who was returning home from Asmara.

Zettie took us to a factory where they processed palm branches into a soft fluffy fiber used in making mattresses. She also drove to a banana garden where the guard gave us a stalk of green bananas for which we were thankful. We had a pleasant stay in Agordat, relaxing and enjoying the wonderful weather. I found time to grade some papers and to read for one of my history classes.

After we visited Zettie for a few days, we persuaded her to take us by car to Asmara instead of the four of us going by bus. Because of a lack of space, we left the bananas in Agordat. We gave Zettie the equivalent of our bus fares to pay for gas. We visited Ruth in Asmara and then decided to return to Decamere by a longer, more scenic route. When we reached Nefasit, our turn-off point to go to Decamere, we decided to continue traveling on the same road and visit a Presbyterian hospital in the town of Ghinda.

After we completed touring the hospital, Arlene and Zettie suggested that we continue on the same road and visit the seaport town of Massawa along the Red Sea. After counting our money to see if we had sufficient, we decided to go. That evening we attended prayer meeting in our mission chapel. The five of us slept in a dorm-like room for $1.20 each in a new hotel not far from the Emperor's Massawa palace. The following morning we drove to a beach along the Red Sea and enjoyed the sea breezes and the sandy beach.

Later that day we headed for Decamere through the coastal lowlands, which were usually arid with sparse vegetation but in January are freshened by rain. At Nefasit we chose the road leading to Decamere, climbed the rugged mountains, and encountered dry, rocky terrain where the rains come in summer.

A few weeks after we returned to Decamere, Zettie sent the stalk of green bananas to us with Mark Budensiek. We wrapped the bananas in a towel. After they ripened, we shared them with others.

New Responsibilities

The next month Victor Glenn and Leslie Wilcox came for our annual spring convention. Each missionary family living in Decamere provided lodging and meals for one or two missionary families who came from other stations. The classrooms at the high school and orphanage became sleeping areas for the nationals.

Ronald and Anna Smith were the treasurer and secretary, respectively, of the Mission in Ethiopia. When they left for furlough in May, Faith and I acquired those responsibilities. That spring Arlene and I moved to the upstairs apartment across the hall from Faith where the Robbins family had lived before they moved to Addis Ababa. A small room at the top of the stairs, with our apartments on either side, served as the office for Faith's secretarial work and my treasurer's work.

Shortly before the Smiths left for furlough, Ronald was the evangelist for revival meetings at the high school. The services continued for two and a half weeks. God manifested His presence, individuals were under deep conviction, in some services there was no preaching, and many sought God. A number of our students repented, confessed their sins, made restitutions, received victory, and determined to do God's will. Some of the staff also found spiritual help.

In early June we had a baccalaureate service and later a school picnic in a nearby forested area. Graduation was held on the 14th for the nine high-school graduates. We were thrilled that eight of them agreed to work for the Mission. Seven joined our elementary teaching staff on the different stations, and one worked in the literature department with Wayne Sanders. At that time a high-school diploma was the government requirement for teaching in the elementary schools.

The summer months were busy for me. I taught a six-week course in social studies for our elementary teachers who lacked certain courses to meet government requirements. We covered a year's work during those few weeks. At the same time those teachers also completed a course in math.

While I taught summer school, Faith and Ruth went to Asmara and attended a three-week course in the Tigrinya language. One weekend

Teachers to whom I taught a six-week summer course in social studies in 1968. They were Kidane, Mehare, Fernando, Manna, Ghide, Kahsai, Bereket

after I completed my summer teaching, I visited the stations of Keren and Agordat. It was a pleasant change for me even though it was very warm.

The Bible school, which had been closed for a few years, was reopened in the fall of 1968. Earlier that year the Mission had purchased property adjacent to our high-school compound. The buildings on the new property were used for Bible school classrooms and living quarters for some of the students. Faith was the administrator that year and taught most of the classes. Leroy Adams taught one Bible class and music. In addition to several high-school classes, I taught a Bible class and current events in which I tried to link the present world affairs with prophecy. I also was responsible for periodic chapel services and several study hall periods each week.

Because of a shortage of high-school teachers, Ruth was transferred from Agordat to help in the high school where she taught English, Bible, and music. She moved into the apartment with Faith.

That fall Ghide Keleta, one of our teachers at the orphanage, married Lemlem Afewerki in our Asmara church. After the ceremony a wedding procession of several cars made the trip of 25 miles to Decamere where the reception was held in the boys' study

The upstairs apartments where Faith, Arlene, Ruth, and I lived on the high school compound in Decamere. Classrooms are in the buildings to the left and right.

hall at the high school. Ghide bore the expense of his reception feast rather than accept the help of his parents who were not believers. If they had helped, they would have served home-brewed beer. We greatly admired him for the stand that he took.

My treasurer's duties included the collecting of charges for the telephone calls for the only phone on the compound. That involved collecting for personal calls and making a monthly bill for each department—the Mission, the high school, and the print shop. Another duty was tallying a grocery list from the missionaries once a month, so we could buy wholesale from a store in Asmara. After the groceries arrived, I sorted them and prepared bills for each missionary. Melvin Adams, one of the missionary children, asked his mother, "Why does Miss Maurer have to pay for all the groceries?" He felt that was not fair. His concern subsided when his mother explained that I took care of the orders, but that each family paid for what they received.

That fall the missionary ladies and the national ladies in Decamere organized an outreach ministry into the community. One Sunday afternoon I went visiting with Shekait, a married, tenth-grade student who was a Sunday school teacher and my interpreter and teammate in our outreach. Our first visit was to the home of a girl who came to Sunday school for two Sundays but then missed a Sunday. She was not home, but we witnessed to her younger sister and her friend and then had prayer.

We next visited in the home of a student whose father was a policeman. The girl was not at home, but we had a pleasant visit

With Shekait, my interpreter and teammate in doing outreach work in the town of Decamere

with her parents. They seemed glad to hear the truth that we read from God's Word. Our third visit was with a girl who recently had started coming to Sunday school and whose father was also a policeman. We sensed a warm welcome in that home.

Teachers in the public schools had a limited amount of resource material for social studies. They knew about the mission high school and sought our friendship, which led to sharing our reference material with them. In early December Mr. Rao, a history teacher in the public school in Decamere, invited Ruth and me for dinner. He and his wife were Hindus from India. He sent his servant to our house with the verification of the invitation. Because of their religious beliefs, they were vegetar-

Mr. Rao, a government history teacher, and his family

ians. They served nine dishes of tasty food prepared with spices and hot peppers. It was interesting to see the various ways they fixed rice and vegetables.

Shortly before we ended our visit, Mr. Rao said, "Let me show you my gods," and led us to the kitchen. He opened a little cupboard full of small images and declared, "These are my gods." My heart ached as I longed to somehow lead that couple to faith in Christ.

Our missionary Christmas dinner that year was at the Adamses' home. The five single ladies including Zettie from Agordat, the families of Mark Budensiek, Maurice Hobart, Meredith Armour, and Wayne Sanders with his parents who were visiting from the States joined them for a delicious meal. Each missionary contributed something. Glenn Griffith had sent money for our Christmas dinner, and we used half of it to pay for our ham. The other half was used to provide meat for the national pastors and teachers in Decamere for their Christmas Day meal, which was January 7.

On December 28 I flew to Egypt, and the Guy Troyer family met me at the airport. They had been able to return to Egypt in the summer of 1968 after the political situation had stabilized following the Six-Day War of 1967. Sunday we attended EFM's church in Alexandria, and I spoke in the evening service. On Tuesday the Troyers took me to visit our pastors in Cairo. From there we went to Girga where I had been living when the missionaries were evacuated the previous year.

While we were in Girga, I preached three times, but we did not go to the village churches because it was not advisable. On the Egyptian Christmas, January 7, the local pastor and I made twenty-one house visits in addition to attending church services. Conditions were too unsettled in Upper Egypt to warrant my return permanently, so I disposed of many of my belongings. I took some things with me, including my trumpet, when I returned to Ethiopia.

It was a profitable three-week visit to Egypt. During that time I visited with all our pastors except one who was in an out-of-the-way village. I returned to Ethiopia and resumed my duties there.

The high-school boarding students were required to work ten hours a week. Ghermai, a seventh-grade boy, was the errand boy for us ladies. He frequently would go to the shops in town or the market and buy supplies. The winter nights in Decamere often became cool with temperatures dropping into the 40s. When it was chilly, he often built a fire in the fire-place in Arlene's room, using kerosene to get it started. One day Ghermai returned from the market and told Arlene he could not find kerosene but that he purchased some *benzene*, meaning gasoline. Arlene was sure that *benzene* should not be used to start a fire and talked with me about it. I also thought there was danger of an explosion and suggested that she check with one of the men missionaries. The boy innocently responded, "We must experiment," but we did not want him experimenting in our apartment. After Arlene checked with one of the men, she did not allow Ghermai to use the *benzene*.

An Outpouring of the Holy Spirit

Victor Glenn and Glenn Griffith arrived in February 1969 for another convention. While the nationals interpreted the messages into the Tigrinya language, it was marvelous to witness God's Spirit upon them as it was on the ministers. One evening about the middle of the convention, Glenn Griffith was preaching a very serious message when it began to rain. The deafening noise on the corrugated metal roof made it impossible for him to finish his message. He suggested that we sing, and when he gave an altar call, several people responded. The Spirit came in mighty power with deep conviction. A melting and humbling took place among the workers and believers, which resulted in many misunderstandings being resolved. Travail of soul fell upon some of the Christians. Such praying!

During the service the next evening, one of the high-school boys suddenly ran down the aisle, singing in Tigrinya, "There is power, power, wonder working power in the precious blood of the Lamb." Everyone started singing with him about the power in the blood. Then Sarah, the wife of one of our former workers, came to the altar where she prayed through to sanctification. Others came running to the altar. God's Spirit fell on us in such a manner that many of us could only praise Him while others sought for spiritual help. Every evening after that the altar was lined, sometimes two and three deep, and often there was no preaching.

A baptismal service was conducted on the last Saturday. Thirteen were scheduled to be baptized, but eight others joined them in making a public testimony that they were living for Jesus.

The next afternoon we partook of the Lord's Supper. It was a blessed time of communing with our Savior. With mighty anointing Glenn Griffith preached a brief missionary message. The altar was lined with young people consecrating their lives to God for service. Simon Abel, one of our teachers, publicly confessed that God had called him to preach several years previously, and now he was willing to obey.

Those days of special visitation of the Spirit were the result of intense praying. Early in the convention some of the men agreed to spend the night in prayer seeking God's help. As dawn approached, God visited the little praying group and assured them that He had heard their petitions. The chapel where they were praying rang with shouts of victory.

We rejoiced in the outpouring of the Spirit. Later Glenn Griffith remarked that it was one of the greatest visitations of the Spirit he had witnessed in 30 years. Revival fires continued to burn at the high school after the convention.

The Flu and a Frightening Encounter

Soon after the convention some of us contracted the Hong Kong flu. Arlene and Ruth were unable to teach their classes. I managed to teach without missing classes because the worst part for me came on the weekend. Although I continued to teach, I had a voice and throat problem with much coughing. At the end of almost every day, my throat was sore. Other missionaries, some of the national workers, and many of the high-school students were affected by the flu.

Shortly after I recovered, I went to Asmara to keep a dental appointment. When the dentist heard me coughing, he tactfully let me know that he was not eager to work on my teeth. He knew that in Asmara the flu was almost at epidemic stage. I said to him, "Oh, if you get the flu, you will blame me."

The dentist replied, "Not only that. I will charge you for the time and loss while I am sick!" I am sure he was kidding; however, I made an appointment for another day.

The ladies who lived in the upstairs apartments at the high school in Decamere: Ruth, me, Arlene, and Faith

Easter in Ethiopia is not usually the same day as in America. Our church in Asmara always planned a special Good Friday service with the speakers focusing on Jesus' seven sayings while He hung on the cross. Each saying was assigned to a different speaker who was to limit his time to 15 minutes. That year I was given the saying "I thirst." Between each speaker there was usually a congregational hymn or a special song. The church was full with many standing. I marveled at the good behavior of the children throughout the three-hour service.

Easter morning Faith, Arlene, Ghermai our errand boy, eight-year-old Melvin Adams, and I left at 7:00 to visit our church in Sorona about forty miles away. It took more than two hours to get there because of bad roads. After service we accepted a dinner invitation to the home of the parents of Yohannes, one of our young teachers who was home for Resurrection Day. Yohannes told us how he got saved and how his father saw the difference God had wrought in his life. His father, not a believer, was so impressed that he sent three other sons to our high school.

The following week I kept my new dental appointment. The dentist surgically removed an impacted wisdom tooth. After the anesthesia was no longer effective, I had to resort to Darvon to get some relief. My jaw swelled until it looked like I had the mumps, but within a week I was feeling better and returned to the dentist to have the stitches removed.

The Leroy Adams family, the high school seniors, and I who was their class sponsor left the high-school compound in Decamere on June 30 to go to Kohaita for a senior outing. The Adams children counted 465 curves on just part of the journey! We found the rugged track that left the main highway but then lost our way. Eventually we found an awesome canyon, but not the one we wanted.

We ate our picnic lunch on a large rock. After we had finished eating, several young freedom fighters (revolutionary forces) approached us. The leader, with his gun aimed at us, demanded, "Hands up!" Of course, we all raised our hands in obedience to such an order. They took Leroy and Berhan, one of the male students, and asked them several questions.

After the men released Leroy, they took all our male students beyond our hearing and spoke with them for half an hour. The boys were very quiet when they returned and never told us about their encounter. The freedom fighters searched the car and found nothing to their disliking. We were relieved when they departed without doing any harm!

Leroy gave each of the five men a booklet of the Gospel of John and spoke to them about preparing for heaven. When the freedom fighters left, we immediately headed for Decamere. We were a sober, quiet group.

Furlough

Ruth, Arlene, Zettie, and I left Ethiopia on July 4, 1969, for furlough. That was two years to the day that the Robbins family, Ruth, and I had arrived in Ethiopia. After several weeks of rest, I started traveling for deputation services for the Mission. From the month of August into early December, I held 52 services in seven states, speaking in churches, camp meetings, conventions, and Bible colleges. On a few occasions Zettie traveled with me.

When I was traveling near South Fork, Pennsylvania, I stopped and had an enjoyable visit with Pauline Keith. She had been a missionary in Eritrea when I visited there in the summer of 1959.

That fall my three sisters and I were able to be together for a Thanksgiving dinner. Eva and Helen with their families came quite a distance to make it possible. It was a special time for us.

Leaving for the States from the Asmara airport with Ruth, Zettie, and Arlene

From January 1970 until the end of the year, I was the speaker in 97 services in 16 states, beginning with a convention in Massachusetts where I ministered four times. The other states included Indiana, Virginia, West Virginia, Kentucky, Tennessee, North and South Carolina, Ohio, Pennsylvania, New York, Michigan, Arizona, California, Idaho, and Washington.

That September I enrolled in Xavier University in Cincinnati for graduate studies in history. I received a Master of Education degree on June 2, 1971. I also completed my last course at the University of Cincinnati and graduated with a Bachelor of Arts in history on August 28 that same summer. Before my course ended, my family notified me that our mother was nearing death. I spoke with my professor about attending Mother's funeral when she died. Because I had

Graduated from Xavier University on June 2, 1971, with a Master of Education with a major in history

maintained a high grade, he exempted me from taking the final exam, making it possible for me to return to Pennsylvania for her death and funeral.

Me on left with two fellow graduates. I received a Bachelor of Arts in history from the University of Cincinnati on August 28, 1971.

During the 1970- 1971 school year, I boarded with Anna Orndorff, a schoolmate of mine at GBS in 1957. We lived near GBS, and Anna worked in the city. On the weekends I represented the Mission in churches that were within a four-hour drive.

Teclemariam Wubneh grew up in the EFM orphanage in Decamere and graduated from the mission high school and Bible school. He was the first pastor of our church in Addis Ababa before coming to the States to attend college in Tennessee.

During Teclemariam's Christmas break he came to Cincinnati, and we had a pleasant time together. He appreciated being in some spiritual holiness churches and having fellowship with conservative Christians. He spoke in my home church in the Cincinnati area and in a couple other churches we attended that weekend. Later I took him to see some of our former missionaries and the EFM headquarters in Bedford.

Cincinnati is a very hilly city, and when the streets are snow packed, driving is very hazardous. It was not unusual for there to be 100 accidents or more during one snowfall. One week there were 300 accidents reported. God was good to me and kept me from having any snow-related accidents.

One Sunday I had two missionary services in Indiana. I decided to drive home after the evening service, a distance of some 50 miles. Roads in places were clear; in other places they were a sheet of ice, and I would slow down to 20 mph. A police car and another vehicle had just passed me on one stretch of icy road in the suburbs of Cincinnati when out ahead of me I saw two cars skidding, blocking both lanes of traffic on my side. The policeman stopped and turned on his flashers to warn traffic behind him. I was able to stop but was afraid that someone would come from behind me and not get stopped in time. Earnestly I asked the Lord for help and to take me home safely. He did, and I gave Him all the praise!

I went to Bedford in September and helped at the mission headquarters while I waited for my visa to Ethiopia to be granted. Soon the visa arrived, and I proceeded with my plans to leave for Ethiopia.

Chapter 8

Second Time in Ethiopia
1971-1975

Flying to Ethiopia

The first part of my return flight to Ethiopia was in a Beechcraft 99 from Allentown, Pennsylvania, to the John F. Kennedy International Airport in New York City. It was November 3, 1971. Frank and Bill Schmidt, two of my nephews, were waiting for me at the Kennedy airport when I arrived. We had enough time to eat a meal together before I boarded a Boeing 707 for my flight to Stuttgart, Germany. On that flight I was seated beside a young Israeli couple who had been born in Russia but now lived in Israel. We had an interesting time of sharing, and they surprised me when they gave me a recording entitled "The Sounds of Israel."

When I arrived in Stuttgart, my connecting flight did not leave until the next morning. Tesfai Asfaha, a former student of mine in Ethiopia, met me at the airport and took me to a delightful restaurant for our noon meal. From there we went to the home of Mrs. Chandler, an American, who earlier had lived with her husband in Asmara where he had worked for the U.S. government. While the Chandlers lived in Asmara, they paid Tesfai's expenses so that he could attend our mission high school in Decamere from where he graduated. They became like a father and mother to him. Later the Chandlers moved to Germany. After Mr. Chandler's death, his widow invited Tesfai to come to Germany and live with her while he furthered his education.

After Mrs. Chandler returned that day from teaching dependents of U.S. military personnel, she served us a snack while we visited. In the evening she took us downtown. After she parked her Mercedes Benz, the three of us walked to a beautiful park surrounded by stately castles that in the past had housed the Parliament. We then went to a lovely restaurant for our evening meal. I was their overnight guest and enjoyed breakfast with them before Mrs. Chandler left for school.

Later Tesfai took me to the airport. When I checked in my two large pieces of luggage, one was slightly overweight, and I was required to pay in *marks*. While I waited, Tesfai rushed to the exchange office and converted my dollars into German currency. We paid the clerk and scurried to the departure gate, bade each other good-bye, and I boarded a Boeing 727 to Frankfurt.

I went through immigration and passport control at Frankfurt and then encountered much difficulty finding my departure gate because I was sent to three different ones before I was directed to the right gate. All the time I was carrying two small heavy carry-on bags plus a garment bag. I quickly became exhausted while rushing up and down stairs and down the long corridors. By the time I arrived at the correct gate, less than two minutes remained before the call came for passengers to begin boarding another Boeing 727 to Munich, West Germany. In Munich we had to deplane, go through passport control, and re-board to continue our flight to Athens, Greece, and Cairo, Egypt.

The Guy Troyers met me at the airport for a one-day stopover in Cairo. During that brief time I attended a revival service in one of our churches and visited three other pastors and their families. I then flew to Asmara, Ethiopia, where several missionaries and national workers met me. When we arrived at the high-school compound in Decamere, I was surprised to realize that the band was playing to welcome me. Students gathered to greet me. High-school classes had begun five weeks earlier, so I quickly got settled in my apartment and started teaching my classes, doing my best to make up for my late arrival.

Pleasant and Unpleasant Experiences

During the 1971-1972 school year, there were three students in our Bible school. Two were Negassi Ghebrejesus and Ghermai Asgodom, who currently is the director of EFM's work in Ethiopia. The third one was Ghermai Yohannes who became blind as a child from complications with measles. A group of American women, whose husbands were in the U.S. Navy stationed in Asmara, learned of Ghermai's blindness and agreed to pay his educational expenses. They bought Ghermai a

High-school students with their teachers during the 1971-1972 school year

braillewriter and a tape recorder. Fellow students recorded his lessons on the tape recorder, and then he typed his study notes with his braillewriter.

Ghermai's teachers also recorded notes for him. Whenever it was time for a test, we recorded the questions, and Ghermai typed his answers by using an English typewriter. He participated in class discussion and was an excellent student. Sometimes we needed to remind ourselves that one of our students was blind. Ghermai was blessed with a beautiful tenor voice, and he sang in the Spirit. Often when he sang specials, God's presence settled upon the congregation, and hearts were blessed. While he served as pastor in the seaport town of Massawa, he often preached on board the flagship of the Ethiopian navy. God used him to minister to many sailors.

Our Thanksgiving Day was marred because our high-school students went on strike. They were not opposing our school or the Mission but were in sympathy with the students at the government school who had struck earlier because of grievances they had against the government.

The faculty met and decided to give our students a break from classes on Friday, but we would resume classes on Monday. We informed the students of our decision. Tekie Mebrahtu, the high-school principal, and the area district officer spoke with the students and urged them not to leave school. Several students from the government school came and urged our students to remain in class and thereby not cause a problem for the Mission.

More than 20 students from grades seven through eleven went home on Saturday in spite of the advice given to them. On Monday nearly 40 students left, including one twelfth grader. The faculty decided that those who left could not return until the government allowed its students to return to classes. A few weeks later the seventh- and eighth-grade students of the government schools returned to classes and most of ours in those grades did likewise. Eventually the government students in the higher grades returned to their classes.

Meanwhile the twelfth grader who left school begged to be allowed to return. He had insisted on leaving, disregarding the advice of his teachers and the pleadings of his classmates. The principal, with the faculty's support, refused to permit him to return because he had missed too much classroom material to be prepared to take the government exams that all seniors were required to take in the spring of their senior year. He returned the following fall and completed his work.

Faith Hemmeter had developed a nervous condition that necessitated her return to the States. There the doctor determined that her problem was caused by an over-the-counter drug she had been taking for another physical condition. I was using the same drug and stopped immediately when I heard the doctor's report regarding Faith.

My teaching load was increased when Faith went home. Another teacher taught one of my social studies classes but I continued teaching that subject for two classes and my three English classes. I also taught church history in the Bible school and was matron of our 27 boarding girls.

All the EFM missionaries in Decamere had Christmas dinner at the Sanders' house on the 25th. We each contributed money so that we could buy ham for the meal, and then each person brought additional food items. Previously we had exchanged names, and after the meal we had a small gift exchange. I received a locally manufactured set of six beautiful glasses with fruit designs.

One interesting part of our Christmas program that year was having Luke 2:8-12 read in seven of the languages spoken in Ethiopia—Amharic, Tigrinya, Tigre, Kunama, Arabic, English, and Italian. On January 7, which is the Ethiopian Christmas, I enjoyed a special dinner of native food with several of our national families.

During the first part of my Christmas break, I graded papers and calculated the grades for that six-week period. The second week I went to the Red Sea Mission rest house in Asmara for a few days of relaxation.

One morning after breakfast someone heard sounds signifying that Emperor Haile Selassie's motorcade was near. The staff and guests rushed to the front gate, and just a few yards down the street, the cars were stopped. The policemen were tussling with a woman who was trying to get to the emperor. He signaled to the policemen to let her come to the car, and he gave her money. Then the policemen lifted two tiny tots to the car window, and they also received money. Slowly the motorcade moved right past us. The emperor exchanged smiles with us and waved at close range. That was a rare opportunity, and I was thrilled to see him just a few feet away.

Barty Riskalla, a former student of mine in Egypt, came as our guest evangelist for our convention in March 1972. We had three services each day for nine days. Barty preached in Arabic twice a day. I interpreted into English, and an Eritrean interpreted into Tigrinya. An Eritrean pastor preached for the other service each day.

Every night there was an all-night chain of prayer with the men from each church taking an appointed hour. The ladies' prayer time was from 6:00 to 7:00 a.m. God honored those prayers by giving us good altar services and definite victories. After

Barty Riskalla, an Egyptian pastor, who came to Eritrea as a convention speaker

the convention Barty's flight schedule gave him a few extra days with us, and he consented to preach in our high-school chapel services.

One of our neighbor boys, who was sixteen, was persecuted by his family after he became a believer. They took him to the police, and under pressure he signed a paper agreeing that he would not attend services in our chapel. Later he felt great remorse for signing the paper and returned to the chapel and sought God's forgiveness. For some time his family did not oppose him even though he kept contact with the young believers at the high school. Eventually someone in his family took his eyeglasses, which he needed for studying, and took him a distance from the home and instructed him not to return. Christian friends came to his aid and helped him to get new glasses. They also provided food and lodging for him. After some time his family returned his glasses but did not welcome him home.

During our Easter vacation Solomon Aregai, one of my former students, who graduated from our high school in 1971, came to visit me. Faithfully he had pastored our chapel in the Decamere marketplace his last two years of high school. While visiting he told me that he never had felt clear about a call to preach, but in the weeks preceding Easter, God made it clear that he was to preach. The news made my heart glad.

A few days before conference began in July, Carrie Boyer and I received the shocking news that Marlin Straub had passed away in the hospital in Danville, Pennsylvania. He was the superintendent of the Evangelical Methodist Church of which Carrie and I were members. Marlin had been a strong supporter of EFM and urged his people to support the Mission.

We held our annual conference on the high-school compound. God graciously met with us during that time, manifesting His special presence until some rejoiced while others sought help at an altar of prayer. Reports indicated that over four hundred had been saved during the past conference year.

One delegate who was a public-school principal and administrator over schools in villages that had a total population of 20,000 reported that his aim was to be different from the people with whom he worked. He tried to be very careful in his conduct because he did not want to be a reproach to either Jesus Christ or the Mission. As a believer he stood alone. He said, "I have been tried and tested several times, but praise the Lord, I have passed the test."

Another delegate told how he had set a goal to win at least three souls to Christ during the year. God helped him to reach his goal by witnessing to his classmates at the university where he attended.

Excursion to Addis Ababa

The Mission encouraged the missionaries to take time to rest and relax and allowed each of us one month of vacation per year. During the summer of 1972, Carrie and I took a three-week trip by car to Addis Ababa. We took three Eritrean young people—Tiblez, Simon, and Berhane—with us. Carrie would be our primary driver, and I would be responsible for planning all meals and providing snacks. Tiblez, the young lady, would be my helper in preparing meals and washing dishes. Simon was mechanically inclined, and he would take care of the vehicle. Berhane was going only to Addis Ababa.

There are two roads from Asmara to Addis Ababa, one longer than the other and more scenic. We chose to take the shorter route and traveled south on a blacktop road that eventually became gravel until we approached Addis Ababa on the third day.

I frequently checked in my travel guidebook for interesting places to visit as we passed through numerous

Tiblez, Simon, and Carrie on our way to Addis Ababa, Ethiopia

small villages and towns. About noon each day we found a convenient place to stop and prepare a simple meal. We made tea and heated our food on our small stove. For the evening meal we tried to find a nice restaurant.

The second night we stayed in a new hotel at Kombolcha. Because the rooms were expensive, we used only three—Carrie by herself, Tiblez and I together, and the men in one. From Kombolcha there was a road to the seaport town of Assab, but when we considered the distance and time involved, we continued to Addis Ababa.

The third day we traveled across the Great Rift Valley and ascended a mountain on the far side. Once we stopped, climbed a small hill, and got a good perspective of the depth of the Valley. It was a spectacular sight to see the Valley stretched for miles. We also stopped at an extinct volcano before we reached Addis Ababa that evening.

For several days we enjoyed visiting interesting places in Addis Ababa, including Africa Hall, the royal palace, and a large Coptic Church where members of the royal family are buried. In the capital city we stayed at a mission rest house that was more economical for us.

From Addis Ababa we journeyed south to the Lake Abiata-Shala National Park, which is located in another part of the Rift Valley. It was exciting to see hyenas, ostriches, zebras, giraffes, and numerous members of the antelope family. We saw several lakes in the area, and for two nights we stayed in a hotel beside Lake Awasa. Our balcony was close enough to the water so that one could fish from there if he so desired. From Lake Awasa we went to Yirgalem so that Tiblez could visit a cousin, and then we returned to Awasa for the night.

After retracing our steps to Addis Ababa, we made a short side trip to Wonji Sugar Estates to visit Bairu and Meharit, one of our Christian couples. Bairu worked on that plantation, which was the source of most of the sugar for Ethiopia. He was grateful for the EFM missionaries who had led him to the Lord while he was a boarding student in one of our schools in Eritrea. Bairu endeavored to minister to his fellow workers by holding Bible studies in his home.

From Addis Ababa we started on our return trip to Asmara, taking the longer, more scenic route. The first major point of interest was near the town of Bahar Dar, situated on Lake Tana, the source of the Blue Nile River. The water flowing from the lake creates the Blue Nile Falls. We drove several miles from Bahar Dar and then walked more than a

The Blue Nile Falls, which flows from Lake Tana near Bahar Dar, Ethiopia

mile to reach the Falls. I bought a walking stick from one of the shepherd boys; it was a good investment! It was the rainy season, and the path was muddy, but the Falls were beautiful.

From Bahar Dar we continued on the gravel road to the historic town of Gondar. The main attraction in that town was the royal compound, which was enclosed by a high stone wall and had more than ten picturesque palaces and ruins. Each powerful king had added to the constructions of the previous kings. Ancient Gondar reached its zenith during the 17th century. Outside the royal compound were other historic buildings, and at one place there were cages that held lions belonging to the royal family. The lion was the mascot of Emperor Haile Selassie I. One of his titles was The Lion of the Tribe of Judah. According to Ethiopian tradition he was a descendant of the Queen of Sheba and King Solomon. Carrie bravely touched a lion cub.

The last historic town on our return trip was Axum, which had been the home of a large empire. It was at its zenith between the third and fifth centuries and was considered equal to the empires of Babylon, Rome, and Egypt. In Axum we saw several interesting sights, including a few stelae, or carved stone pillars used for commemorative purposes

After Axum our next town was Asmara and then to Decamere. We had traveled over 1,500 miles during those three weeks without serious problems. At times we had to contend with heavy rainfall and muddy roads, but we enjoyed viewing the many waterfalls cascading down the mountainsides. It was a refreshing vacation as we visited interesting places in Ethiopia.

Later Happenings

Prior to the beginning of the 1972-1973 school year, L.W. Barbee came to speak in our fall convention. He was greatly loved by the missionaries and nationals because of his practical messages. We had a good convention, and two times there was no preaching. The Holy Spirit came and brought both blessing and conviction, and the altar filled with seekers. In every service during the ten days, whenever an invitation was given, souls sought help from the Lord.

That year my teaching assignment included 10th grade English, 11th grade English and social studies, 12th grade English and geography, and a Bible school class on Hebrews through Revelation. There were four new students in the Bible school, making a total of seven. I was also matron for the 31 energetic girls in our dormitory and supervised the students who worked to beautify our compound by tending the flower beds in front of our classrooms and the boys' dorm.

One assignment for my 10th grade English class was a composition involving a study of past continuous tense. Four sentences with blanks for the verbs were in a set, and four verbs were given, each verb to be used only once. Some students gave correct answers but others included the following amusing sentences: "She was cooking my sweater." "She was mending my meal."

To make the chapel services more interesting that year, each teacher was assigned a topic. I spoke once every two weeks, and my topic was the book of Revelation. Another thing that we did differently was to urge all the teachers to speak personally with three students every week about their spiritual condition. Our one-on-one dealings proved to be an effective way of helping the young people become established in the grace of God.

One evening in October the missionaries gathered for cake and ice cream at the Armours' home to celebrate the fourth birthday of their daughter Rebekah. The children were telling us about playing hide and seek on the Bible school compound. They mentioned several good hiding spots. Then five-and-a-half-year-old Rosanne Smith, said, "There are three other places to hide."

We wondered where, and an adult asked her, "Where?"

She answered, "By the tree down on the front part of the compound."

When one of us questioned her, "Where are the other two places?"

She quickly replied, "There are three trees!"

We all had a good laugh.

During the last weekend of our Ethiopian Christmas vacation in January, I attended the revival services in our Asmara church where Carrie was preaching. It was thrilling to observe how active Yemane Ogbaslasie was in the church. He sometimes led the singing, was a good altar worker, and was the pastor's right-hand man. Yemane had been saved during a revival in the church in 1967 when I was the evangelist. From that time he considered me to be his spiritual mother.

Saied Ibrahim, an Egyptian pastor and a former student of mine, came to Ethiopia for our annual convention in February. I interpreted his messages into English a few times, and then he decided he would rather preach in English even though English was his second language. He found it difficult to wait for two interpreters—from Arabic into English, and then English into Tigrinya. Carrie was the other evangelist. We had a wonderful convention with many seekers, several of them testifying to a clear experience of grace. One evening there was no preaching but two altar services. We were reluctant to leave the sanctuary because God's presence was so precious. A baptismal service was held on the second Saturday, and 13 were baptized, including Weini our maid.

That spring we faced a water shortage. Our water was supplied by the municipality of Decamere, but water came only part of the day or night. Sometimes I stayed up at night and waited for the water. When it came, I filled kettles, buckets, bowls, teakettles, washtubs, and our bathtub. I tried to get extra water so that the girls in the dormitory would have enough to do their laundry. We began to pray for rain, and although it usually did not rain in that area in the month of May, we praised the Lord for sending us several good showers.

Our schools closed on July 7. The following week was filled with activities. First, our annual conference convened at the high school. On Friday we attended a graduation program in our Asmara church for our Bible school graduates. The next morning we attended the wedding of two of our Asmara believers. After the wedding we drove 12 miles outside the city to attend two wedding feasts—one provided by the groom's family and the other by the bride's family.

Faith returned to Ethiopia in September 1973. She had gone home two years previously because of physical problems and then had remained home for her furlough.

In addition to my regular duties for the new school year, I gave ten beginner students piano lessons. They used the piano in our high-school chapel for their lessons and practice times. That piano had been repaired repeatedly and was not worth fixing again. My family sent money toward the purchase of a good used one. The high school and the church located on the high-school compound paid the balance. It was delightful to have a nice replacement.

In our fall revival Ronald Smith served as the evangelist. He preached good messages which contained vital truths that were applicable to our students' needs. Nearly all who had spiritual needs sought the Lord during the revival. There was no preaching at least twice when God came in a wonderful way. Students earnestly prayed and many made restitutions. The last evening there was not sufficient room at the altar for those who came to pray, and the overflow knelt either on the platform or at the front seats. It was wonderful that some students were able to go home for Christmas with Christ in their hearts for the first time in their lives. We gave all the glory to God.

Political problems in Eritrea, the northern province of Ethiopia, were escalating. In January the fuel truckers went on strike, and no fuel was transported from the seaport in Massawa to the highlands. Because of a shortage of fuel, the local power plant turned off its generators from noon until 4:00 p.m. The strike was short-lived, and we were relieved to have electricity again for 24 hours a day.

We faced other inconveniences as the political situation worsened. Mail service was stopped for a while. We could neither send letters to the States nor receive them from there. Then traveling became dangerous, and for a short period we were unable to go to Asmara. Throughout that time of uncertainty, we had God's promise of Deuteronomy 33:27a, "The eternal God is thy refuge, and underneath are the everlasting arms."

The evangelists for the 1974 spring convention were Tekie Mebrahtu, our high school pastor, and Emil Massaoud, one of our Egyptian pastors. Tekie faithfully preached on holiness. When Emil preached, two interpreters were needed, but the truth was effective, and there were many good altar services. A few of our young Christian mothers carried a burden for souls and prayed fervently in the Spirit. In one of the services, eleven-year-old Samuel, the son of our chairman, Tesfai Debas, got saved and went to the platform to testify. God sealed his testimony by sending a sweet atmosphere on the service.

During the convention Emil stayed in the small apartment on the second floor of the apartment building on the high-school compound. One morning he came across the hall to our apartment for breakfast and said, "*Mabrouk*!" which means "Congratulations!"

I interpreted what he had said to Faith. Both of us wondered why he was congratulating us. He replied in Arabic that our cat had kittens in a large basket in the bathroom. We were surprised because we did not own

Bible school teachers and students in 1974. Students: Araia, Kahsai, Worede, Solomon, Fernando, Ghermai, and Simon. Teachers: me, Tekie Mebrahtu, Tesfai Debas, Ronald Robbins, and Faith Hemmeter.

a cat. We followed him to his lodging and, sure enough, there we found a cat and its soft furry kittens in the basket! Unbeknown to us, a stray cat had gotten into the apartment through an open window and found a comfortable place to give birth to her litter of cute little kittens.

Carrie moved to Decamere that September. The fighting between the Eritrean freedom fighters and the Ethiopian government troops was increasing in the lowland area where she usually lived. She willingly served as matron for the girls, relieving me of that duty. I was kept busy with my treasurer's work and classes in the high school and Bible school.

Because of the deteriorating situation in the country, our missionary staff slowly dwindled. As the missionaries returned to the States, they entered other fields of service.

When we gathered at the Adamses' home for our Christmas dinner on December 25, the Adams and Robbins families, Carrie, Faith, and I were the only EFM missionaries remaining in Ethiopia. Previously we had drawn names for a gift exchange. Dennis Robbins had my name and gave me a woven bread basket made in southwestern Ethiopia.

Later that day we three single ladies learned that our eight Kunama students, who also celebrate Christmas on December 25, had no special treat for Christmas. We invited them to our home and gave them cookies, a drink similar to Kool Aid, and small individual gifts that they greatly appreciated.

A few days before the Ethiopian Christmas, I invited the eleven-year-old son of a poor family with whom Faith had been doing personal evangelism to come to our apartment. I supplied him with colored strips of paper and a stapler and showed him how to make paper chains for decorating their home. He was delighted and took home with him two long chains. We gave each family member a small gift. They invited us to their place for a special Christmas dinner, but the mother received news of a death in her family and was unable to have us come.

Speaking in the preachers' convention in Egypt in February 1975 with Riad Atallah interpreting

However, she prepared *zigganey*, a native food, before leaving for the funeral and sent it to us.

On the Ethiopian Christmas Eve, we ladies entertained a poor widow and her six children by serving them refreshments and giving each of them a gift, which made them happy.

Ethiopian Christmas Day was a busy one for us. First we had a dinner of hot, spicy chicken *zigganey* in the home of an Ethiopian woman in a nearby village. In the afternoon we had tea and fellowship at the orphanage with the missionaries and national workers who were living in Decamere. In the evening we ladies invited the 17 high-school students and our only lady Bible school student to our house for popcorn, tea, and gifts. Those students were unable to go home for Christmas.

I enjoyed the 1974 Christmas season immensely because of the privilege of giving to others. I did not know then that it would be my last Christmas in Ethiopia.

The congregation that attended one evening service during the preachers' convention with me on the right

Convention in Egypt

One of our Eritrean pastors was scheduled to speak at the annual convention in Egypt in February 1975. Because of the political situation, it was not wise for him to leave the country. I had served in Egypt; therefore, I was asked to go in his stead. As the time for my departure approached, tensions between the Eritrean freedom fighters and the government troops continued to increase in the highlands. Tesfai Debas, the national director, and Ronald Robbins, the missionary director, took me to Asmara on January 31 for an evening flight to Cairo. That night fighting began in Asmara, and my flight was canceled. We were ordered to spend the night in the airport, which was about seven miles outside the city. It was winter and at an altitude of 7,000 feet, it was cold in the unheated building. I got a bad cold that bothered me for some time.

On Saturday morning while I waited to board the plane, there was shooting on the edge of the city. We could hear the loud booms of guns firing and see the spiraling clouds of dust. Then the loud rumble of a bomber was heard overhead. By that time the airlines officials became quite excited and hurried the passengers to the plane. I was overloaded with carry-on bags because the Troyers had requested that I bring them some commodities that were scarce in Egypt. Seeing my plight, a Pakistani young man grabbed some of my bags and carried them to the plane for me. Soon I was safely on my way to Cairo and was happy to find the Troyer family waiting for me at the airport.

The convention was held in Cairo, which at that time was a sprawling city of more than 7,000,000 people. Our Egyptian conference leaders rented the English Church and hostel in Old Cairo for the convention. God came and helped in a gracious way during those meetings. Immediately following the convention, a telegram arrived from our mission leaders in Ethiopia instructing me to remain in Egypt until further notice.

Chapter 9

Later Egyptian Years
1975-1981

Traveling to Upper Egypt

While I waited in Cairo, Barty Riskalla, a young preacher, had to go to Girga, Upper Egypt, to make arrangements to have his furniture moved to Cairo where he was going to pastor. At that time there was freedom to travel in Egypt, and with the encouragement of Guy Troyer, I accompanied Barty, because that would give me an opportunity to visit our churches and believers in that part of Egypt where I had worked from 1958 to1967.

Barty and I went by train from Cairo to Sohag, arriving late Monday night. We stayed with our pastor and his family overnight and continued to Girga the next day. In Girga we stayed with Barty's brother, Shukry, pastor of our church there.

During the few days Barty and I were in Upper Egypt, we used public transportation to travel to several of our churches. I was privileged to minister in Sohag, Girga, East Zuouk, Kombadar, and Hawawish. It was a great delight to see people whom I had not seen during the previous seven and a half years.

Early on the following Monday, Barty and I traveled by a horse-drawn carriage to the train station where we took the 4:20 train to Cairo. By then Barty had made arrangements to have his furniture shipped by truck to Cairo.

Tuesday morning I spoke in the weekly women's meeting in our Shubra Hafzeea church in Cairo, pastored by Saied Ibrahim. After the women's meeting Saied, another pastor, and I visited the mother of a young believer who had been killed instantly when a tractor trailer struck him while he was leading a blind man across the street. The blind man was seriously injured. Endeavoring to comfort the mother, we read from

God's Word and had prayer. That evening I returned to the Troyers' residence where I was living.

After we knew that I would not be returning to Ethiopia, Guy asked me to teach his Bible school classes. To make it easier for me to work and travel in Egypt, I obtained a work permit.

Women's Meetings and Home Visitations

My time was occupied with teaching in the Bible school, doing home visitation, and speaking in our churches in Cairo. Later that summer a lady asked Saied and me to visit her sister-in-law. We were not given any hint of the woman's circumstances and were shocked when we were greeted with the words, "I decided this morning to give up belief in God and to curse the messengers of religion."

In tears that mother told of her anguish that seemed unbearable. The family had been blessed with a good income derived from a trucking business until the father developed heart problems and could not work. They hired a man to drive the truck, but their income decreased greatly.

The oldest child had lost her speech when she contracted a childhood illness, and now she worked in a factory where she earned a meager income. Her future looked bleak because she probably never would get married. The second child, another daughter, had lost an eye and her other eye was weak. Also she had developed psychiatric problems. Thankfully, the third daughter had no physical deformities or emotional problems. The youngest child was an undisciplined son who kept the family in turmoil.

The children wanted to continue their high standard of living, and the mother could not convince them that it was impossible. She was blaming God for her troubles. After the mother poured out her heart to us, we counseled her and had prayer. When we finished, she exclaimed, "Now I know God loves me because He sent you my way."

Bible school classes ended in June, and I began speaking in women's meetings in some of the Cairo churches. On the days I went for the women's meetings, I stayed and did house calling in that area. Sometimes the Troyers and I went visiting together. In some homes we found signs of poverty while in others there were indications of luxury. Everyone gave us a warm welcome.

One day a pastor and I made nine calls in one area. Our last visit that day was in the home of Aziz, a backslider. Although he had stopped attending church nearly 40 years before, several members of his family came regularly to our services. A few years later he became addicted to cigarettes. I told him the story of a man who had been in the last throes of alcoholism and a slave to tobacco but who was converted and found deliverance.

As the pastor and I encouraged Aziz to seek the Lord, he told us to pray for him but that he was not going to pray. I told him that unless he personally sought the Lord, he could not be saved. I suggested that we pray together. While we prayed, God gave us special help. After prayer Aziz gave the pastor a partial package of cigarettes to destroy. He also found forgiveness!

In addition to helping in the women's meetings and home visitation, I gave a series of studies on the book of Hebrews in one of our Cairo churches and piano lessons to beginners. Mixed in between all those activities, I studied Arabic.

During the first two weeks of July, our pastors rented a YWCA campsite in Alexandria where they had an extended convention. The first week was for families and the second for youth. The days were filled with Bible studies and discussions on practical issues relating to the Christian family and Christian living, sessions for teaching new songs, times for fellowship, and evangelistic services. God's presence was with us and much good was accomplished. One young man found forgiveness after earnestly seeking God for restoration.

Several weeks after the convention, one pastor reported that he was seeing positive results from those services—a few young men from his congregation visited the barber shop, and some of the young women lengthened their skirts. Saied and his congregation gave extra time to prayer. God heard and rewarded them with souls getting saved, some of them from deep sin.

When Bible school classes began that fall, I taught English, Hebrews, and a class on holiness. I spent an hour a week with three pastors who were learning to interpret from English into Arabic. They came for their lesson to the church where we were teaching the Bible school classes. I also helped Deborah Troyer, who was home schooled, with her English and social studies.

Besides my teaching responsibilities, I was translating my notes on Hebrews into Arabic. With all those activities I had to curtail my involvements with the women's meetings and home visitations.

L.W. Barbee and Joe Vernon came from the States in September for two weeks. They preached in our churches in Cairo and ministered in a four-day convention to the pastors and missionaries. God blessed their ministry among us.

One day after Joe Vernon had preached, the national chairman said, "Maybe Miss Maurer or Mr. Troyer told the evangelist about the situation here." Both Guy Troyer and I assured him that we had not. The chairman then replied, "It had to be from God." The Holy Spirit knew what was needed and directed and anointed the minister.

The following February L.W. Barbee and Leonard Sankey came to Egypt for special services in Girga. Shortly after they arrived, Leonard received word of a terrible earthquake in Guatemala. He immediately returned to the States to coordinate relief for Guatemalan victims. L.W. and our pastors from the Delta proceeded to Girga for the convention.

Pastors who attended the conference in Girga in 1976

A few months before I left Egypt for furlough in May 1976, Barty and I visited one of his neighbors, Abou Nagi, who was ill. He had gone to a doctor who had discovered that Abou Nagi had dangerously high blood pressure. The doctor feared a stroke or a brain hemorrhage, so he sent the man home with instructions that he stop all his addictive habits. Those words were like a bombshell to the man because he had used cigarettes, alcohol, and opium for 40 years. The seriousness of his situation caused him to quit using opium and alcohol, but he struggled with his cigarette addiction.

Abou Nagi's wife was a believer who was praying for her husband's salvation, and God was showing mercy to him. His wife told us he was praying for God to save and heal him. We prayed with him, and after he earnestly sought God, he testified to deliverance and peace in his heart. Barty and I continued to visit the man weekly. As we witnessed the change in Abou Nagi, we praised God for deliverance from the habits of sin!

Easter Customs

Members of the Orthodox Church refer to Christmas as The Little Feast and to Easter as The Big Feast. There is a period of fasting prior to both feasts with more celebration taking place during the Easter season.

The fast before Easter is a period of 55 days when adherents to the Orthodox Church practice self-denial by abstaining from all foods of animal origin. During that time many members attend the church services and go to the confessional more frequently than usual.

On Good Friday the people do not eat or drink until after 3:00 p.m. They go to their churches for a solemn service, and instead of referring to it as Good Friday, they call it Sad Friday. Saturday night many people attend a lengthy service at the church, climaxed at midnight with a symbolic resurrection of Christ from the tomb. Their long fast is then broken, and they eat whatever they desire.

Sunday is called the Feast of the Resurrection, and that day is observed with feasting and visiting. Many people serve their guests tea and homemade cookies. All who can afford new garments buy them for their families.

Easter Monday is a national holiday and is called *Shem en Nessim*, meaning smell the fresh air. It is a celebration to welcome spring. The day is spent in merrymaking with loved ones and friends. Many people rise early and take a walk, sometimes carrying a breakfast of bread and moist salted fish, which is traditionally eaten on that day.

Furlough and Return

After the school year ended, it was time for me to return to the States for another furlough. I flew from Cairo on May 27, 1976, and spent the night in Frankfurt, Germany. The next day I continued to Philadelphia and then to Allentown, Pennsylvania, and met my family. They took me to Shamokin, Pennsylvania, where I lived in Doris' upstairs apartment during furlough. The Mission granted me the months of June and July to visit my family and get some rest before starting deputation services in August.

Before I arrived in the States, Lester and Helen had invited me to accompany them on a trip to the West. They wanted to visit their two sons, Joseph and Durwin, who lived in Idaho and Colorado respectively. Lester and Helen came from Vineland, New Jersey, to get me.

The first place of interest was the Corn Palace in Mitchell, South Dakota, decorated with mosaics made from ten different colors of corn and various grasses. Each fall the interior and exterior are redecorated with new murals. The first Corn Palace was built in 1892.

In the same state we saw the majestically sculptured heads of George Washington, Thomas Jefferson, Theodore Roosevelt, and Abraham Lincoln on a granite cliff at Mount Rushmore. The head of Washington is as high as a five-story building.

Joseph, me, Helen, and Lester at Glacier National Park in 1976

Lester and Helen had arranged to meet Joseph at Glacier National Park. The park boasts about sixty glaciers and hundreds of mountain lakes. The immensity of the peaks and lakes astounded me. Oh, the grandeur of God's creation! The Psalmist said, "The heavens declare the glory of God; and the firmament showeth his handiwork" (Psalm 19:1).

My visit to the park was so refreshing after keeping a very busy schedule for over four years in Ethiopia and Egypt!

Next we went to Hayden Lake, Idaho, where Joseph lived. Mr. Carnegie, his friend, took us on an interesting tour of a lumber yard where he worked.

After we met Durwin at the airport in Spokane, Washington, Joseph took us to his place of employment at Heritage Homes, a company that manufactured pre-fab homes. New technology had made it possible to do computerized drawings of house plans, and Joseph was sent for training for the job. The same work that had required several days could now be done in a half day.

From Hayden Lake our next stop was Coeur d'Alene Lake and a mountain peak by the same name in the background. After we left Idaho, we visited the large copper mine, two miles in diameter, near Butte, Montana.

Our travels took us to Yellowstone National Park in Wyoming. What a thrill to watch the water cascading down spectacular falls. We stayed long enough to see Old Faithful, the famous geyser that spouts tons of boiling water about every hour to heights equal to a fifteen-story building.

Traveling south we stopped at the Grand Teton National Park with its beautiful snow-covered Teton Mountains, considered by some people to be the most majestic mountains in North America. The highest peak is 13,766 feet above sea level. We saw Jackson Lake, the largest lake in the park. Water from that lake is used to irrigate areas of Idaho.

We continued to Colorado Springs, Colorado, to take Durwin home. From there we headed east across the grain belt of America to Bedford, Indiana, home of Evangelistic Faith Missions. I was thankful to Lester and Helen for a memorable vacation.

I remained in Bedford a few days before driving to Pennsylvania using a mission car. I then began traveling and speaking in missionary services. My schedule took me to several services close to my home in Shamokin.

On one of my trips, I was driving the mission Ford Maverick and knew something was wrong with the car. When I explained what was happening with the vehicle to my nephew Bob, who was a mechanic, immediately he knew that the problem was the master cylinder for the brakes. He took the car to the garage where he worked and made the necessary repairs. I felt safer as I continued my travels.

I enjoyed Thanksgiving Day near Elizabethville, Pennsylvania, with Hilda Straub, widow of Marlin, in the home of her sister Ruth Shaffer, and some of their families. Mesgun Tedla, an Eritrean who was studying at Kansas City College and Bible School in Overland Park, Kansas, joined us. His winsome personality added to the holiday atmosphere.

While representing the Mission in January, I was stranded in Cincinnati, Ohio, because of a snowstorm and icy roads and had to cancel some services. Providentially, I was visiting with Anna Orndorff. I stayed with her until road conditions improved.

At the end of February, I met the EFM board in Bedford, Indiana. The members decided that I should return to Egypt in June because the Guy Troyer family would be coming home in July.

In March I had a missionary service at the Calvary Holiness Church in Philadelphia, Pennsylvania, where William Rosenberry was the pastor. I was entertained in the home of Anita Brechbill, who worked as a lab technician at the Episcopal Hospital in the city. In later years she became the founder and director of Rope Holders, a prayer-support

Anna Orndorff, a friend from GBS days, with whom I sometimes stayed during my missionary travels

ministry for missionaries, and is associated with Mission Helps, Lititz, Pennsylvania.

After a year of traveling for deputation services, visiting family and friends, and replenishing my wardrobe, I returned to Egypt in June. I bade farewell to my family at the Allentown airport and flew to the John F. Kennedy International Airport in New York City. Before we departed from Kennedy airport, the ground crew discovered that our plane

Family and friends who bade me farewell on June 21, 1977, from the Allentown airport in Pennsylvania

had a flat tire, and they replaced it. We had a smooth flight to Paris and then to Cairo. No one was assigned to my row of seats from Paris to Cairo, which allowed me to recline and sleep.

When I stepped off the plane in Cairo, I felt the extreme heat of an Egyptian summer day. Guy was involved in the annual conference with the pastors, so Dana and Deborah Troyer, Carrie Boyer, and Mary Lou Lorimer, a neighbor of the Troyers, met me. Carrie had left Ethiopia because of the political situation and was helping in Egypt until time for her furlough. The following month the Troyers returned to the States.

Living in Cairo

During my previous years in Egypt, I had lived in Alexandria along the Mediterranean Sea and in Girga, Upper Egypt. Although I had visited Cairo many times, I never had lived there. However, I soon found that living in Cairo was more challenging than living in either Alexandria or Girga. Trips into the heart of the city for business and shopping required stamina, patience, and grace. Walking during the day in the extreme heat was exhausting. Sometimes we were forced to walk because taxi drivers refused to take anyone for only a mile and often buses were not available.

On one occasion shortly after my return, Carrie and I needed to go shopping. That time we went to the bus terminal and located the bus that would take us to our destination. There was standing room only, so we climbed aboard and stood near the driver. I wanted to tell him where to stop because we were not going far. When we got there, I notified the driver and then worked my way past several people to get to the door.

The driver kept asking in Arabic, *"Khalas, khalas?"* meaning, "Finished, finished?" a free translation meaning, "Are they off now?"

I kept answering, *"Lisa, lisa,"* meaning "Not yet, not yet." I had little trouble exiting the bus, but Carrie had difficulty squeezing through the crowd. When she was at the door, the bus started to move, and I hastily grabbed her arm and pulled her off the bus! If I had not helped her, she would not have known where to go or how to get back home, and to make matters worse, she did not speak Arabic. Neither of us enjoyed riding the buses in Cairo.

Ronald and Margaret Robbins with their children, Timothy, Dennis, and Rachel, returned to Egypt in November 1977. Part of my duties for that school year was tutoring Timothy in math. I also gave piano lessons to beginners.

After the Egyptian Christmas in January, Dale Yocum came and preached in our churches for three and a half weeks. We were blessed by his scholarly, yet humble ministry. He also conducted a workers' convention in Cairo during that time. Later Nabih, a man who often interpreted for the missionaries, translated Doctor Yocum's book *This Present World* into

Dennis Robbins and me with our instruments

Arabic. The translating took several months. I spent many hours with Nabih at the Robbins' home reviewing the translation and comparing it with the English edition.

Pastors and workers at the preachers' convention in Cairo in 1978. Dale Yocum was the special speaker.

I wrote the following to my family in May: "My! It is hot here these days—ever since last Friday the 26th. Saturday it was 105 degrees in the shade. Nights have been cool except last night when there was no breeze. I tossed and perspired, basically until the morning hours when a slight breeze came in my window for a while before the hot sun rose again around six o'clock. One hates to go outdoors, but our work requires it. Today I had to come to the heart of the city for a committee meeting. I expect to stay tonight at Rev. Saied's home and speak at the women's service tomorrow morning."

Dale Yocum again visited our work in February 1979. For six days we had two services a day in Cairo. The morning gatherings were for the pastors, and Doctor Yocum preached enlightening messages on the Holy Spirit from the book of Ephesians. The evening evangelistic services were well attended by people from our seven local churches and other visitors. One night the service ended with individuals seeking God at the altar.

After the meetings in Cairo, the Robbins family and I took Dale Yocum to Upper Egypt for a week of ministry. The day services were for our pastors from that part of Egypt, and evening services were held in our various churches. Much good was accomplished for God's kingdom during those meetings.

With rejoicing we opened a new church in Cairo in April. The first Sunday I was there, the attendance was about fifty for both the morning and evening services. On various occasions I filled the pulpit on Sundays because no pastor was stationed there until conference time in the summer.

In early May I was invited for dinner to the home of a widow who attended our Shubra Tag church in Cairo. Her husband had died in a freak accident more than 20 years previously. While he was walking down a sidewalk on a windy day, a window shutter of one of the houses broke from its hinges and fell, killing him. His wife, about twenty-three years old, was left with three small boys—William, Samy, and Aziz. She grieved bitterly, and to add to her sorrow, she contracted tuberculosis. God was merciful, and through His help and the kindness of her brothers and church friends, she recovered and reared three fine sons.

After completing mandatory military service, William became a public school teacher, and Samy became a bank clerk. Both were saved and were active in the Shubra Tag church. They were present for dinner that day. The third son, who was not present, later became a Christian medical doctor.

While with them I met Soliman, who was orphaned of both parents when quite young. Out of pity the widow "adopted" him. At first he fought and cursed, but under Christian influence, he soon changed his behavior. When he was 12 years old, he gave his heart to the Lord in Sunday school and proved to be a blessing to others. Before I left the home, we sang some songs and had prayer.

I was exhausted continually from my duties as the mission administrator and the tensions of living in the crowded, noisy city of Cairo. In the early part of 1979, I received permission from Victor Glenn, the president of EFM, to return to the States for two months of rest.

Before I could leave, there were several things that required my attention. The licenses for the three mission vehicles had to be renewed in person. It was necessary that I attend the annual conference in June. I also needed to renew my visa and work permit in July.

I left Egypt on July 11 and flew to Allentown. After two months of rest and visits with my family and friends, I returned to Egypt.

In March 1980 the Robbins family returned to the States because Ronald was having physical problems. That left Carrie and me as the only EFM missionaries in Egypt.

For the 1980-1981 school year, I went three mornings a week to another part of Cairo to teach in our Bible school. I taught two English classes and a theology class and gave piano lessons to five of the students. The rest of the week I prepared for my classes, visited our churches, spoke in women's meetings, and gave piano lessons to children and young people in some of our Cairo churches.

Soon after classes started in September, Tekie Mebrahtu, national director of EFM's work in Ethiopia, visited us for several days. He spoke to our pastors in the morning services and in some of our Cairo churches in the evenings. His ministry was greatly appreciated by the Egyptian people. Tekie and I along with Ishak, an Eritrean studying medicine in Cairo, enjoyed the fellowship and prayer times we shared.

In Egypt it was not customary for women to speak in the regular worship services. However, when we had women's meetings, they were free to express themselves and to tell us their needs. As a result many women found spiritual help during our weekly women's meetings in our Cairo churches.

Labiba, a village woman in her fifties, came to one of those women's meetings. She was visiting her son in the area, and a neighbor woman invited her to attend. Her heart was touched as she heard the news of salvation for the first time. She opened her heart to the truth and responded by asking how she could be saved. At first she did not understand, but with additional explanation during the following days, she came to comprehend what was required of her to know the Lord. That precious woman broke down in tears and said, "I want the Lord to forgive me." She did not know how to pray, and we helped her to pray a simple prayer. She soon began pleading with God for forgiveness. Finally she said, "No one has to tell me that Jesus has forgiven me. I feel it right here," she exclaimed, pointing to her heart.

Several weeks later Labiba returned to visit her son. Everyone was interested to know how she was doing spiritually because she could not read, and there was no evangelical church in her village. Someone asked, "Labiba, how is it with you spiritually?"

Smiling and pointing to her heart Labiba replied, "Jesus is keeping me. When I say or do anything that is displeasing to Him, He speaks to me, and I go and make it right." We rejoiced with her regarding her obedience and constant victory.

Eventually my duties became too much for me to continue with the women's meetings, so Carrie took that responsibility. I often accompanied her in the evenings and gave piano lessons in our churches nearby.

One evening in November Carrie and I, accompanied by Saied as our interpreter, were on our way to a women's meeting and piano lessons. We had vehicle problems with our Peugeot 504. Saied went in search of a mechanic, but because it was closing time, he could not find a mechanic who was willing to come. He and Carrie went by taxi to the women's meeting, and I stayed with the vehicle. Fortunately the Peugeot stalled in front of the Nile Hilton Hotel, and by the lights of the hotel, I could see to write several letters. After service Saied and Carrie returned with a mechanic who fixed the car.

Thanksgiving Day was not a holiday in Egypt, so I left our house early to go and teach my Bible school classes. I returned home by mid-afternoon to join Carrie for our Thanksgiving dinner of chicken, dressing, potatoes, vegetables, cranberry sauce, and freshly baked pumpkin pies.

One of my interesting duties during those later years in Egypt was to serve on a bookstore committee. Faith Missions had joined with the Free Methodist mission and the Church of God (Anderson) mission to operate bookstores in Alexandria, Assiut, and Cairo. I was part of the committee that had oversight of those stores.

Another Visit to Upper Egypt

In the spring of 1981, Carrie, Saied, Pastor Shukry's wife and youngest son, and I made a trip by car to Upper Egypt, which was 350 miles south of Cairo. We had good roads most of the way. In the afternoon we had a flat tire, but thankfully, we were in a town and close to a tire shop where we had it fixed. After we made a stop in Sohag to see our pastor about the service arrangements, we continued to Girga, which was to be headquarters for our stay.

The following morning I spoke in the women's meeting at the Girga church. There was a good spirit and many hands were raised for prayer. For the next five evenings, we had services at either the East Zuouk church or the Kombadar church. Those meetings were well attended, and there were many seekers. A boys' youth group and a children's group sang special songs at the Kombadar church.

Sunday was a big day. Carrie preached in the Sohag church at an 8:30 a.m. service with Saied interpreting. Saied and a friend then went to Kombadar for a service that morning. Carrie, our Sohag pastor Fawzy Malona, his teenage son, and I went to our Hawawish church where I spoke in Arabic in the morning. Our group made more than twenty house calls in Hawawish in the afternoon, and Carrie preached in the evening service. Many children were in the services that day, and it was a privilege to minister to them.

A young man from Sohag who led the singing at Hawawish invited Carrie and me to his home. His family, who were complete strangers to us, were gracious hosts for our overnight stay and provided breakfast the next morning.

After breakfast we returned to Sohag, and Fawzy and I made several house visits. One visit took us to friends who had lived in Girga. The husband was 80 and an invalid because of a stroke and diabetes. We found him cheerful and bearing his suffering well. His wife, a little younger than he, took care of him. They were grateful for our visit.

On Monday afternoon Saied, Carrie, and I went to the train station in Sohag to meet Emil Massaoud. He came to be our interpreter for the second week of our visits in the Girga area. We went to the home of Fawzy for dinner before departing to Hawawish for the evening service. That night Carrie and I lodged with the same family with whom we stayed the previous night. We returned to Girga the next morning where both Carrie and I spoke in the women's service before going to West Zuouk for services on Tuesday and Wednesday evenings. Attendance was good, and God gave help.

Carrie, Emil, and I returned to the train station in Sohag on Thursday to meet the mother and brother of our pastor in Girgaris. We were surprised to see that part of their baggage was a crate of pigeons, which they used to prepare delicious meals for us. We stayed in Girgaris about one hundred miles north of Sohag for two nights. One evening I observed a lady with a shawl over her hand as she greeted us. I learned that she was a leper who loved the Lord.

Our group, composed of Emil, Shukry's wife and youngest son, Carrie and me, left for Cairo on Saturday morning. About two hours from home, we developed car trouble. We had work done on the car, but that did not correct the problem, so we were handicapped and drove apprehensively the rest of the way. Again the Lord was good to us and gave us a safe arrival.

Final Furlough from Egypt

Carrie accompanied me to the States in July 1981. We stopped in Germany to visit Tesfai Debas and his family who had fled from Ethiopia during the war. Our schedule allowed us to be with them for a few days, and we enjoyed our visit. Tesfai had been the national director in Ethiopia in 1975 when I flew from Ethiopia to Egypt for a convention and was unable to return because of the ongoing political instability.

The summer months are busy times for deputation. Because we arrived in the States at the peak of the camp meeting season, immediately Carrie and I began speaking in those missionary services. We enjoyed traveling together that summer and fall. It was a privilege to meet many friends of long acquaintance and also to make new ones. When I returned to overseas work, Carrie remained in the States and traveled for the Mission until her death in February 1999.

Chapter 10

Beginning Missionary Work in Bolivia
1982-1984

Going to Bolivia

Frank and Leah Klassen and their daughters, Carla, Kelly, and Rhonda, were due for furlough from Bolivia in June 1982. That would leave Faith Hemmeter as the only EFM missionary there. A few months before they were to leave, Faith wrote asking me if I would consider coming to help her. I prayed, "Lord, if you want me to go to Bolivia instead of returning to Egypt, let the request come from the home office."

One evening in April Juddie Peyton, the new president of EFM, called and asked if I would be willing to go to Bolivia to be with Faith until the end of her term in 1983 because there was no one to replace the Klassens. That phone call assured me that God wanted me in Bolivia. A medical checkup indicated that I was well enough to work in the high altitudes of Bolivia, giving me additional assurance. That short term was extended several times until it became 17 years!

The Saturday evening before my departure, we had a family gathering at Doris' home in Shamokin, Pennsylvania. While we were there, the phone rang. Faith was calling from Bolivia to tell me that she and all the Klassen family had typhoid fever. My immediate thought was, *Oh, no*!

Monday morning I called the Geisinger Medical Center in Danville, Pennsylvania, and inquired if they had inoculations for typhoid fever. They did, so I borrowed Doris' car and left for Danville.

On my way the car in front of me suddenly stopped on the road. I slammed on the brakes which caused me to swerve, and my car turned a half circle and stopped against the guard cables along the highway. While I was heading for the guard cables, the thought came to me, *I am having an accident, and I am to leave for Bolivia tomorrow.* The car behind me stopped, and the man came to me and said, "Be calm, and I will get you out of there," meaning he would get my car away from the cables. After he did, I thanked him for his help, drove to where I could turn around, and headed to Danville again.

When I arrived back at the car that caused me to swerve, I stopped, went to the wife, and said, "Your husband stopped right on the road."

The wife replied, "Yes, the hood flew up, and he could not see." I returned to my car, thanked the Lord for His protection, and continued to the medical center where I received my shot.

One of the tires was losing air, so I went to a garage and had air put in it before leaving Danville. When I arrived in Shamokin, the tire was soft again, so I went to a garage where a man removed the gravel that was causing the slow leak. At the garage I locked the car keys inside the car and had to walk a few blocks to my sister's house to get a second set of keys.

Later that day Doris took me to Allentown where I stayed overnight with Eva. The next morning, May 19, Eva took me to the Allentown airport for an overnight flight to Bolivia, via Atlanta, Georgia; San Juan, Puerto Rico; Bogotá, Colombia; Lima, Peru; and finally La Paz!

When our plane arrived in Lima, the passengers were informed that the Bolivian government had declared a state of siege, which included a curfew, and we would have a layover in Lima to avoid reaching La Paz before the lifting of the curfew the following morning. I went to the rest room to comb my hair, took off my sweater and laid it aside, and failed to take it with me. After a while I saw a cleaning lady pushing a cart that held her cleaning supplies. I was shocked to see that she had my sweater on the cart. I approached her and told her that it was my cardigan and that I had left it by mistake in the rest room. She accepted my claim and gave it to me. Again I was made aware of God's unfailing love and care for me.

It was exciting to see Faith with Frank and Leah Klassen and their daughters at the La Paz airport. In immigration I was given a visitor visa. Faith and I flew immediately to Cochabamba, situated at 8,500 feet and much lower in altitude than La Paz, which is 12,000 feet above sea level.

Faith and I stayed at the Baptist Mission rest house in Cochabamba for eleven days while I became acclimated to the altitude, and Faith continued her recovery from typhoid fever. Strong winds from the South Pole brought unusually cold weather. Most of our days began and ended cold, and our room was chilly all the time because the building was not heated. We were really cold the first few nights even though we were under a sheet, a spread, and a heavy woolen blanket. We requested more blankets and the housekeeper gave each of us a lightweight woolen one that we doubled and added to the other bedding. Realizing that we still needed more covers, we bought shawls made of alpaca and llama wool that were very warm and draped them over our upper bodies. In the yard a thin layer of ice formed on the birdbath, and a taxi driver had to clear the frost from his windshield the morning he took us to the airport to fly to La Paz.

La Paz is the highest capital in the world. It has the highest airport and the longest runway in the world. It also has the highest five-star hotel in the world.

Getting Involved in the Work

The Klassen family was waiting at the airport for us, and soon our luggage was loaded into the mission Toyota Land Cruiser, and we headed to the mission house in Bosque de Bolognia, a zone of La Paz, where I would be living with Faith. As we left the city, we traveled on a paved road heading southeast. From there we turned onto a cobblestone road and climbed to a pass in the Andes Mountain range before descending into the river basin where Bolognia, the local name for Bosque de Bolognia, is located. Later that day Carla and Rhonda helped me clean my cupboards, unpack my boxes, and put things away.

The next morning the Klassen family left for the States. They later went to Australia and served two years working for EFM there.

Bolognia was a clean, pleasant community and reminded me in many ways of Asmara, Eritrea. The part of the city where Faith and I lived also reminded me of the Garden of the Gods near Colorado Springs, Colorado. All around us were steep, rugged, eroded mountains and permanently snowcapped peaks in the distance. Stone walls were used to keep rocks from sliding down the mountainside onto the road into Bolognia.

Our rented, white-stuccoed house was inside a red iron fence. On three sides were rose gardens and grass. In one side yard were flowers, clotheslines, a storeroom, and a place to park the mission vehicle. A black German shepherd named Cinder, which guarded the property, was a challenge to me. Cinder was a good friend with Faith and Cecilia (Cici), our maid, but I was a stranger. I began making friends with her by giving her food, and, eventually, I succeeded.

With Cinder, our German
Shepherd

The days were pleasant, but the nights were colder than we had encountered in Cochabamba. In addition to a sheet, a doubled sheet blanket, and a quilt, I used an electric blanket to keep warm. My head cold developed into a chest cold and infected sinuses that bothered me for several weeks. Finally, I saw a doctor who prescribed steam inhalation and treatment with antibiotics and sulfa drugs that cleared my cold and sinuses.

In addition to adjusting to the cold, I had to learn to pace myself because of the high altitude of Bolognia. I had to rest more frequently, which was a change of lifestyle for me. A major challenge was learning Spanish, the official language of Bolivia. Because I planned to be there only a short time, I did not go to language school but endeavored to learn Spanish through my daily contacts with the people. Very few Bolivians knew English, so Spanish was my only means of communication.

My first responsibility was helping Faith with the treasurer's work. Eventually I became the mission treasurer and relieved Faith of that duty. I also gave beginner's piano lessons to several children and young people who came to our house for their lessons.

At the time I arrived in Bolognia, our missionaries were holding services in Spanish in the living room/dining room of the mission house. Most of the people who attended were descendants of Spaniards. After the Klassens left, the services were moved to a larger room in the house that the Klassens had used for a classroom for their daughters. On Sundays our schedule included a morning service, an afternoon Sunday school for children, and an evening service. Tuesday evenings we had Bible study, Thursday evenings prayer meeting, and Saturday afternoons a youth service.

The Mission also was conducting services in Collana and Chacoma among the Aymara Indians about seventy miles from La Paz. Those villages are two of the many located on the vast, arid high plains of Bolivia that stretch for miles. Because of the high altitude of 13,500 feet, there are few trees, but the area is covered with tufts of stiff grass and low shrubs. Whenever the rains start, the people plant grains and potatoes, which are the major part of their diet. More than two hundred varieties of potatoes are grown in Bolivia.

It was several weeks before I adjusted enough to the altitude to be able to visit those two places of worship. Aymara men pastored those churches, one of whom was Manuel Paco, who served as director of the Indian work. Although those Indians knew some Spanish, they used their Aymara language in the church services. Whenever a missionary preached, he spoke in Spanish, and someone translated the message into Aymara.

An organization in Bolivia called the National Association of Evangelicals (*Associacion Nacional de Evangelicos en Bolivia* – ANDEB) assisted missionaries in getting visas, drivers' licenses, and other legal documents. Dennis Farah, the son of a Wycliffe missionary couple living in Bolivia and operating a rest house for missionaries, was the director of ANDEB.

Faith and I visited the ANDEB office on June 29 and asked to see Dennis, who had been working on my legal papers. We were shocked when the clerk replied, "Dennis is dead." A few days earlier we had met Dennis at a bus stop and had taken him into La Paz.

We learned that Dennis and two of his missionary friends were working with chemicals to make fire crackers when there was an explosion, and Dennis was killed. Another man lost a hand and an eye and had internal injuries, but he lived. The third one was not hurt. Faith and I drove across the mountain to the Farah home to give our condolences to the grieving family.

A few weeks later Faith and I were on our way to the doctor's office when we were involved in an accident. A doctor failed to stop at a traffic circle where we had the right-of-way and hit our Land Cruiser on the back left side. He tried to blame Faith, but the policeman indicated that the doctor was at fault, and he finally admitted he was in the wrong. We were thankful that our vehicle was not damaged, and that the doctor's vehicle had only minor damage.

By August I had my residence visa, identification card, and driver's license. I was not eager to drive in the extremely congested traffic in La Paz where some drivers showed a lack of courtesy, but the work required it. Faith helped me with that challenge by having me drive first on the high plains where there was less traffic.

The next month we had special weekend services in our Collana church before the farmers began their spring plowing, which started in early October. Because there was no electricity in the village, we borrowed a loudspeaker system that operated from a car battery. We played music over the loudspeakers for forty-five minutes before the afternoon services to notify the people that we would begin the service soon.

We drove to Collana and returned after the service, taking food with us for our return trip. The days were lovely on the high plains, but they became cold after sunset. One evening on our way home, we encountered snow flurries but had no difficulty traveling.

On Sunday people from our Chacoma church, twenty miles away, came for the morning and afternoon services. The Bolivians love to sing, and it is not unusual for them to sing for forty-five minutes to an hour before the message. They shared their food for the noon meal, placing it on colorful blankets laid on the ground. Because of the danger of contracting typhoid fever and at the recommendation of one of our Bolivian men, Faith and I ate our own food. We provided two cakes so that each individual could have a small piece, which they greatly appreciated. The services proved to be very encouraging to our people, most of whom were new Christians.

The Aymara Indians have an interesting custom that is different from that in the States. Whenever they arrive at church, many of them go to the front and shake hands with the pastor and any special speaker. Even if they arrive after the service has started, they do the same before going to their seats.

A young, Hispanic, holiness preacher was our evangelist in October for revival services in our chapel in Bolognia. The two Saturdays during the special meetings we held street meetings. Faith played her accordion and I my trumpet. Several of our believers testified, and the evangelist gave a message. Because Saturday was the day for open market in Bolognia and people from other zones as well as the local people came to buy food, many people got to hear the messages. It was a wonderful opportunity to preach God's Word. In the nightly meetings in the chapel, seekers came forward to pray in every service. Claudina, a precious Aymara lady, and Sandra, a young Hispanic lady, sought to be sanctified, and God met their hearts' need.

A Time of Relaxation

In early November Faith and I drove 100 miles northwest of La Paz to the town of Sorata to enjoy a time of rest. It was a small town at 9,000 feet nestled at the base of Illampu, towering to 21,490 feet, the second highest mountain in Bolivia. The majestic, permanently snowcapped peaks filled us with a sense of awe as we beheld the greatness of God's creation. We reached the village by a series of switchbacks and horseshoe curves on the mountainside. The contrast between Sorata and La Paz was interesting. The scenery in Sorata was gorgeous, and the mountains were lovely with green vegetation while the mountains around La Paz were barren. Also in Sorata the farmers were able to plow and plant crops farther up the steep mountainsides.

We arrived on Monday evening and found a quaint old-fashioned hotel that was operated by a Hispanic-German man and his Bolivian wife. They had a sweet baby girl named Helga. Our room had a balcony that overlooked a large flower garden. It was a beautiful and refreshing sight, but because we were weary, we ate food we brought with us and retired early. The next morning we were served hot drinks, butter, jam, and crackers. Bread was not available because of a shortage of flour in the country.

The day we arrived was All Saints' Day. The Spaniards observed it by putting flowers on the graves of their deceased loved ones. Many Aymara Indians believed the spirits

The Spanish-German man and his Bolivian wife who operated the hotel in Sorata

of their departed ones returned, so they often bought stalks of sugar cane to serve as canes for the spirits. They prepared food, and on the holiday they took it to the graves or set it somewhere for the spirits of their loved ones. Finally the living relatives ate it. They ended their celebration with singing and drinking strong drink.

With Faith on the hotel balcony that overlooked
a large flower garden in Sorata

We took a table, chairs, a camp stove, and food supplies with us, hoping to have cookouts at quiet places in the area. However, because of the inclement weather, we were unable to implement our plans, so we prepared some meals in our hotel room, and others we ate in a nearby restaurant. A meal including Pepsi cost us each 60 cents (U.S.). We had brought a package of filet mignon steak but could not cook outside, so we offered it to the couple operating the hotel to prepare a meal for all of us. They greatly appreciated our offer as meat was not always available in Sorata because of economic problems in the country.

When we went to Sorata, I had a slightly infected finger. It became worse, and I went to the local health center to have it examined. The doctor did a thorough job by removing the skin around the infected area, cleaning it well with peroxide, putting iodine over the whole finger, and applying an antibiotic ointment. Because I had a slightly elevated temperature, the nurse gave me a shot of penicillin. By Friday morning my finger was much improved.

It was quiet and peaceful in Sorata with spring-like weather. By the end of the week, we were refreshed and ready to return to Bolognia.

Added Responsibilities

After Faith and I returned to Bolognia, we received a letter from Juddie Peyton asking us to extend our stay in Bolivia until the summer of 1984 because there was no one to replace us. Faith contacted her parents and Gertrude Campbell, the lady who was caring for Faith's invalid mother, and they indicated that an extension would be all right with them. I also agreed to stay.

Before Christmas the brethren at Chacoma worked hard and poured a cement floor in the new church. They also stuccoed and white-washed the front exterior. The first day of the revival services in early January, the men painted the interior, and during the revival they poured a cement porch out front. In the mornings Faith held a Daily Vacation Bible School (DVBS) for the children, giving lessons on the Christian soldier based on part of Ephesians 6. Saturday morning most of the 37 children present gave their hearts to the Lord. The evening services were well attended, and almost every night people sought help from God.

New responsibilities were added to my schedule in March and April of 1983. During the first week of March, Faith returned to the States to be with her dying mother. That resulted in some first-time experiences for me.

The first Sunday that Faith was absent, I dedicated Daniela Martinez, one of my godchildren. I found a baby dedication program in Spanish in a church manual, and with some practice I used it. One of the men read Scripture and prayed.

The last Tuesday evening of the month was Bible study. It was my first time to give a Bible study in Spanish. The previous night I spent about four and a half hours translating twenty-five questions into Spanish for our study. The Lord faithfully helped me.

Easter was April 3, and that weekend was a busy time. After I taught my Bible Institute classes in Jocopampa on Wednesday evening, the Bolivian teachers and I returned to Bolognia on Holy Thursday. Manuel Paco and I went to the hospital in Miraflores, a zone in La Paz, to visit a mother who attended our Collana church. She had been brought by ambulance on Wednesday morning because of complications with the birth of her tenth child. Eventually she had the stillborn baby by cesarean section.

In those days in Bolivia, the hospitals provided nothing in the area of medicine. It was customary for the family to purchase all medicines and medical supplies, even buying pins for bone fractures. The doctor had ordered medicine for the mother, but it could not be found in a nearby pharmacy. When Manuel and I arrived, we took the husband in search of the medicine. Most of the pharmacies and stores were closed on Holy Thursday, but we finally found the medicine and returned to the hospital.

The family wrapped the baby in an Aymara Indian woolen blanket. Because of their poverty, there was no coffin or funeral. I drove the mission Land Cruiser and took Manuel and several family members to the city cemetery to inter the body. That experience was another first for me.

Faith attended her mother's funeral in Michigan, made living arrangements for her father, and then returned to Bolivia on Thursday following Easter. Cici and I did extra cleaning to have the house a little cheery for Faith. We were happy to welcome her home.

On Saturday I used four cake mixes to make a wedding cake for Giullermo and Otelia, a young couple of our Collana church, who were getting married the next morning. Faith beautifully decorated it. The couple did not know we were making it for them. The bride's eyes sparkled when we presented the cake along with flowers to decorate the church as our gift to them. After attending the wedding and the traditional five-course meal, we returned to Bolognia just in time to get ready for our Sunday evening service.

About two weeks after the wedding, I became sick with paratyphoid. We assumed I had contracted it by eating some of the food at the wedding. My symptoms included a dull headache, low temperature, and physical tiredness. A few days later Faith became sick. Lab tests indicated she again had typhoid fever. She probably got it at the wedding because we learned later that the father of the groom had died, possibly of typhoid fever. Before I was well, I contracted the flu and developed chest congestion. The doctor gave me two shots of penicillin to check the congestion quickly and instructed me to continue with the treatment for paratyphoid.

On a Sunday morning I sprained my lower back while moving a light-weight table in our chapel. Monday I was confined to bed with back pain. Faith continued to suffer from typhoid fever symptoms but was able to make breakfast that morning. Cici contracted the flu but recovered before we were well. She was a big help with preparing the meals and agreed to stay Friday night with us to help with some of our Saturday duties.

During the time of our illnesses, we received word that our city water was contaminated with typhoid bacterium. Immediately we began boiling our water for 30 minutes instead of 20. One morning I got out of bed, felt much better, and did not need extra bed rest. God had touched me in response to the prayers of His people.

Drought, Starvation, and Inflation

Because of a lack of rain, the potato crop for the growing season that ended in April 1983 was a total failure for some of the farmers on the high plains and a partial failure for the others. The farmers on the high plains depend on their potato crop to supply food for their families and cash to buy other necessities. By June some of the families, especially in the Chacoma area, were facing starvation. Not only was there a failure of the potato crop but also the lack of water and pasture caused some of the farmers to lose one-fourth of their flocks of sheep.

In one of our churches a father with five children told me that his children were crying because they were hungry. Roasted kernels of grain and noodles were all they had to eat.

Friends from the States provided funds so that we could purchase food items—rice, corn, carrots, turnips, cooking oil, fava beans, other vegetables, and noodles—for needy families. One Wednesday we gave aid to 30 families in Chacoma.

In spite of the famine conditions, we dedicated our church in Chacoma on July 3. We had special services from Thursday through Sunday, and people came from Jocopampa and Collana for the Sunday services.

ANDEB began collecting food items in large quantities to give to destitute communities. Evangelistic Faith Missions was a member of ANDEB, so we obtained more supplies through them than what we had been able to purchase.

In addition to the families in the Chacoma area, we received aid for families in Jocopampa and Collana. By August we were helping 80 families. As a result of that effort, our churches saw increases in attendance, and some people prayed and found salvation. In January of the next year, we gave aid

Food aid for families in Jocopampa in 1984

to 102 families in Chacoma. ANDEB provided help until the next potato crop was ready to harvest in March.

Economical and political problems were worsening. Between May 1982 and January 1984 inflation increased by 1,500 percent. Later, according to a newspaper in the United States, spiraling inflation in Bolivia reached 23,000 percent.

In February 1984 I wrote the following to Eva:

> This country is in deep, serious economic, and consequently, also political problems. We sort of live from day to day. We cannot plan ahead too much, for there may be a strike of one sort or another—transport, banks, all shops and government offices, or buses. Then there are shortages of food items, gasoline lines where you waste time waiting your turn to get gas, long lines to get a limited amount of bread or coffee, ... sometimes no sugar or flour, etc. It is difficult for the people—soaring prices all the time and salaries not increasing proportionately ... and sometimes no bread at all, and it's a basic food of the people, more important than bread is to us. This morning in the center of the city, we could not get past a certain intersection because Aymara women were sitting on the street blocking passage. We had to turn around in the street and leave the center of the city.

At one point the post office went on strike for more than a month. We were unable to send or receive mail.

Preparing to distribute food for a
work-for-food program

Food for the Hungry, another organization that provided food for the struggling families, gave commodities in return for work on a community project. They required each head of the family to work for a total of 68 hours to qualify for food. The men from Chacoma dug a stream bed to allow more water to flow off the mountainside into the village where they made a reservoir for the water. The men of Jocopampa dug a canal for irrigation. That organization had difficulty getting enough food brought by trucks from the seacoast to meet all the needs. The situation in Chacoma was desperate, so they received their food immediately. The people of Jocopampa had to wait for their food allotments.

Plane Crash in the River

One day in September 1983, I was in our backyard and heard the sound of an airplane. Looking up I saw that it was flying very low. I yelled to Faith, "I am afraid that plane is going to crash!"

Faith nonchalantly replied, "Maybe they are doing some stunt like they did in Costa Rica." Then there was a loud bang, causing our windows to rattle.

A young lady in the street exclaimed, "A plane just crashed into the river!"

Quickly Faith and I got into our vehicle and drove up the street to where we could see the river. We were told that an engine had fallen from the plane, and the plane crashed as the pilot attempted to make an emergency landing in the river. The other engine caught on fire and several local people were trying to extinguish the flames with buckets of water from the river. Soon soldiers arrived from the nearby military college and made a semicircle around the forepart of the plane to keep people away. After an hour a fire truck arrived from the airport and the firemen made sure the fire was extinguished.

The plane was a DC-3 that was used for transporting meat from El Beni, a tropical part of Bolivia where many cattle are raised. It was going to the airport in El Alto when the engines overheated. The pilot realized he could not reach the airport and headed for the river. Along the way the

The DC-3 that crashed in the riverbed near Bolognia

crew threw large pieces of beef out an opened door to make the plane lighter for the emergency landing. The pilot had radioed to the military college and notified them of his emergency landing plan and requested an ambulance. After impact the crew of six men jumped to safety without serious injury. A newspaper report indicated that it was the third plane crash the pilot had survived.

The lower hull of the plane had been destroyed during the crash and the plane was left in the river for some time. E.D. Coxon and his wife came from Michigan to visit the EFM work in November, and we took them to the river to see the plane.

We looked forward to having a new missionary family join us to help with the responsibilities. Sonny and Judy McNear finished language school in Santa Cruz, Bolivia, and moved with their daughters, Elizabeth, Christina, and Melanie, to La Paz in early December. Faith was suffering with pancreatitis, and two days before Christmas she returned to the States for medical help. Because it was time for her furlough, she remained in the States for one year. When she left Bolivia, I became administrator of the EFM work and filled that position most of the time until I returned home in 1996 to retire from overseas missionary work.

Chapter 11

Continued Ministry in Bolivia
1984-1990

Brief Furlough Interrupted

I left Bolivia on April 12, 1984, for a three-month furlough. Faith was still in America for furlough, but Sonny and Judy McNear and their girls were living in La Paz and would oversee the work in my absence.

A few days after I arrived in the States, a friend made it possible for me to fly to Egypt to take care of my household goods that I had left there when I came home on furlough in 1981. While in Egypt I also attended to some mission business.

At the time of my visit, the government of Egypt was making it extremely difficult to build evangelical churches. It also had closed our Ameeria church in Cairo, but the congregation continued to worship in various homes. Eventually the government allowed them to reopen their church for services. In spite of the government opposition, our largest EFM church in Cairo, the Medan Victoria church, had received government permission to operate a kindergarten/child care center. They were ministering to over 300 children. It was a joy to observe the children, visit our churches in Cairo, and fellowship with our pastors, believers, and their families.

I returned from Egypt on May 24, making it possible for me to attend the graduation of my niece Mary from medical school in Philadelphia. It was a special occasion, and two of my brothers and my three sisters came also. Later I saw my other brother who lived near Shamokin. It was a great delight to see all my siblings again.

The next weeks were crowded with deputation services, but my schedule was shortened because Judy McNear became seriously ill and needed to return to the States. I quickly changed my plans so that I could return to Bolivia to care for the McNear girls—Elizabeth, 13; Christina, 10; and Melanie, 7. Judy and Sonny left for the States before I returned, so friends of other mission organizations took care of the girls until my arrival on July 5.

When I arrived, I discovered that the country was partially paralyzed by a general strike. Uncertainties were the order of the day. I went to the mission house, ate some soup, and changed some items in my suitcase. Then Duane Erickson of the Bolivian Holiness Mission took the girls and me to the airport to fly to Cochabamba. What a dilemma we experienced when we were informed that our flight had been canceled! I was told to call at 5:00 the next morning, so we returned to our house in Bolognia.

Soon a sister from the church came to welcome me. Our doctor's mother, who thought we would be having prayer meeting, arrived shortly thereafter. She shared teatime with us. Meanwhile, Antonia, another sister from the church who was staying at the McNears' house in their absence, arrived to greet me. Together we read the first chapter of John and had prayer.

I called the next morning at 5:00 and was told to call again at 6:30. I called and was advised to be at the airport by 7:20 for an 8:20 flight. Adding to our dilemma our vehicle would not start. Providentially a taxi was in our community, and the driver consented to take us to the airport. When we arrived, we were informed that the flight was not confirmed. They kept putting us off until about 1:30 that afternoon when we finally boarded for the 25-minute flight to Cochabamba.

At the Canadian Baptist Mission rest home where we stayed, the girls did not find any playmates, so I entertained them. We often went for walks or visited the local shops. One day we climbed to the top of a hill where we could see the city and watch the planes coming and going at the airport.

On the hilltop was a statue of the heroines from the Battle of Cochabamba in 1824. During that battle the women had joined the Resistance, a group that was fighting for independence from Spain. The Resistance was victorious, partly because of the help of the women. Bolivia gained her freedom from Spain and on August 6, 1825, became an independent country.

Another day we went to an exceptionally large market in the morning, and in the evening we took a half-hour walk to a pizza place for supper, which the girls really enjoyed. The general strike ended while we were in Cochabamba, and everything returned to normal. We flew back to La Paz on July 18, and I continued caring for the girls until their parents returned three weeks later.

New Experiences

Bruce Johnson, a missionary with the Central Friends Mission, came to Bolivia in September for a two-week business trip. He needed to go to the Yungas, a part of the province of La Paz that has valleys and mountains covered with tropical foliage.

Neither the McNears nor I had been to the Yungas, so we asked Bruce if we could go with him, and we would use our mission vehicle. He gladly agreed. We left Friday morning and returned Saturday evening. Overnight lodging in the highland town of Chulumani was $1.00 (U.S.) including breakfast and a private bath. My dinner and supper cost slightly over $2.00 (U.S.).

The dangerous road to the Yungas, a part of Bolivia that has valleys and mountains covered with tropical foliage

Oh, such beauty! But, oh, such a treacherous road! That road is considered the most dangerous road in Bolivia. I was glad I went, but one time was enough.

EFM President Juddie Peyton and missionary evangelist L.W. Barbee came to visit our work in October. We had services for our Spanish-speaking people in our Bolognia church and several people sought God for help. Our five Aymara Indian congregations gathered at Jocopampa for Sunday services. One day during Juddie and L.W.'s visit,

With Faith and Cici beside Lake Titicaca

we took them to beautiful Lake Titicaca for a picnic. At an altitude of 12,507 feet, it is the highest navigable lake in the world.

In December 1984 I was bitten by a large German shepherd that belonged to the McNears' neighbors. There was no anti-rabies vaccine in Bolivia, so my doctor asked me to call the mission office in Bedford, Indiana, and have them send vaccine. A pharmacy in Miami, Florida, sent it by courier service on the first flight to La Paz. When I was notified by Eastern Airlines that the package arrived, it was nighttime, so the McNears went with me to the airport. The package was marked with big letters, "LIFE OR DEATH." Thankfully, friends in the States helped to cover the expenses involved. The vaccine required seven shots, which were administered at intervals for several weeks.

During the Christmas season I was privileged to attend a performance of Handel's *Messiah* in English at the La Paz Community Church. We welcomed Faith when she arrived in late December after a one-year furlough. In mid-January she flew to Cochabamba to readjust more easily to the high altitude and to attend the annual meeting of ANDEB on the 25th. I needed a respite from my busy schedule, so later I flew to Cochabamba to attend the same meeting. Both of us were refreshed when we returned to Bolognia three days later.

For some time Faith had been sensing the need to open a Bible school to train nationals for the ministry. In February her vision became a reality when she and Manuel Paco began classes at the Jocopampa church for our Aymara Indians. Fifteen men enrolled, and they met each Wednesday and Thursday evening for classes. By using the Theological Education by Extension (TEE) program, the students were able to live at home, work during the day, and study at night. Many of them were farmers who had sheep. Most of the men lived near Jocopampa; however, one lived in Huancarani and another in Chacoma, and they walked two hours each way to attend classes.

Whenever Faith went to Jocopampa to teach, she stayed in a two-room dwelling on the property. There were no sanitary facilities, no electricity, and no pure water; thus, it was necessary for her to take a kerosene lamp, candles, and jugs of boiled water. Usually our maid went with her to keep her company and to help with kitchen chores those two days a week. Manuel and his wife, who were pastoring that church, stayed nearby in a room they rented from one of the brethren. In the classrooms they used pressure lanterns, and the men sat on backless benches.

That month I attended my first funeral in Bolivia. I had helped to bury an infant in 1983, but there was no funeral on that occasion. Feliciano, a believer from our Jocopampa church, passed away. He had been saved from a drunkard's life about a year and a half before his death. Because he wanted his funeral to testify that he had found the Lord, he had asked his sons not to practice any of their former pagan customs. His widow and two of his sons were also believers who attended the church faithfully, and they honored his request.

The financial situation worsened as inflation continued and prices soared. It became almost impossible to find basics like bread, rice, sugar, cooking oil, flour, and macaroni. The Lord was always faithful to provide for us. Hilde, a European lady who had a grocery store, gave me some flour and butter; I provided milk and yeast; and our maid, Cici, made homemade bread. We shared the bread with Hilde, who really enjoyed it.

God continued to bless our work in Bolognia. A dentist who was the father of some of our teenage believers began attending services. A few years previously he had opposed his children going to our services. However, he saw the change in their lives, and then in his wife's life when she was saved later. Soon after he started coming, he sought God and experienced His transforming power. Several other young people and adults were saved or reclaimed during that time. Among them was Margot, a young lady who was attending teacher-training college and began bringing a girlfriend who was interested in the gospel. Consuelo and her daughter, Fabiola, also claimed to get back to the Lord. They began attending the Sunday morning services when Consuelo's schedule as a nurse permitted. Sometimes her sister Rosario, a policewoman, and baby girl, Daniela, came.

A general strike that occurred in March lasted for 15 days. The city of La Paz was filled with 10,000 angry miners, who descended on the city to demonstrate. They made road blocks in the streets and at times set off dynamite. Finally the government called in the army to keep the streets open for traffic. After many sessions between the government and the labor leaders, an agreement was reached, and the miners returned to their homes and work. During such situations it was difficult for us to travel, and often it was prudent to stay at home.

Later that year we had a week of meetings in Chacoma. Faith conducted a DVBS during the day for the children, and we had revival services in the evening. The public school teachers heard about the DVBS and brought their 69 students for the last two days. One of the teachers said, "If you come again, let us know ahead of time, and we will bring our students over every day for DVBS." We praised God that there were victories among the children and among the adults in the evening services.

In September the price of gasoline per liter increased from 45,000 *pesos* to 300,000. That made gas more than $1.00 a gallon, which was high for a country that produces petroleum. Not only did the price increase drastically but also gas was rationed, and that resulted in long lines at the gas stations. One day Faith waited in line for three hours and was allowed to buy only 30 liters or about eight gallons. The next time she waited three and a half hours for another 30 liters. The following day I waited in line for one and a half hours and received 40 liters. By then we had enough gas to take a load of building supplies to Jocopampa. The gas shortage lasted nearly six weeks.

Faith and I went to the city of Sucre for a few days in November. Sucre was founded in 1538 and had a colonial atmosphere. The city was lovely, clean, and tranquil. Most of the buildings were painted white, and it was recognized as the White City of Bolivia. Our days there were very refreshing. We visited the building where Bolivia's Declaration of Independence was signed and saw their cracked Liberty Bell.

Before Christmas 1985 the Christian Ladies Book Club to which Faith and I belonged gave a Christmas tea to the girls in the government orphanage in Obrajes across the mountain from where we lived. On the appointed day we took homemade cookies and tea. With club money we had purchased Christian literature and gave each of the 90 girls a New Testament, a tract, and a storybook. The girls were delighted and thankful.

A Christian dentist in the States sent money for us to provide shoes for the Indians in our churches on the high plains. We hired a man from one of our churches and a relative of his to make sandals of various sizes from used vehicle tires and inner tubes. With other gift money we bought popcorn and sweet limes. Those were probably the only Christmas gifts most of them received.

Immediately after Christmas, Faith and I went to Jocopampa. We conducted a DVBS during the day and revival services in the evening.

We planned for most of our Daily Vacation Bible Schools to be held during the summer months, December to March, while the public schools were on vacation. We also held a few during the three-week winter break the last week of June and the first two weeks of July. That is the coldest time of the year in Bolivia, and because the public school buildings are not heated, school is not in session.

Children in the DVBS in Jocopampa with their handicrafts

The Church at Jocopampa

In January 1983 Manuel and I conducted a service at a new location on the high plains. One of the men of Jocopampa had invited us to come and preach to them. Our first service was with the village women's club on a Thursday using a classroom in the public school building. There were nearly seventy present for that service. At the close several prayed for forgiveness. We continued having services on Thursdays until June when we started services on Sunday afternoons, which made it easier for the men to attend. We conducted a Sunday morning service at Chacoma and then went to Jocopampa for an afternoon service.

Delores, who had been saved six weeks previously, died of tuberculosis in June. She left behind her husband, Alberto, who was also a new believer, and three small children. We were thankful that God led us to start services earlier that year in Jocopampa.

The growing congregation had a desire to build their own church. The Mission bought land to help them. The men immediately began work and dug by hand a 36-foot deep well in order to have water to make adobe bricks, which are mud bricks used for building. While the men dug, the women scoured the fields and collected stiff grass that grew on the high

Men in Jocopampa making adobe bricks for their church building

plains to make the bricks. During the next several weeks, the congregation made 17,500 of them. It was quite a task because they had to draw the water from the well, loosen the earth, add water and grass, press the mud into molds, and lay the bricks in the sun to dry.

On November 23 about thirty men and forty women gathered for their groundbreaking service. At the close of the service, the men used string to mark the foundation and then dug the trenches. Large stones had been delivered previously by truck, and now the women carried them to the site for the men to lay the foundation. They were a happy people that day because they had a mind to work.

After the men completed the foundation, they started building the walls. When Manuel and I went to Jocopampa in early December to distribute food, we found the church people working on the structure. Men, women, and children were swarming like busy bees. Some were mixing soil and water for mortar; others were carrying the heavy adobe bricks to the six masons. It was inspiring to see them working so diligently.

Pablo, one of the new believers, was a tremendous blessing. He worked part time in construction, so he was able to give valuable direction and help to the men as they built the church. He guided them in the building of two reinforced concrete pillars to support the roof.

Women in Jocopampa carrying the bricks during the building project

Soon the walls were finished, and we purchased doors, windows, and materials for the roof with gifts from friends in the States. When the roof was completed, the men nailed lathing onto the bottom of the rafters and added chicken wire. Above the wire they placed grass from their fields and neighboring mountain slopes, creating a surface to which the plaster could adhere. Ralph and Pauline Stuck, a couple from Pennsylvania, who was celebrating their fiftieth wedding anniversary, gave a gift that covered the cost of plastering the ceiling and the inside walls and laying a concrete floor.

The congregation did all the work to avoid labor costs. They used hand tools even to cut the iron rods for reinforcing the concrete. They worked many hours in the bone-chilling winds, rain, and cold on the high plains and sometimes under the scorching sun.

The dedication service took place on Easter weekend. They had two special services on Good Friday and then the dedication service on Sunday, April 7, 1985. Faith went to Bolognia on Saturday, and Easter morning the local congregation there enjoyed their first communion service. She returned to Jocopampa for the afternoon dedication service. For that special service believers came from our churches in Chacoma, Collana, Huancarani, and Alto Patacamaya. There were about two hundred in attendance, and the local congregation provided the noon meal of baked mutton, cooked potatoes, fava beans, and salad.

Dedication of the Jocopampa church on April 7, 1985

Later the men constructed a two-room building on the property. Then a third room was added and the three rooms were used as a house where the missionaries could stay whenever they had revivals and Daily Vacation Bible Schools in the churches on the high plains. Eventually another building was built with two large rooms for Bible Institute classes and a third room for a caretaker and his family. A gift from one of my sisters-in-law helped to cover the expenses of that project.

Anna Ramos' Burn Experience

Fourteen-year-old Anna Ramos was severely burned in her village of Huancarani in February 1986. She and her sister were lighting a lamp in their bedroom, and the lamp exploded. Anna's clothing caught on fire, and she ran outside. Her brother quickly wrapped his coat around her, extinguishing the fire.

The following day when Faith and I went for Bible Institute classes, Anna's family flagged us down, and we took her to the government hospital in La Paz. Anna had first-, second-, and third-degree burns from head to waist including her arms. At first she was unable to feed herself, so Anna's sister who lived in the city, Faith, and I took turns going to the hospital to feed her. We often took food to her because the hospital did not supply much meat or fruit. The hospital did not provide medicine, so we also helped the family to purchase the medical supplies she needed.

Anna had skin grafts for the third-degree burns on her chest and arms. We were able to help pay Anna's medical bills through a generous gift from Jacqueline Wheary, a high-school classmate of mine. Anna's folks

did well to pay bus fares to come the 70 miles to visit her. She was released two months later. However, her burns were not healed completely, and because of severe infection that developed on her back, she had to return to the hospital for another month. When I took her to the doctor, her mother wanted me to ask him how long she would have to stay. With firm emphasis he replied, "Until she is well."

With Jacqueline Wheary, who gave a generous gift to help Anna, a burned girl

Anna's father, Tuborico Ramos, was the lay pastor at Huancarani. Partly as a result of Anna's accident, other members of her family began attending church. Her sister Trinidad and two older brothers, Pablino and Felix, with their spouses became believers.

Brief Visits to the United States

I returned to the States in July for another brief furlough. During that time I attended my family reunion near Shamokin, and all six of my siblings were present. Leonard was suffering with terminal cancer, and we knew it probably was the last time that all of us would be together, so we had a studio picture taken that day. Even though my time in the States was short, I was happy to travel for deputation services.

In 1986 with my siblings—Charles, Leonard, Earl, Doris, Eva, and Helen

When Leonard's condition deteriorated, I received permission from the Mission to stay home until after his death. During his last weeks in the hospital, I was able to speak to him on a few occasions about his need of a personal relationship with Jesus Christ. God gave special help during one of the visits, and Leonard prayed to be saved. He passed away on November 30, and at his funeral I shared about the special time we had had in the hospital a few weeks previously.

While I was in the States, Jerry and Jacqueline Kwasigroh with their children, Jessica and Jonathan, arrived in Bolivia. They had been in language school in Costa Rica.

Getting ready to return to Bolivia was no small task. Because I was returning for what I thought would be a four-year term, I had many items to pack for myself and also some used clothing for the Bolivians. The pieces of luggage piled up until they looked like a small mountain. I arrived at the airport in Allentown on December 11 with five suitcases and five duffle bags. Piedmont Airlines did not charge me for the extra bags nor for any excess weight. However, when I was ready to fly out of Miami, Florida, Eastern Airlines informed me that a new regulation allowed me to take only two pieces of luggage. I explained that I was not notified of such when I purchased my ticket nor when I left Allentown. With the clerk in my favor, the manager called to the pilot, who by that time was preparing for departure, and received permission for me to take the ten bags. Praise the Lord for His never failing help!

When I arrived in La Paz that night, it appeared that I might need to leave my luggage at the airport and go through Social Action because of the used clothing that I had brought with me. Again, the Lord intervened, and after a brief inspection of two of my bags, my luggage was released without needing to pay any customs.

The following week I spent most of two days at the customs office obtaining clearance for a Honda 2200-watt generator, which had been sent by air freight. The Great Lakes District of the Wesleyan Holiness Association of Churches had purchased the generator for our work in the countryside where there was no electricity. I finally paid import fees and the generator was released from customs.

I received an urgent phone call in May from Doris, asking if I could come home for a month to help her while she recuperated from a physical and emotional problem that was caused by a chemical imbalance. The Mission granted me a six-week visit to the States.

In September Doris urgently needed me again, so I took an indefinite leave of absence to help her with her problems that had continued. She paid all my travel expenses and the amount of my support both times. During my absence Zettie (Finch) Cotton, a former EFM missionary to

Ethiopia and a widow at the time, went to Bolivia to help Faith until I returned.

Doris and I observed both Thanksgiving and Christmas at the home of her son Bill and his wife, Marylea, in New Jersey. On Christmas Eve we went to their town square and sang carols with hundreds of other townspeople and then to a church for a candlelight service before returning to Bill and Marylea's home. My niece Mary and her husband came for the holiday, and we sang carols accompanied by Mary on her violin. Lester and Helen arrived about noon on Christmas Day. After dinner we sang carols again with Mary playing her violin, Helen the guitar, and Lester the mandolin. It was a joy for me to be with members of my family for the holidays.

Various Mission Activities

Doris was well enough so that I could return to Bolivia on March 2, 1988. Shortly thereafter the Kwasigroh family moved to the *Departamento* of Cochabamba, of which the city of Cochabamba is the capital. They pioneered works in the mountain villages of Churo and Larati and in F. Tropical, a small community in the jungle.

Faith and I helped with special weekend services in June at Villa Tunari that culminated in the dedication of the property purchased while I was in the States. The buildings on the property provided facilities for church services, Sunday school classes, and Bible Institute classes. Visitors came from our Collana and Jocopampa churches. Several groups of young people sang and played special songs, and Faith preached the dedicatory message.

My Sunday responsibilities usually involved going to one of our churches in El Alto or on the high plains. For example, one Sunday in July, I arose at 5:00 and had a time of prayer. After breakfast I packed a previously prepared lunch. At 7:15 I left for Chacoma on the high plains 75 miles away. Humberto Mamani and Manuel Paco's wife with her four youngest children were with me. Humberto preached at Alto Patacamaya and Belén, while Manuel's wife and children went with me to Chacoma.

At Chacoma I accompanied the singing, taught the Sunday school lesson, and preached. After a quick dinner our group went to the Gran Poder church. There I provided music on the keyboard, taught the children's Sunday school class, and preached. After that service I took the Bolivians to places near their homes, and I returned to Bolognia, arriving at 6:00. I was weary but glad that I was able to work all day for Jesus. Faith, who was the pastor of our Bolognia church, spent Sundays in Bolognia.

A few Sundays later I preached in one of our churches on the theme, "Your Life Depends on Where You Look." I talked about not looking backwards, not looking at our difficulties or around us, and not looking to ourselves, but rather looking to Jesus for salvation and help. After service a little fellow about six years of age asked me, "*Señorita*, may we look like this?" and he rolled his eyes. I realized that he had thought of all those points of my message like looking with our physical eyes. So I explained to him and his little sisters that I was talking about behavior that affects our spiritual lives and not the manner of moving our physical eyes. Sometimes we do not know how the minds of little children grasp our messages!

We began teaching Bible Institute classes at Villa Tunari in August with 14 students. Our Bible Institute had been started at Jocopampa on the high plains in February 1985, but that was too far for the men from Villa Tunari to travel. We continued classes at Jocopampa on Saturday mornings and began teaching at Villa Tunari on Wednesday evenings. Because of the wide range of schooling the Bible Institute men had, they were divided into two groups. All would cover the same material, but one group would take three years and the other six. It was my responsibility to teach those whose Spanish was limited, and Faith taught the other group.

The school year had ended and on December 15, 1988, Faith went to the States for a three-month furlough. That began a pattern of a three-month furlough every three years for her. I never took another three-month furlough because I was planning to retire from overseas missionary work. However, with a shortage of missionary personnel, it never became convenient for me to retire until November 1996.

As Christmas approached, there was a sense of joy and excitement among our congregations. For most of our churches, it was their first time to present a Christmas program. The programs were scheduled at different times so that the missionaries could attend each one.

I celebrated Christmas on December 22 with our people in Chacoma. Pedro, a student in the Bible Institute, gave the message, and I made a few remarks about Jesus and Christmas. At the close each one received a bag of Christmas goodies. The next evening the Bolognia church held their Christmas program, and afterwards a tea was served in our house for about fifty people with each family bringing snacks for the occasion. I went to Jocopampa to share Christmas Eve with the congregation. After their program I gave a brief yuletide message, and then they served bread with hot chocolate made with water. It was after 1:00 a.m. before I got to bed.

Christmas Day was an extremely busy day for me. I went with pastor Humberto and his wife to Belén for their program, and I gave a brief message. Afterward we drove to Collana, and near noon we began their Christmas program. I made a few remarks based on two appropriate verses of Scripture. We shared dinner in the churchyard, sang a song of praise, prayed, and then hurried to El Alto for service at Grand Poder. My last activity of Christmas Day was the evening service in Bolognia. I was exhausted by bedtime.

Sandra and José Luis Bohorquez accompanied me on New Year's Eve to our Villa Tunari church. We worshiped with singing, scripture reading, special songs, and recitations. Before I gave the message, the young people presented a gift of twenty chairs to the church, and they also presented a certificate of appreciation to me for the encouragement and help I had given to them that year.

On my way to minister to our people in Chacoma on New Year's Day, I left Humberto at Belén to be in charge of the morning worship service. Taking his wife and son with me, I drove to our Chacoma church to preach. Immediately after the service we hurried to Belén to conduct a baby dedication service after which the parents served a delicious meal. From there we went to Jocopampa and attended the last of the special services that Pastor Macario was conducting. Our group, including Macario, returned to El Alto where I left those who were with me, and I went to Bolognia and attended the evening service.

Following the two months of summer vacation in December and January, I began teaching the Bible Institute classes at Jocopampa. I also taught Faith's classes until she returned from furlough on March 15, 1989. After she returned, we started classes at Villa Tunari.

The annual celebration of Carnival took place in Bolivia shortly after we started the Bible Institute classes at Jocopampa. The Carnival is a time of drunkenness and immorality for many. In an effort to help a young believer who was recently married so that he would not be tempted to slip back into sin during Carnival, we arranged special services for our people at Collana. Not only did the young man come but also his wife and his in-laws. It was worth the extra effort to drive to and from Collana those two days. Some of the church folks received spiritual help, and one was weeping while he testified that he sometimes sold things on Sundays. The Lord had punished him for it, and he promised never to do it again. In the last service I dedicated two baby boys.

The Mission had leased the property where we were living since 1984. In February 1989 the Lockmers, who were living in California, decided to remain in the States, and they agreed to sell EFM the property we were leasing. Mrs. Lockmer came to Bolivia to do the legal work involved. We also took official procedures to buy their telephone line to the house because it was difficult to secure telephone service.

In addition to working on the legal papers for the property in Bolognia, I was working with the architects on the church building projects at Gran Poder and Villa Tunari. I continued visiting the churches in El Alto and in the *campo* or the countryside, taking care of mission accounts, teaching in the Bible Institute, and attending mid-week services in Bolognia. I was amazed at what God helped me to do.

We entertained our first Touching Lives for Christ (TLC) team in June. That ministry is an outreach of the Hobe Sound Bible Church in Hobe Sound, Florida. We wanted to show the team the tropical area of

Road to the Yungas where one vehicle had to wait for the oncoming one

Bolivia, so we took them to the Yungas, a lush green area between La Paz and Carnavi. At places the road was just a ledge barely wide enough for one car along the mountainside, and sometimes the bottom of the precipice was not visible. There were places where one vehicle had to wait for the oncoming one to pass. I had traveled that road in 1984 and thought I never wanted to travel it again. After we returned from the Yungas, the TLC team helped us conduct Daily Vacation Bible Schools and revivals in our churches in Sixilla Baja, Bolognia, Jocopampa, and Collana. The men in the group also painted the exterior of the mission house.

That fall our two co-pastors and the young people of our Villa Tunari church conducted a Child Evangelism project sponsored in part by a children's Sunday school class in Shamokin. Every other Saturday they had an afternoon service, after which they played games in the churchyard, and enjoyed rolls and hot chocolate. As many as 200 children attended on some Saturdays. From that effort two new families began attending services, and some of them found spiritual help.

During that Christmas season we gave our church people 520 bags of goodies that contained popcorn, cookies, and hard candy. A few of our Bolognia young people prepared 320 bags in our dining room, and the Villa Tunari church people prepared the other 200. Monetary gifts sent to us made those treats possible. We also gave each family a gift of rice, sugar, and cooking oil.

Our new year began with excitement. On the first Friday in January 1990, we had two accidents in our kitchen that could have been serious. Faith put potatoes in a pressure cooker and placed it on the stove. While she waited for the pressure to rise, she took some dishes to the cupboard in the dining room. Just as she was ready to enter the kitchen, the cooker exploded! The lid blew off hitting the refrigerator and damaging the door in two places. Tiny pieces of potatoes were splattered on the kitchen walls, ceiling, and furniture.

That evening Cici opened the freezer door of the refrigerator, and it fell to the floor apparently because of the damage received from the pressure cooker lid. Fortunately, the door did not hit her. James and Grace Fulton with the Central Friends Mission were visiting, and he repaired the door. We thanked the Lord for protecting us in both accidents.

On Easter over 300 people attended the special services at Jocopampa. People came from nearly all our churches in the La Paz area. Some walked for two hours, and two young women and a little boy walked for four hours over the mountains from Sixilla Baja. The local congregation and the Mission provided food for the noon meal.

While the Kwasigrohs were on furlough, Faith and I made periodic visits to the works they had been pioneering in Churo, Larati, and F. Tropical in the Cochabamba district. One Friday after Easter, Faith and I with José Luis and his sister Alejandra from our Bolognia church drove to the Cochabamba area to visit our work in Churo. Sergio, the pastor at Churo, walked down the mountains for several hours to take tests for his Bible Institute classes. He then urged us to go to Churo that same afternoon. We thought it was a wise idea because municipal elections were to take place the next day and driving on the highways would be forbidden during voting hours. After a delicious fish dinner, our group gathered our sleeping bags, blankets, warm clothing, food, hot tea in our thermoses, and bottled water and began a two-and-a-half-hour drive over several mountains to reach Churo.

When we arrived, Sergio took Faith, Alejandra, and me to the public school building where we stayed overnight in the one-room, teachers' dwelling. The school was closed for summer vacation, and the teachers, a married couple, were spending the summer in Cochabamba, so the room was available. The bed was made of boards set on mud bricks and a mattress filled with dried, tough grass. The men brought more blankets to make sure we would be warm during the night. We three ladies snuggled into our sleeping bags and lay crosswise on the bed with the blankets on top of us. We were warm and had more blankets than we needed and feared that maybe the others were cold, having sacrificed their blankets, but they were fine. We had a fitful night of sleep. José Luis slept in the Land Cruiser.

After the service on Saturday evening, we met with some of the villagers and gave them money to buy roofing for a new classroom under construction. Friends back home had given us special offerings for such situations. On Sunday morning when the believers gathered for worship in a long narrow classroom with a thatched roof, most of the village elders joined them. The elders may not have come to worship, but we were thankful for the opportunity to preach the gospel to them. After the service they thanked us for the money and expressed their gratefulness with a handshake and a tap on the shoulder, a typical highland Indian greeting.

A tasty meal was provided by Sergio and his wife; then we visited two homes where we had been invited. Following those visits we had another service. There was a ball game in progress on the school grounds, but the players continued quietly until we finished our service. We appreciated their gesture of respect.

We hurried back to Cochabamba after the service, hoping to get down those mountains before dark. On the way we saw scraps of wood and metal from a truck that had gone over a precipice, killing several people. We arrived in Cochabamba about 8:00, thankful for another safe trip.

In the second week of July, Pastor Raimundo's only grandchild, a one-year-old girl, died after falling down the stairs. The young father, Raimundo's son, could not afford to bury her in the city, so we took the body to the village cemetery. Raimundo and one of his sons dug the grave; then the grandfather laid the body to rest until the resurrection morning. The custom among the Aymara Indians is to eat cookies and drink alcoholic beverages at the grave site, but our believers eat cookies and drink soft drinks. I am glad that the redeeming power of Jesus changes lives!

A small independent congregation in Santiago II in El Alto joined our work later that month, giving us a work in both Santiago I and Santiago II. A few weeks later I dedicated seven children to the Lord at Santiago II and gave the morning message on "The Christian Family." It was a precious service because the Holy Spirit was there giving help.

We attended the wedding of Sixto and Anna in August in the village of Belén. Anna was the young lady who had been burned badly in an accident in her home. Although she had bad neck scars, God healed her face beautifully.

The wedding was performed by Pastor Raimundo in the front yard of the bridegroom's parents. A tarpaulin made a canopy to accommodate the bride and groom and their attendants. When Raimundo asked Sixto, "Do you take this woman to be your wedded wife?" Sixto replied, "I do with my whole heart." After the ceremony we played Christian music until it was time to eat. It was a good way to witness to the unsaved at the wedding.

That year I was showered with celebrations for my 66th birthday. On my birthday, August 23, Faith prepared a chicken dinner and decorated a small cake that we shared with three older ladies of our Bolognia church. In the afternoon a few missionary friends came to have cake and ice cream.

The Monday following my birthday, Celia invited Faith and me to her home where she served us a Bolivian chicken dish to celebrate both of our August birthdays. Then on the first Sunday in September, we were invited to the home of a church family in Bolognia to enjoy a fried chicken dinner with our church people. One of the young ladies had made and decorated a gelatin cake. A few days later the Teófano Bohorquez family invited us to their home for an elegant tea.

Chicken was the meat that urban, middle-class Hispanics often served to their guests and ate on special occasions in their homes. The main meat of the rural Aymara Indian was mutton. Our congregations in the high plains often served it for Sunday dinner when holding or hosting conventions and anniversary revival services in the La Paz district.

I marvel at God's continued watchful care as I have served Him in foreign countries. One day while I was riding in a taxi to the city of La Paz on business, another car crossed the thoroughfare and collided with the taxi. The other driver was at fault because he did not have the right-of-way. Even though my left leg was injured, I was thankful that I had no broken bones.

Two months later I was involved in another incident while I was standing on a street corner in La Paz waiting to cross the street. A young man who was walking rapidly down the sidewalk and was not watching where he was going ran into me and knocked me into the street in front of a car that was stopped for a traffic signal. The man was kind enough to come and help me back to the corner before the traffic light changed, and I retrieved my purse before it was stolen. Although it could have been more serious, I received only a bruised knee. Thank the Lord for His protection!

During November we held a weekend meeting in Cosmos '79 in El Alto. Faith and three ladies from our Bolognia congregation had gone early and distributed 400 invitations in Cosmos '79 and Quishuaras, a nearby housing development. Faith and some of the pastors did the preaching. I was unable to help them because of a sore throat. On Sunday people came from our other churches in El Alto to rejoice with the local brethren in the dedication of their little chapel. We were encouraged when a new family began attending the services as a result of that weekend meeting. A few years later we built a church on the property, and the little chapel was used as a Sunday school classroom

The week after Christmas, Faith and I held Daily Vacation Bible Schools and evangelistic services in Collana and Jocopampa. It was a blessing to stay in our little house on the property in Jocopampa. I held a three-day DVBS in Collana in the mornings with twelve children, and about eighteen people attended the afternoon evangelistic services. Several received spiritual help, including a young mother who asked forgiveness of the church. It was not convenient to hold night services in Collana because there was no electricity in that area, and the people were scattered and lived far from the church, making it unsafe for them to walk home at night.

At Jocopampa where Faith ministered, the people lived closer together, and we could have night services. We climaxed the week with a watch-night service at Jocopampa. About sixty people attended, representing 18 families. Our hearts echoed the words of the psalmist: "Thou crownest the year with thy goodness" (Psalm 65:11a).

Chapter 12

Renewal and Advancements
1991-1995

Enjoying a Mini Vacation

In February 1991 Faith and I took a much-needed vacation. Elena, Celia, and her granddaughter Daniela went with us for part of the time. We took the night train to Potosi where we stayed for two days. Elena grew up there and took us to see her childhood home. She knocked on the door with some misgiving, not knowing what the reaction of the present owner of the house would be. When Elena told her who she was, the owner graciously welcomed us inside. While in Potosi we saw *Cerro Rico* or Rich Hill, the mountain where silver was discovered in 1545. Lead, tin, and iron were also bountiful in *Cerro Rico*. We then visited a nunnery and the Royal Mint, which was established in 1562.

From Potosi our group took a minibus to Sucre and spent a couple, enjoyable days with the Allen McVeys, friends from the Immanuel Missionary Church Bolivian Mission. In Sucre we visited the building that had housed the first government seat of Bolivia. After a long struggle with Spain, Bolivia declared her independence on August 6, 1825.

We then flew to Tarija in southern Bolivia and visited Richard and Mary Smith and Marjorie Hall, missionaries who were starting a new work for the Emmanual Mission of Bolivia. From there our Bolivian friends returned to La Paz. The Smiths and Marjorie made plans to take Faith and me to Jujuy, Argentina, a country we had never visited. We drove to Villazon where we received visas from the Argentine Consulate and planned to cross the border. However, Bolivia was experiencing an epidemic of cholera, and at the border, we were required to be seen by a doctor in the customs area. Because the doctor was not present, it was necessary for us to return overnight to Villazon.

In the morning we returned to customs and met the doctor. When he released us, we joyfully continued on our way. We arrived in Jujuy about midday and found a restaurant. Because Argentina is famous for its beef, several of us enjoyed delicious steaks for our meal. On the return trip I saw a sign along the road that read The Tropic of Capricorn. Excitedly I told the others about it. We returned to the sign and followed a road to the monument where we took photos. That evening we stayed in the border town of La Quiaca, Argentina. Early the next morning we resumed our journey to Tarija, reaching there in time to refresh ourselves and have lunch before boarding our afternoon flight to La Paz. We had been

The monument marking the Tropic of Capricorn

away for about two and a half weeks, and it was good to be home, renewed, and ready to return to our work.

Sundry Endeavors

During the week preceding Easter, we were in revival services at Jocopampa. The atmosphere was filled with excitement as almost three hundred people gathered on Sunday to celebrate our annual Easter convention. The majority of them came on chartered buses from our churches in El Alto. The Kwasigroh family and 52 people from our work in the Cochabamba area made the long trip of about two hundred miles on a chartered bus. The Indians in Cochabamba speak Quechua; the Indians of La Paz district speak Aymara; and all speak Spanish except small children and most of the older women. In the morning service the preacher spoke in Spanish, one of the Aymara pastors interpreted into Aymara, and a brother from our Bolognia church interpreted into Quechua. Regardless of the time involved in all the interpreting, many prayed at the close of the message.

Shortly after Easter we started Bible Institute classes in Villa Tunari and Gran Poder, two zones on the opposite sides of El Alto. The few students who lived in the countryside came to Gran Poder for classes.

* * * * *

We had notified Francisco, our pastor in Sixilla Baja, that we would visit them Saturday and Sunday, June 8 and 9. After we finished Bible Institute classes in Gran Poder, we began our journey that afternoon, accompanied by Rubén and Marcela Verastegui and their four children. In spite of rain and snow in our area, we reached Sixilla Baja safely before dark. Rubén's family set up their tent in the pastor's patio, and Faith and I made our bed in the back of our Land Cruiser.

Besides our group of eight, 40 people came for the morning worship service. In the afternoon attendance was also good. We rejoiced that people sought the Lord in both services.

It was already 4:30 when we started for home. It had rained the previous night, and the narrow road in the valley was muddy. We were concerned because there were about sixty small log bridges over irrigation ditches that we had to cross. After crossing the valley we started ascending the mountain. It was dark when it began to snow and get slippery. We were glad that Rubén, a very good driver and a mechanic, was driving and that the vehicle had four-wheel drive.

At 8:00 we stopped on the high plains to eat a snack we had with us. Susana, the eight-year-old daughter of Rubén and Marcela, had never touched snow. She and her two older sisters asked their parents if they could feel the snow which had begun to accumulate at the side of the road. When Susana got back into the car, she said to Faith, "When I touched the snow, it felt like cotton, but when I squeezed it, it felt like water." Although the weather was inclement, we felt God's presence and thanked Him for giving us a profitable, safe trip.

* * * * *

Many of the people in the Santiago II church, including Pastor Cruz, were originally from the village of Quillcoma on the high plains. There was no evangelical church in their village, and a burden grew on them to get the gospel to their people. They asked us to help them get a church started there. The community had recently set aside a section of farm land to be used for housing and had designated a lot for an evangelical church and a lot for a Seventh-day Adventist church. However, the newly elected village secretary of justice, who had an evangelical background, thought that a lot on a nearby hill was a better site for an evangelical church. He convinced the village authorities to allow the Mission to buy it from the public school for a small amount of money. We already had told Pastor Cruz and others of the village that the Mission would not have the money to help them build a church for some time. With that in mind, some of the local men immediately began making adobe bricks for building a small chapel.

By February the men had made 700 bricks, and we encouraged them to start building the chapel to shield the worshippers from the rains, the cold temperatures, the fierce winds, and the scorching sun. They had been worshipping in the open air since September. They bought the window frames and panes and paid

Mixing mud to make adobe bricks for the Quillcoma chapel in 1991

Seven hundred bricks ready to be used to build the chapel in Quillcoma

part of the cost of the door. The Mission paid the other part and gave them some used roofing. In just a few weeks, the chapel was completed and dedicated on March 15, 1992.

＊ ＊ ＊ ＊ ＊

For several years Marcela Verastegui was hired to prepare the materials for our Daily Vacation Bible Schools. Between mid-December 1991 and the end of January 1992, she and several young people conducted seven Daily Vacation Bible Schools. The workers presented the illustrated story of Pilgrim's Progress and Bible stories using felt figures. The children were captivated with how the figures stuck to the flannelgraph board, and some were curious enough to come forward and touch them. The theme for that year was "The Bible." They learned the chorus "The B-I-B-L-E" in Spanish and sang it with all their hearts and shouted *Biblia* with great joy and enthusiasm. For their memory work they were to learn the names of the books of the Bible. Some learned only the books of the Old Testament, others the books of the New Testament, but several succeeded in learning all of them. The names were impressed upon their minds by singing the names to the tune of the chorus "If We All Work Together." By repeating them over and over with the children, I learned them in order in Spanish for the first time.

Two of those Daily Vacation Bible Schools were held at Jocopampa and Collana with revival services being conducted in the evenings. The first was at Jocopampa and the second at Collana. Raimundo, Rubén and Marcela Verastegui with their three girls and baby boy, a young relative of theirs, and I lodged in rooms on our property at Jocopampa. With help I prepared our meals in the kitchen in the little house. Raimundo, Rubén, and I did the preaching. Attendance was very good, and several sought the Lord.

During the DVBS at Collana, it rained parts of every day, but the Lord answered prayer and always gave us sunshine over the dinner hour. The food brought by the church families varied slightly from day to day and consisted of *chuños* or *tuntas*, corn, little cakes of cooked *quinua* that was a nutritious cereal grown in the Bolivian highlands. Sometimes we had a small bowl of a hot spicy sauce to add flavor. The food was placed on a colorful shawl on the ground, and those present squatted or sat on the ground, taking handfuls until they were satisfied.

Chuños are potatoes that are laid on the ground to freeze at night. The farmer and his family then extract the water from the potatoes after they thaw by stomping on them with their feet. That process is repeated at least three times; then the potatoes are left on the ground until they become very dry and can be stored for several years. When the Bolivians want to eat the potatoes, they soak them in water for a couple days to reconstitute them. If water is plentiful, they change it several times. They then cook them in clean water before eating them.

Another process to preserve potatoes is to place them in a pond, lake, or a slow-flowing stream for some time. The potatoes become coated with a white film, probably lime. After they are recovered from the water, they go through the same process of stomping as they did the *chuños*, and then they are dried and stored. These also keep for several years and can be reconstituted by soaking them in water like the *chuños* before being cooked. These are called *tuntas*.

On New Year's Eve we were preparing to go to bed when a truck pulled into the yard. Ernesto Lima of Belén had come seeking our help. That evening his young son Rubén, with one of his siblings, was house-sitting next door for his mother's sister Anna and her husband Sixto, Ernesto's brother. Rubén found a firecracker and lit it, causing the firecracker to explode. He lost some of his fingers and needed emergency care. Marcela stayed with the children while Rubén V., Ernesto, and I rushed the boy in our Land Cruiser to the children's hospital in La Paz about a two-hour drive away. Praise the Lord, the child survived and learned to live without some fingers.

* * * * *

Shortly before Lyndal and Rebecca Black with their daughters Alecia and Leah arrived in June, I had a shocking experience. I was in the city of La Paz during evening rush hour to make the final payment on a bathtub we had ordered for the Blacks' apartment. Finding a place to park was a problem, so I parked in a place reserved for taxis. The shopkeeper sent one of her helpers with the tub to the corner where I was parked. I did not know the helper, nor did he know me. He asked, "Are you the lady who is to get the bathtub?"

About the same time another man came to the Land Cruiser and said, "Senora!"

"Do you belong to this store also?" I asked.

I had the back doors open to lay down the second seat to make a place for the bathtub, and I was getting anxious because a taxi was waiting to park where I was. In the midst of the confusion, the man who said "Senora" stole my purse! I did not miss it until I reached for it to pay the balance due on the bathtub.

I moved the Land Cruiser and then went into the store and told the owner that someone stole my purse. Faith was at Pastor Nano's house in Bolognia for prayer meeting. I contacted her by phone, and she confirmed that we had sufficient funds at the mission house to pay for the bathtub. The store owner sent her helper with me to receive the payment.

I made sure that the young man got on the right bus from Bolognia to return to the store.

The extent of my loss immediately hit me. My purse contained my Bolivian driver's license, my I.D. card, important papers for the Land Cruiser, almost $100.00, plus other items of lesser importance. When I applied for a new driver's license, I received a courtesy license that needed no renewal as long as I was working there with the Mission. My new I.D. card had the same number as the stolen one, and a lawyer helped us acquire new documents for the Land Cruiser. Even in that difficult situation, God was faithful to take care of me.

The Blacks came to replace the Kwasigrohs who were returning to the States. They went with the Kwasigrohs to Cochabamba for two weeks to become acquainted with the work in that area. The Blacks then came to Bolognia and lived in an apartment above the chapel on the mission property. They studied Spanish at home with a private tutor for a few months before moving back to Cochabamba at the end of November to oversee the mission work there.

In November we concluded our academic year of Bible Institute classes at Gran Poder and in December those at Villa Tunari. That completed our seventh year of Bible Institute classes. We had two graduates from Villa Tunari—Florentino Paco and Arturo Chambilla.

Faith and me with the Bible Institute students on the last day of school in Gran Poder in 1992

Five days before Christmas 1992, we went to Cochabamba to spend Christmas with the Blacks and to visit our work in F. Tropical, Larati, and a new outreach in Villa Barrientos between Cochabamba and Sacaba. José Luis helped Faith pack our luggage in the carrier on top of the Land Cruiser. In El Alto we stopped to get Florentino, his wife, and daughter to go with us. While we tended to a problem with our luggage, two women from our Cosmos '79 church came and greeted me by the driver's side, and two men, unknown to us, appeared. One of them tried to sidetrack Faith, telling her that our tire was losing air, but she saw a man near the front door of our vehicle on the passenger's side, apparently planning to steal our purses. She hurriedly got into the vehicle, closed the door, and locked it. When the would-be thieves saw that they would not be able to grab the purses, they walked away. Had they succeeded, we would not have been able to go to Cochabamba. Again our heavenly Father was watching over us; praise His wonderful name.

I was past the age that is considered retirement age and was making plans to retire from overseas mission work in December 1992 or January 1993. However, those plans did not materialize because there was no one to replace me in Bolivia.

* * * * *

For several months some areas of Bolivia had experienced drought and a shortage of food. In March the Food for the Hungry organization gave us three tons of food to be distributed to our Aymara Indian people in El Alto, Sixilla Baja, and Huarcamarca. We received cracked wheat, sugar, salt, white flour, and a mixture of corn meal and soy flour. Faith, Nano, who was a gifted young pastor, and a few volunteers weighed most of the commodities for distribution. Nano and I delivered the supplies to the churches in El Alto. We sent the food to Sixilla Baja by truck, and the Huarcamarca people took theirs when they came for special Easter services. The recipients were very appreciative. We received food aid again in May and July.

A few months later a small group of us from Bolognia went to Sixilla Baja to hold a DVBS and conduct revival services. One of the highlights of the revival was helping an elderly woman who desired to make a clean break from witchcraft. One morning while Faith and Damian, a believer from Bolognia, were in DVBS, Pastor Francisco and I walked down to the lady's house. We removed a stone from her property that was part of her pagan worship and discarded the ashes of a sacrifice that her family had made. Then we dedicated the entire property to the Lord and asked Him to protect the family from all evil. That was an outstanding victory! Another triumph was the salvation of two couples. One was a young couple without children; the other couple had twelve children.

Our congregation in Sixilla Baja desired to build a church and worked hard collecting stones and sand from the riverbed when the water was low in the dry season. During one of our visits, we took Francisco to a neighboring community to the offices of a European organization that was working in the area to improve the living conditions of the people. The pastor requested that they send a driver with one of their trucks to transport the stones and sand to a site near our property to save our people from transporting them by wheelbarrows. The request was approved, and it was a great blessing to the congregation. They made abode bricks, purchased cement for the floor, and soon started building a church.

In October we dedicated two of our churches. The first one was at F. Tropical in the Chapare, a hot steamy jungle region. With no suitable

Village boys washing the Land Cruiser beside the river. We were going to the Chapare to dedicate a church.

lodging for us in F. Tropical, we stayed in a small hotel in the community of Villa Tunari about nine miles away. It was common to have screened-in openings instead of windows in the rooms. The room we were given had no locks. We bought a latch to secure the inside, and the owner gave us a padlock to put on the outside. The grounds were dotted with lush, tropical foliage, making the place serene and restful. Several whole stalks of bananas had been cut and were hanging on the grounds for those lodging there to enjoy. Damian, Faith, and I conducted revival services that week. Because Damian spoke Quechua, the language of the Indian people of that area, he did most of the preaching. However, one evening he came to me during the service and asked if I would preach in his place. He had left his glasses in the hotel room and could not read without them, so I complied. On Sunday morning Faith preached the message for the church dedication.

The second dedication took place two weeks later at Sixilla Baja. Our group from Bolognia went there on Saturday and arrived in time for the evening service. One lady in her sixties who did not have money for bus fare walked alone across fields and mountains for approximately eight hours on Saturday to attend the dedication service. We made sure she had money to return home by bus. One of our young pastors brought his wife and baby daughter by bicycle and was accompanied by his wife's brother and an uncle on their bicycles. They left at 8:00 a.m. and rode down the mountains and across the valley to Sixilla Baja, arriving at 6:30 in the evening.

It was dusk when we gathered for the Saturday evening service. When they tried to light the kerosene lantern, it malfunctioned. We always carried flashlights with us, and they were useful for those who sang the special songs and preached that evening. In the semidarkness God met with us in a gracious way.

Sunday morning Nano preached the dedicatory message. During the prayer that followed, we stood on the earthen floor covered with dried stiff grass called *paja*, a contrast to what we are accustomed to in the States. How happy the people were to have their own church building after worshiping for several years in a small room. Elva Lutz, a Christian lady in Florida, had given money in memory of her husband who had been a pastor. We purchased five windows plus the roofing of the church as a memorial to him.

After the Sunday afternoon service, the young pastor asked me to take his wife and daughter back to their home. We already had a full vehicle, but I could not refuse because the little one was ill. We left the three men to make the long, weary trek pushing their bikes up the mountains. They arrived home exhausted about 3:00 on Monday morning.

* * * * *

In our Daily Vacation Bible Schools in early 1994, our lessons were about Old Testament patriarchs, men who believed God and obeyed Him. The day I used Felt-o-Graph to tell the story of Noah, some of the children stood on the benches and others craned their necks and listened with rapt attention. I also told them of Jesus, our Ark of Safety, and mentioned that He is returning to earth soon to take to heaven those who have given their hearts to Him. The children were deeply convicted, and most of them came forward to pray.

A few of the days were rainy. Even on those days the children came, walking in the muddy streets and getting wet because of lack of rainwear, but their spirits were not dampened.

* * * * *

We received a phone call with shocking news in February 1994, informing us of the death of seventeen-year-old José Luis. Cirilo and Aurelia, his parents, had moved from Jocopampa to El Alto and were attending one of our churches. José had been sick for about twelve days with a fever, diarrhea, and hemorrhaging from his nose and mouth. We suspected that he may have had cholera or typhoid fever. At the funeral the father told us that a few hours before José died, he asked his parents' forgiveness, asked God's forgiveness, and testified that God had forgiven him.

After a brief funeral service in the parents' yard, the casket was placed in the mission's vehicle, and I drove to the cemetery. We had a missionary friend visiting us with her twin boy and girl, so they sat in front with me because we laid down the second seat to make room for the casket. Faith and two men of José's family sat beside the casket. Other family members and friends took public transportation and joined us for the burial. José's testimony to being saved helped to make the family's grief more bearable.

Two days later we received another phone call from one of our pastors in El Alto informing us about a tornado that had struck the previous afternoon. He told us that the house of one of our brethren was destroyed except for the kitchen, and they were temporarily living in it. They wanted me to come and visit them, perhaps with hope that I might provide financial aid. The next day I went and saw their plight. My heart went out to them, and I gave them financial help from the Mission to rebuild some of the destroyed rooms.

* * * * *

As was customary, we held our quarterly pastors' retreat on Good Friday at Jocopampa. That was followed by special Easter weekend services. During the evening services Raimundo and I did the preaching. A man named Cipriano, who was paralyzed, was brought to those services by his wife, sometimes in a wheelbarrow and other times in a small cart on wheels. He had fallen from a building two years previously and just recently became paralyzed. We rejoiced when he sought the Lord and found forgiveness.

A couple weeks later there was an explosion from a leaking gas tank in the home of Pastor Cruz. He had opened a small bakery in his home, and his young son was lighting a gas lamp when the accident occurred. The son had not secured the lamp well enough to the gas tank before striking a match to light the lamp. Pastor Cruz was not at home, but his wife was able to enter the room and pull the flaming tank outdoors and prevent serious damage to the house. Neighbors heard the explosion and came to help. One of them courageously dragged the tank to the street where the flame eventually fizzled. We were thankful that God had spared the boy from injury, and that no extensive damage was done.

* * * * *

In June a TLC team came from Hobe Sound, Florida. That was the fifth team that came to help us with projects, Daily Vacation Bible Schools, and revivals. We conducted the schools during the day and revival services at night in our churches in Sixilla Baja and Gran Poder. Faith and the ladies of the team went to Sixilla Baja and the rest of us went to Jocopampa to lodge. From there we drove to Sullcavi each day where the four young men helped to lay the foundation for the church. The entire team helped in the DVBS and revival at Gran Poder. Later they also went to the University in La Paz and distributed tracts.

After the team left, I visited Sullcavi and was thrilled to find 36 families busily involved in building the church. By the end of that day, the

Building the church in Sullcavi in 1994

men had erected the walls to a height of six feet and finished them later that week. The roof was completed by the end of August and the congregation used the church for services even though the inside was not plastered nor the outside stuccoed.

* * * * *

Faith and I needed to leave the high altitude for a few days, so in August we drove to Cochabamba to join the Blacks and other missionaries for a retreat. We were privileged to sit under the ministry of Winfield Poe, director of the Holiness Pilgrim Mission in Haiti and also mission work in Ukraine, whose messages were very encouraging and challenging.

On a spring day in November, we had a baptismal service in the countryside near Sullcavi. Attendance was good, and 31 were baptized, including an 80-year-old man and a few elderly women.

Twelve days before Christmas Faith left for a three-month furlough to the States. Lyndal and Rebecca Black with Alecia and Leah came from Cochabamba to be with me during the holidays. We observed Christmas Eve together by reading the Christmas story, singing carols, and exchanging gifts. The Black children added to the excitement of the evening. On Christmas Day we worshiped with our people in Bolognia; Lyndal preached in the morning service and I in the evening. I spent parts of the next two days preparing food and supplies for us because we would be gone for a two-week stay in Jocopampa to hold Daily Vacation Bible Schools and revival services there and in Collana.

We first conducted the DVBS and revival services in Jocopampa. We also attended their watch-night service. Sunday we held only an afternoon service after which Pastor Pedro gave us a typical Bolivian meal consisting of *chuños*, two kinds of soup, and fava beans.

From Jocopampa we went to Collana on January 2 for their DVBS and revival. Lyndal and Raimundo did the preaching there as they had done in Jocopampa. Sunday morning was the closing service of the revival, and two small boys were dedicated to the Lord. At the end a man sought salvation. He rose from the altar and shook hands with several people joyfully saying, "The Lord has forgiven me! The Lord has forgiven me!" That was worth the whole revival, and we rejoiced as we returned to Bolognia.

* * * * *

Later that month I visited our Cosmos '79 church in El Alto. After the morning service some of the church people and I made a visit and had prayer in the home of Hilarion and his wife, Catalina. She was suffering with terminal cancer but did not appear to be desperately ill. Three days later I received word that Catalina had died that morning. What a shock! I hastened to their home. The family was destitute and did not have money for funeral expenses, but donations from the neighbors and the Mission were enough to cover those needs. I took a few of the neighbors and Paula, a daughter, to obtain a casket, a death certificate, and documents for the burial.

I learned that Paula had not eaten all day because the family had no money to buy food. On our way back to her home, we stopped and bought something for her to eat. By the time we returned, some of our pastors and neighbors had gathered in the home to hold the wake by singing hymns, reading the Word, and praying. I stayed with them into the night until I felt it was necessary for me to leave for home, over an hour's drive away. The following day her grieving family and caring neighbors took care of her burial.

Chapter 13

Chile, Huarcamarca, and Farewell
1995-1996

Arica, Chile

Faith returned to Bolivia from furlough on March 16, 1995. The next week she and I flew to Arica, Chile, a city of 150,000 people situated on the edge of the Atacama Desert and along the Pacific Ocean. We wanted to take a brief time to relax before starting all the Easter week activities and the opening of our Bible Institute that followed. I had not left the high altitude for seven months, so it was wonderful to walk at sea level without getting short of breath as I did walking the hills of La Paz!

Arica, called the City of Eternal Springtime, is an important seaport for both Chile and landlocked Bolivia. One day we hired a taxi to take us on a tour of an archeological site where Indians had made *geoglifos,* drawings on the hillside by using stones. The drawings were of great height and could be seen from far away. We visited an archeological museum that had

pre-Spanish artifacts and then went to Morro, a bluff overlooking the ocean, where a famous battle took place on June 7, 1880, between Chile and her enemies Bolivia and Peru. Chile won the war and gained control of Arica, which had belonged to Peru. We stood on the bluff and had a magnificent view of the ocean and the city.

With Faith beside the Pacific Ocean in Arica, Chile

Along with twelve other people, Faith and I took a one-day tour with the Tarapaca Expedition tour company to Lake Chungara, a well-known tourist attraction in Chile. On the way we saw an old church and cemetery that remained from the first Catholic parish in Arica, candelabrum cactus, a pre-Hispanic fort, and at Putre we viewed two active volcanoes with snow-covered slopes. Finally we reached Lake Chungara at an elevation of 14,819 feet with Mount Sajama in the distance, a mountain peak visible on a clear day in Chacoma, Bolivia. The air was thin, and we had to walk slowly at that altitude. On the return trip the group stopped in Putre for our afternoon meal.

Because there is plenty of seafood in Arica, the local people feed fish to the chickens. Consequently the chicken served in the restaurants has a strong fish taste. So if you visit Arica, my advice is to order a fish platter rather than chicken!

For 25 cents each we could ride a bus that took us to the different beaches in the area. We visited several of them and enjoyed watching the pelicans and the rolling sea, hearing the rushing and splashing of the waves, and feeling the wonderful sea breezes while we relaxed. We often bought a soft drink at a pavilion. Faith prepared materials for the upcoming Daily Vacation Bible Schools, and I wrote letters, read, and did some work on a scrapbook for one of my godchildren.

Our room at the *pensione,* a small hotel, was spacious, had a private bath, and cost us each $6.00 a night. It was operated by a woman and her son Pepe. The hotel provided breakfast that consisted of a bread roll, butter and jam, and tea. Sometimes instead of jam, liver paste was on the roll. To add to our breakfast, we splurged and bought a large box of Corn Flakes and dry milk. The hotel owners allowed us to use their refrigerator, microwave, and stove for preparing some of our meals. Other times we bought either a sandwich or a full-course meal at a restaurant. Ten days of

Eating a meal at a restaurant in Arica, Chile

vacation had a wonderful effect. We were rested and ready to return to La Paz.

Continuing Our Ministry

The following week J. Stevan Manley, the new president of EFM, arrived in Bolivia to be with us for Easter week. It was his first visit to Bolivia, and later he shared some of the indelible memories he had of that visit:

> As our plane flew over Bolivia, I was amazed at the breathtaking beauty of the Andes as the snowcapped peaks glistened in the sunshine. Another thing that caught my attention was the altitude of the airport in La Paz that was over 13,000 feet and made it difficult to do normal tasks such as carrying one's own luggage.
>
> The national dress of the Aymara Indian ladies is unique. Their colorful full skirts and derby hats are not seen in any other country where I have traveled. When I was taken to visit Lake Titicaca, I was awestruck at the dazzling beauty of the highest navigable lake in the world.
>
> The thing that touched my heart the most was the commitment of Faith Hemmeter and Irene Maurer. They had labored faithfully for Christ in Bolivia for nine years without an official visit from the home office of EFM.

Ordination service during President J. Stevan Manley's first visit to Bolivia

During President Manley's visit he met with the pastors for a retreat on Good Friday. On Sunday morning he preached to over 300 who attended our Easter convention in our church at Jocopampa. His text was "Blessed are the pure in heart: for they shall see God" (Matthew 5:8). Many hearts were touched by the Holy Spirit and nearly one hundred sought help at the altar. During his visit we discussed plans for the future of the work. We deeply appreciated his visit.

I again made plans to retire from missionary work in the summer of 1995. The Blacks, who were living in Cochabamba, were planning to move to La Paz to help Faith. However, before they moved, Rebecca developed serious physical problems, and they returned to the States in late April. Again my plans to retire were put on hold!

We received a wonderful blessing in October. The municipality completed a project that gave water 24 hours a day to our zone and other nearby zones. After having our water rationed for several years, it was wonderful to have it all the time! However, we continued to filter or boil our drinking water.

The Blacks were unable to return to Bolivia because of Rebecca's illness, so Lyndal and a friend came soon after Thanksgiving to take care of their personal belongings and mission business. When the men went to Cochabamba to take care of mission furniture, Faith and I followed in another vehicle to select some of the furniture to be trucked to Bolognia. While we were there, one of the believers, a lady, came to us and implored, "We have no place to go to church. What shall we do?" It was decided that her husband, who had worked with the missionaries, would take responsibility to open a new work in Sacaba, a small town a few miles from the city of Cochabamba.

The day before Christmas we worshiped with our Bolognia congregation for both services. About 11:00 p.m. we went to the Abán family's home to celebrate Christmas Eve with a meal, according to Bolivian tradition. It was that family's custom to have a time to worship together by singing Christmas carols, reading the Bible, and praying before partaking of the meal. About midnight we were served slices of beef in a tasty sauce, cooked potatoes, corn on the cob, and jello for dessert.

In late February 1996 we went to Cochabamba to attend a special meeting of Evangelicals in Bolivia. Because we were close to our work in Sacaba, we stayed and attended several services with them. We held what I believe was the first Sunday school that those children ever attended, and they enjoyed it very much.

When our Bible Institute started in 1996, we had classes in three locations. For the Aymara Indians we met at Gran Poder and Villa Tunari. Faith also taught classes in Spanish at our house in Bolognia.

Teaching in the Bible Institute in Jocopampa in 1994

The Church at Huarcamarca

Faith and I with Florentino Paco, his family, and brother-in-law made a trip in September 1989 to the mountain village of Huarcamarca. It is near the border of Peru and is more than 14,000 feet above sea level. At that altitude it was above the tree line, tundra-like, and too cold to raise garden vegetables or chickens. Hardy grains, potatoes, and a legume called *tarwi* were grown. The view of 21,490-foot-high, snow-covered Mount Illampu in the distance was breathtaking.

Although the distance between Bolognia and Huarcamarca is only 143 miles, the trip took seven hours by vehicle, including a stop to eat our prepared lunch. Most of the roads were rough like an old-fashion washboard, which the Bolivians call *calamina,* the word in Spanish for corrugated tin roofing. That first trip began the fulfillment of Florentino's vision. He was a Bible Institute student who was attending our church in Villa Tunari and desired to establish a holiness church in the village where his mother lived. We left the main road at Vila Cala and drove the mission Land Cruiser as far as we could, and then on foot we slowly wound our way for 30 minutes down the steep slopes that led to his mother's home.

First service held in Huarcamarca in the yard of Florentino's mother in 1989

We conducted an afternoon service in Florentino's mother's yard. The local people who had gathered sat in a semicircle, and Faith played the accordion while we sang. I gave a message in Spanish, and Florentino interpreted it into Aymara, the language of the Indians in the high Andes of Bolivia. Following the service we met with the village elders, and they invited us to open a work in their village. We left literature to help them spiritually until Florentino could visit them again. After we said

good-bye, we climbed, huffing and puffing, back to the parked vehicle and returned to Vila Cala where we spent the night. Faith and I slept in our sleeping bags in the back of the Land Cruiser and Florentino's family stayed with his wife's brother, who lived in Vila Cala.

Florentino, his wife Benancia, and their daughter, Marlene

At first Florentino made periodic visits to Huarcamarca, but eventually it became possible for him to make biweekly visits. Every other Friday he, his wife, Benancia, and their young daughter, Marlene, joined others on top of the cargo of a large truck. They traveled about eleven hours through the cold to reach the main village of Vila Cala where Florentino and his family spent the night. The following morning they walked down the mountain trail to Huarcamarca. They ministered to the people and then repeated the bone-chilling trip back to La Paz, leaving Vila Cala shortly after midnight on Sunday.

Periodically Faith and I accompanied by Florentino's family visited Huarcamarca. On a few of our visits, our group had some interesting experiences. In September 1990 before we reached the village of Vila Cala, it began to snow, making the road slippery. We arrived safely, and I fixed a snack for us while Faith made a bed for the two of us in the back of the Land Cruiser. The next morning the windows were covered with ice, but we had kept warm with hot water bottles inside our sleeping bags—thanks to Benancia who had heated the water for us. Sunday morning we made our way to Huarcamarca and again held the morning and afternoon services in the yard of Florentino's mother. The skies grew dark and threatened to rain, but it only drizzled while we worshiped.

After the service some of the brethren kindly carried our musical instruments and bags to the vehicle. I had all I could do to climb the steep trail at that high altitude and was forced to rest several times. Back in Vila Cala we ate sandwiches, and a hot drink helped to warm us. It was about 6:00 when we started for Bolognia. At times the fog was so dense that I could not see the road, and Florentino and Alex, one of Raimundo's sons who was with us on that visit, walked in front of our vehicle to guide me. In El Alto we took Florentino and his family to their home, left Alex near his place, and drove to our home in Bolognia, arriving about 2:00 a.m. We were tired, yet rejoicing because we had been privileged to preach God's Word to a needy and a responsive people.

Florentino was employed by a building contractor as supervisor of workers in La Paz. A little over a year after the opening of the work in Huarcamarca, he oversaw and helped in the building of a church there. It was dedicated in September 1991. Later some rooms were built on the church property providing a room for Florentino and his family and a place for Faith and me so that we all could stay for two or three days at a time.

Part of the congregation for the dedication service at Huarcamarca

Eating a Bolivian meal after the dedication service

Faith, Florentino and his family, and I visited Huarcamarca in May 1993, and we had vehicle difficulties. On the way to the village, a hose from the radiator began to leak and the motor overheated. We got water from a river to fill the radiator. Before we left Huarcamarca on our return trip, we filled it again. About every hour on the first part of the journey, we stopped to cool the motor and fill the radiator. As the night got colder, the problem of overheating diminished. In addition to a leaking hose, we had a flat tire. When we reached La Paz, our gas gauge registered empty. We found a gas station that was open at 3:30 Monday morning. If all had gone well, we would have been home by midnight, but we arrived at 4:00. Thank the Lord He saw us through our difficulties! We had good services on Sunday, and souls sought for a pure heart. It was worth the problems of the journey! I rested for an hour before eating breakfast and making preparations to take the Land Cruiser to the garage early so that the mechanic could have it repaired by midweek when we would need it.

Just before the end of the dry winter season in September, we made another venturesome trip to Huarcamarca for their weekend anniversary services. We had good times of prayer, and the Lord's presence was precious. About sixteen people, including three children, gave their hearts to the Lord. Faith held three sessions of DVBS with 36 children attending. It was the first one for those children. How they enjoyed it even though for two of the sessions they sat in the yard of the church with fog so heavy it was misty! They all asked Jesus to come into their hearts. On the way home we got into heavy fog again. Sometimes it was so dense I could not see the road in front of me and had to stop to see where the road was. The Lord was with us and protected us.

We visited Huarcamarca the following May and received what appeared to be good news. The pastor's wife told us that the community and church people had worked on a new road that turned off the main road before reaching Vila Cala. She said that now it was possible for us to drive within sight of the church, and we would have only a ten-minute walk compared to the previous thirty-minute walk. When the new road would be completed, it would go past the church and the government school. We decided to try the new road. However, we learned to our dismay that there were some very narrow places, and the clutch got hot on our descent. At one point the road was so narrow that I said, "Faith, I'm afraid I'm going to scrape the vehicle."

On Faith's side there was a drop-off, and she exclaimed, "Scrape it, Irene, just scrape it!" At the foot of the hill, the men had used two oil drums with the ends removed to make a bridge over a stream. Right by the stream we faced another sharp curve. I negotiated that curve with extreme caution to make sure the wheels were on the bridge.

Farther on, to widen the road and make it passable, the road workers had built a section with stones and dirt, but the road was not wide enough for the wheels. Everyone in the car except me got out, and Florentino and another man with us adjusted the stones so that I could drive past that place. We reached the end of the construction, and I said, "Faith, we are not going back this way."

The men adjusting the stones to make the road wide enough so I could drive past
that place

In a few moments Faith replied, "Oh, yes, we are. There is no other way to get out of here but to turn around and go back the way we came!"

Realizing that she was right, I turned the vehicle around in the widest space available and parked. We took our supplies with us and walked the short distance to the rooms near the church.

On our return Sunday afternoon, the clutch overheated again, but we reached Vila Cala where we stopped to get some things Florentino wanted to take to La Paz. When we went to leave Vila Cala, the clutch would not work. We pictured ourselves stranded with the need to send one of our young men to La Paz to get a new clutch and bring a mechanic who could install it. I suggested that we wait a half hour to let the clutch cool and to see if it would work. We prayed. When I tried the clutch again, it worked, making it possible for us to return to Bolognia. We thanked the Lord for His help and mercy. Oh, what a loving, caring God we serve!

While going to Huarcamarca in the spring of 1995, we had a flat tire near the town of Carabuco. Pastor Pascual and a Bible Institute student who were traveling with Faith and me tried unsuccessfully to remove the lugs with the wrench Faith gave to them. We flagged down a man on a motorcycle and asked him to help. He asked if we had a different lug wrench, and I remembered another one in the Land Cruiser. He used that one to loosen the lugs and went his way. Faith then showed our men how to change a tire because it was their first time to do so.

When we reached the village of Escoma, we found a shop that fixed flats. However, the owner damaged our inner tube but managed to make it useable; unfortunately there was no place to buy a new one. Some miles beyond that village we had another flat. By then it was dark and drizzling. The men did not have warm jackets, so we loaned them our winter coats. They changed the tire without our help and were pleased with themselves.

I tried to start the engine, but there was no battery power. We were parked on an uphill grade with an open curve behind us and a blind one in front of us. We realized that we were stranded in a desolate area and would need to alert all oncoming vehicles.

After a while we heard a truck coming from behind us. When it got near, the two men and Faith got out and, using a red emergency light, tried to get the driver to stop, hoping there was a mechanic with him who could help us. The truck stopped but people on top of the load began yelling excitedly in Spanish, "Fire! Fire! Get down! Get down!" We thought that the truck had caught on fire, but nobody got down.

Pascual remarked, "There must be thieves." The men and Faith quickly returned to our vehicle, and we locked our doors. I prayed and moments passed, but no thieves appeared. Soon the truck started and passed by us quickly. Finally Pascual spoke again, "You know what? I think the people in the truck thought that we were thieves." What he said made us laugh, and several times that night some one would break out with laughter. We learned on that trip that thieves in that area often wore long coats to hide their weapons when attempting to hold up passersby. The two men with us still had on our coats! No vehicles came for the rest of the night.

By morning we had decided it was not wise to continue our trip to Huarcamarca. The driver of the first vehicle to come was able to start our Land Cruiser and turn it around for us. But it soon quit. The next driver got it started again but for only a short time. A white man and his chauffeur were in the third vehicle. The chauffeur was unable to get our Land Cruiser started, but at our request they took Faith and Pascual to a telephone. Pascual got into the bed of the pickup, and Faith sat in front with the two men.

Faith told us when she returned that evening that she was uncomfortable sitting between the two men, but she courageously witnessed to them. Eventually the white man suggested they listen to some music, which Faith said was acceptable. Finally they found a phone miles away at the town of Carabuco, and Faith was greatly relieved. She offered to pay the men, but the white man graciously declined.

Faith contacted Mark Frink, a friend whose mission had a Land Cruiser. He brought a spare tire and a charged battery, stopped for Faith and Pascual at Carabuco, and they reached my student and me just before dusk. The charged battery was the answer to our problem. Pastor Pascual and the Bible Institute student continued their journey on foot to Vila Cala near Huarcamarca, our original destination. Mark followed Faith and me until we reached our home safely about midnight.

The last Sunday of October 1995, we again visited Huarcamarca. During our return trip on Sunday evening, the motor suddenly stopped, and we had no lights. Some of our passengers started to exit the Land

Singing group from the Huarcamarca church

Cruiser to check under the hood, but we heard men talking and shouting. We thought they might be drunken men or even robbers, so everyone stayed in the vehicle, and we locked the doors. After a few minutes we decided they were drunken men. Even so, we were fearful and remained in the vehicle. The men soon left, and some of us ventured out of the vehicle and looked under the hood. The continual bouncing on the washboard road had knocked one of the battery cables off the post. Pastor Pascual replaced the cable, and we were on our way, praising the Lord for His protection and help.

We were returning home from Huarcamarca the following spring and had to take a detour because the government was improving the main road. When we returned to the main road, the clutch on the Land Cruiser did not want to work but finally did. In El Alto we took Florentino and his family to their home and started for Bolognia. When I slowed for a speed bump on a four-lane highway at the entrance to the air force base, the clutch quit working.

We called to the guards at the entrance, and they pushed our vehicle off the highway and onto their property along the outside of their high wall. Because it was late at night, Faith and I felt it was not safe to take a taxi to our house. I asked the officer in charge at the base for permission to use a phone to call a friend. He allowed me to enter the base, and an airman took me to a phone that was in a small room where a few men were sleeping on the floor. A missionary friend, Gordon Elliott, came and took us to our house.

Before we left the air force base, we told the officer we would return in the morning and get our vehicle. The next day we called the Toyota garage, explained our problem, went to the garage, got one of their mechanics, and took him with us in another mission vehicle. He replaced an auxiliary cylinder for the clutch system, which solved our problem.

I thanked the officer on duty for allowing us to park the Land Cruiser on their base overnight. He asked if we found our vehicle in good condition, and I assured him we did. I was then asked to sign the logbook. The record indicated that two missionary ladies had permission to park their vehicle on their property overnight and that they found it in good condition the following morning. I gladly signed the logbook and thanked him for their help.

Final Months

Lloyd and Ruth (Franklin) Gordon came to Bolivia in May 1996 and stayed almost a year, giving us much needed help. They had a private tutor to help them learn Spanish. Lloyd was a handyman and did plumbing repairs, electrical work, and maintenance on the mission Land Cruiser. Ruth assisted in our services by playing the piano and accordion and did the bookkeeping after I returned to the States in November.

For some time Faith and I had felt the need to have our national brethren involved in the decisions of the work. In our pastors' retreat in June, we presented our plan to them, and three pastors were elected to work with Faith and me on our first executive committee.

A thirteen-member TLC team came from the States to be with us from June 18 to July 9. Their sponsor, LyNan (Coker) Redman, had lived some

Part of the TLC team from the States with their sponsor LyNan (Coker) Redman (back row second from right)

of her teen years in Central America where her parents were missionaries with Evangelistic Faith Missions. She married Dale Redman, and later they with their two young daughters became missionaries with EFM in Honduras. Now these daughters, Jennifer and Rebecca, were members of the TLC team, and an added bonus was that the mother and daughters could communicate in Spanish. Other members included Peggy Cisneros and Stephen DeLong, who both knew Spanish, Brandon Hamilton, Christina Bickel, Annalisa Patrick, Stacy and Brian Cantrell (siblings), Erica Osborne, April Mills, and Christopher Dewhurst.

The day after the team arrived, we took them to Cochabamba. With their help during the week, we held a DVBS in Sacaba. Some of the team members were excellent story tellers and held the attention of the children. A number of those children continued to attend the worship services after we left. In the evenings we held revival services. Because there was no preacher on the team, Faith and I did the preaching.

For the weekend we chartered a small bus belonging to the owner of the house where we held services in Sacaba. The owner's brother-in-law took us and the 13 team members to the Chapare about four hours away where we visited the F. Tropical church. Our visit was an encouragement to that congregation. They provided the Sunday noon meal for all who stayed for the afternoon service.

Preparing a meal at F. Tropical

After we returned to La Paz, the team helped to conduct three Daily Vacation Bible Schools. Faith took two members and Damian and went to Sixilla Baja to have a DVBS and revival services. I took three with me to our new work in the countryside at Villa Ancara to hold our first DVBS there. Marcela, our helper, took the remaining team members and held a DVBS in our Gran Poder church in El Alto. A result of that DVBS was that 30 children started attending the church, increasing the attendance to 50.

In August I celebrated my 72nd birthday. A few days before my birthday, Faith made a beautiful cake for me, and she and Ruth fixed a delicious chicken dinner. In the afternoon James and Grace Fulton joined us for ice cream, potato chips, and cake. On the 23rd, which was my birthday, we were in Huarcamarca. We took another cake with us and shared it with the people who were present.

Three days later we were invited to a baked pork and chicken dinner at Celia's home to celebrate the birthdays of Faith and me. With the meat they served baked bananas, potatoes, sweet potatoes, another kind of sweet potato called *oka*, tossed salad, and fruit salad. Birthday celebrations are happy occasions and at times include multiple courses in the meal.

Celebrating my 72nd birthday. Faith made a beautifully decorated cake.

The next day the Bolognia church financed another dinner held at the home of Claudina and Leonardo in Bolognia to celebrate the birthdays of Ruth, Faith, and me. They served *sajta de pollo*, a favorite dish made of *tuntas* and chicken cooked in a slightly hot *picante* sauce and topped with raw chopped tomatoes and sliced onions. They also prepared a ground meat sauce to serve over the potatoes. For dessert we ate a chocolate flan and a delicious cake iced with whipped cream. Lloyd and Ruth Gordon and Faith gave me a new carry-on piece of luggage for my flight to the States.

The following month three pastors began a new outreach for the Mission. They prepared two half-hour weekly radio broadcasts. The one that aired on Friday nights was in the Aymara language and reached into the countryside. The other one, aired on Saturday mornings, was in Spanish and was on FM. Time was purchased from Radio Southern Cross, a Baptist Mission radio station in La Paz. The men were able to maintain those broadcasts until 2004.

November 24 was a special day with our people and pastors from many of our churches gathered at our Cosmos '79 church for the dedication. The pastors and missionaries also had planned for it to be a farewell service for me. It was an emotional time as a number of our congregations presented gifts to me–sweaters, *chuspas* that were knitted or woven by hand and used to carry one's Bible and hymnbook, and a pewter plate with the pastors' names engraved on it. We shed tears as we embraced and said our farewells. The occasion lingers in my memory.

With mixed emotions I left Bolivia on November 25, 1996, the country that had been my place of labor for the past fourteen and a half years. I knew I would miss the people and the work, but I felt that it was time for me to retire from overseas missionary work.

Chapter 14

My Surprise Return to Bolivia
1997-1999

Deputation Services

After I returned to the States, I settled in Shamokin, Pennsylvania, and lived in one of Doris' upstairs apartments. Mrs. Walter Faust, one of the teachers in the children's Sunday school department of the church that Doris attended, had inspired the children to save their pennies for EFM. That money helped to finance the children's Happy Hour that was held weekly in our Villa Tunari church in El Alto, Bolivia. One of my first deputation services in 1997 was speaking to Mrs. Faust's Sunday school children.

I spoke at the local chapter of the Christian Women's Club about a week later. They listened with interest while I shared about my work on the mission fields.

I also participated in three weekend missionary conventions. The first one was at the Calvary Holiness Church in Columbus, Ohio. I flew

from Harrisburg and our plane stopped at Pittsburgh, Pennsylvania, where we were delayed by an ice storm followed by rain. I was grateful when the plane finally landed safely at Columbus.

President Manley and Carrie Boyer were present to help in the services. It was a pleasure to work with them and with Amos and Ruth Tillis, the pastor and his wife. The Tillises had attended

With Carrie in a missionary convention

God's Bible School years earlier when I was there. They also were missionaries for a short time in Eritrea.

That weekend Tekie Mebrahtu and his wife, Elsabet, and Stephanos Tesfu Almedom and his wife, Sahlu, and their two daughters came to one of the services. Those Eritreans had worked faithfully with EFM in their homeland before immigrating to the States.

My next convention was with the Manleys at the Wesleyan Holiness Church in St. Louis, Michigan. By Saturday evening the goal was reached of raising $3,000.00 to purchase 45 Spanish Thompson Chain Reference Bibles for our pastors and students and also study books for our pastors in Bolivia. Our hearts were blessed while we sang praises to the Lord for helping them meet their goal. On Sunday morning the Lord was present in a special way.

At the Crystal Park Wesleyan Church convention in Canton, Ohio, the enthusiasm for missions was contagious as the congregation made their generous pledges and rejoiced in the Lord. The Crystal Park congregation has supported EFM for many years.

Later I spoke in a chapel service at Penn View Bible Institute in Penns Creek, Pennsylvania. A number of students prayed about God's will for their lives. Before I left the campus, I met Mesgun Tedla, an Eritrean living in America, who just arrived for revival services.

A Visit to Egypt

At the request of the EFM Board, I visited Egypt in March because there was no resident missionary there at that time. A couple from Doris' church took Doris and me to the home of my niece Mary in McLean, Virginia. Later that day Mary took me to the Dulles International Airport near Washington, D.C., from where I flew on Lufthansa Airlines to Frankfurt, Germany. There were two terminals at Frankfurt, and I was concerned about making my connections. In God's providence a young American lady on the same flight who worked for Lufthansa and was familiar with the airport offered to help me reach the right terminal for my departure. It was the same terminal where my nephew Bill was arriving in Germany on business. Before we left the States, we had arranged that I would meet him at his arrival gate. Bill and I enjoyed breakfast together before going our separate ways.

From Frankfurt I flew to Cairo, Egypt, where the national field director, Saied Ibrahim, and some of his family met me. We went to their home, and by the time I retired that night, it had been 25 hours since I was in bed.

The next day was Saturday, and I was able to rest. That evening I preached to a young ladies group at the Medan Victoria Church in Cairo where Saied pastored. I spoke twice at the same church on Sunday. At the end of the evening service, a number of people prayed.

The following week was a busy one. I attended business sessions with the field executive committee, ministered to our pastors, and was present for a special conference during which time God graciously met with us.

Mother's Day is celebrated on March 21 in Egypt, and that week I spoke in two Mother's Day services. First I spoke to nearly two hundred women in the Medan Victoria Church, and later in the week at Ard es Shirka, another of our Cairo churches. Saturday was again a day of rest for me. On Sunday I spoke in two other churches in Cairo. The pastors had been my students in the Bible school in the 1960s. It was a joy to fellowship with them and their families.

Early the next morning Saied's son Stephen took me to the train station where Magdy, a young pastor, met me and accompanied me by train to the university city of Assiut, Upper Egypt. That evening I spoke in our village church in Qurqaras with the village police guard present. Because of attacks of some radical Muslims on churches and evangelicals, police guarded churches around the clock and provided an escort for foreign visitors traveling in Upper Egypt. The next morning Magdy, his wife, and I returned by taxi to Assiut, then went to Sohag, and finally East Zuouk where I spoke in their Mother's Day service. During the service one young woman quoted the passage from Proverbs 31, describing the virtuous woman. After dinner we traveled by taxi to West Zuouk where Magdy was pastoring. I sat in the back seat of the taxi with an armed police guard on each side of me. The government had stopped that church in a remodeling project, so in the evening I spoke to a large group under the stars because there was no roof on the church. Later the government allowed them to complete the project.

The next few days I continued to have police escort while I traveled by taxi to preach in three village churches. It was a mutual delight to meet individuals from past years. I visited with our Sohag pastor and his wife and enjoyed a delicious meal with them.

Friday I returned to Cairo and then went by train to Alexandria on Saturday afternoon where I spoke in our two churches on Sunday. Monday morning three pastors and a believer took me beyond Alexandria to a large conference center that belongs to our work in Egypt. We visited our new church in Kafr el Dawar, and I spent the night with the pastor and his family. The next day we visited Abou el Matamir where we saw their newly erected church building. We also visited our new outreach at Anani and found some of the brethren plastering a part of their church. Saied met me in Abou el Matamir and after visiting with the pastor and his family, we returned to Cairo by taxi with other passengers. For nearly three hours our driver drove rapidly, making it a scary ride for me. I prayed silently much of the way. Thank God, we arrived safely!

During the rest of that week, I spoke in several of our Cairo churches and another outreach work. I was privileged to attend the 28th anniversary service of the Medan Victoria Church.

By the time I left Egypt, I had spoken 24 times in 24 days. God had given me strength for all the traveling and speaking engagements. It was a delight to visit the country of my first missionary labors, and I thanked the Lord for the opportunity to share the gospel with the Egyptians and to see several of them seek the Lord.

An Unexpected Development

I returned to the States and began traveling in deputation services, most of the time with Carrie Boyer, who was living in Bedford. We used the mission house where she lived for our home base. Our first tour took us to churches in West Virginia and Virginia.

Lloyd and Ruth Gordon, who had been in Bolivia with Faith, returned to the States in April for business reasons and did not return. At the same time Faith came home from Bolivia for medical treatment and stayed with us in Bedford. Carrie, Faith and I attended the Interchurch Holiness Convention (IHC) in Dayton, Ohio. The services were uplifting, and we enjoyed meeting with many friends. In late May I returned to Shamokin and attended the alumni reunion of the Shamokin High School, which marked the 55th year since my graduation. It was the only one I ever attended.

The following month we three ladies attended the memorial service for Lorene Smith at the West Virginia Training School in Point Pleasant, West Virginia. She had been the business manager there for many years.

With Faith beside the mission house in Bedford

Carrie, Lorene, and I were all members of the Evangelical Methodist Church in Lavelle, Pennsylvania, and Faith was her step-sister.

When Faith returned to Bolivia in July, I realized that because she was the only EFM missionary there, she would not be able to fulfill all the responsibilities. I spoke with President Manley about the situation and offered to return to Bolivia. He indicated that he was very reluctant to permit me to return because of my age. He thought that I had served beyond the call of duty, and he could not ask me to return. I replied. "You are not asking me. I am volunteering." He realized there was no one else who could go and said that he would present my offer to the Board. After consultation the members approved my return.

Carrie and I attended an alumni reunion of Intercession City Biblical College that was held at Toccoa Falls, Georgia, in July. We enjoyed the fellowship and met classmates whom we had not seen for 47 years. I spoke about missions during the reunion, and they gave a good offering to EFM.

My sister Helen and her family had moved from Vineland, New Jersey, to Colorado Springs, Colorado, while I was in Bolivia, and I had not seen them for 10 years. In August I spent a week with them. My nephew Richard Moser used his frequent flier miles to purchase my plane ticket. During my time there my great-niece Eunice Bump took me to tour the headquarters of Focus on the Family and the Air Force Academy, my first time to visit both places. Helen took me to The Navigators headquarters in Glen Eyrie for a special tea and a tour. I enjoyed a picnic in the Garden of the Gods with Lester and Helen. Doris sponsored a breakfast at the famous Broadmoor Hotel for Helen, some of her family, and me. Because my visit concurred with my birthday, Helen invited family members and friends to her house to celebrate with cake and soft drinks.

After an enjoyable visit I returned to Bedford and soon left for Camp Gilead in Ohio to represent EFM on missions day. I went to Shamokin from there and began preparations to return to Bolivia. My last missionary service was at the Wesleyan Holiness Church in Portage, Pennsylvania. Ronald and Anna Smith lived there, and they took me back to Shamokin.

In Bolivia Again

When I flew to Bolivia on September 23, I was permitted to take two extra pieces of luggage without paying any fee. Sandra Miller, who was going to Bolivia to help EFM for a short time, met me at the airport in Miami. I was surprised that Grace Fulton, a missionary friend of mine in Bolivia, and two of her friends were on the same flight. Faith, Sandra, and I went to Cochabamba for a few days so that Sandra and I could adjust to the altitude. While in Cochabamba we drove to the Chapare and had two good services in our F. Tropical church.

The road from Cochabamba area to Churo

Previous to Homecoming Day in 1997 at God's Bible School in Cincinnati, Ohio, Darrell Stetler, president of the Alumni Association, called me in Bolivia and told me that I was being honored as the Alumni of the Year. On Homecoming Day he interviewed me by phone so that all present could hear our conversation. When Leonard Sankey came to Bolivia a few weeks later as the evangelist for our first camp meeting, he presented the Alumni-of-the-Year plaque to me.

Leonard Sankey presenting me with the GBS Alumni-of-the-Year award in 1997

Leonard's ability to speak Spanish well was a great blessing during the camp meeting because he was able to preach without needing an interpreter. God met with us during those services, and souls found definite victory.

Pastors and Leonard Sankey in our first camp meeting in Bolivia.
Leonard came to be our guest speaker.

After the camp meeting, Leonard, Sandra, Cici, Faith, and I picnicked beside Lake Titicaca. The next day all of us except Cici went to Cochabamba. Leonard preached in our F. Tropical church and the following day in our outreach in Sacaba where hungry hearts bowed in prayer. He flew to the States from the Cochabamba airport, and we ladies returned to Bolognia.

During the time that remained of that school year, I taught a six-week music theory class to some of the Bible Institute students. We customarily took our students on an excursion near the end of the school year, and that year at their request we took them to the zoo in La Paz. After we visited the zoo, we found a quiet park to relax and eat our picnic dinner. Although it rained some in the morning, the day ended well.

In November Faith and I attended a baptismal service held by our churches at Peñas, a few miles from La Paz, where 18 people were baptized. For the noon meal each congregation sat in a group on the grass by the stream and enjoyed their lunches. In the afternoon Faith preached the Word in the open air, similar to Bible times.

On December 19 Faith and I flew with James and Grace Fulton to Riberalta, El Beni, Bolivia. It was raining, and I became tense when the plane skidded as it touched down on the unpaved runway. We went to visit James and Eunice McBryant, their five children, and Lessie Green of the Central Friends Mission. Lessie had known Faith since she was just a child in Cleveland, Ohio.

Riberalta is in the northern jungle area of Bolivia where two tributaries of the Amazon River join. Oh, it was hot! One day it was 100 degrees in the shade with 70 percent humidity. The Sunday evening service was at 8:00 because of the heat.

Manuel Rojas and his wife, parents of Absalom, of

With Manuel Rojas, his wife, and their son Absalom in their bamboo house

the local Friends church, invited the missionaries to their home for Christmas dinner. He was also celebrating his 80th birthday. Their house was typical of those in that area. The roof of their living room was layers of palm branches, the walls were split bamboo branches, and the floor was split bamboo logs. There were open areas on each end of their living room to give relief from the oppressive heat. From one end we had a splendid view of the Beni River flowing through the lush tropical foliage. In another section of their home, they had a long table spread, and with us and their extended family, 30 people ate a tasty dinner. Each plate was filled with rice cooked with small pieces of beets, potatoes, chicken, and wild duck. For dessert we had birthday cake and soft drinks.

The day after Christmas, Faith and I rode a bus for two hours to Guayeramerin, a town on the wide Mamoré River, a tributary of the Amazon River. We took a taxi to the river and then in a small boat, seated on backless benches, we crossed the river to Guajará Mirim, Brazil. I was concerned when I noticed that there were not enough life preservers for the 15 passengers. We did a little shopping in Brazil and then returned. Men who worked in logging floated many huge logs down the river, and the boats had to ply the waters with caution. The motor of our boat stalled in midstream. I mentally pictured one or more of those floating logs colliding with our boat and tossing us into the river. Thank God the pilot got the engine started, and we reached the Bolivian shore safely. While on our way back to Riberalta, the bus had a flat tire, but it was quickly replaced with the spare. The day turned out to be a memorable one!

Faith and I attended the birthday party of the McBryants' oldest daughter, Elizabeth, on their spacious back patio a few days later. Her Hispanic girlfriends from Sunday school were present.

When it was time to leave Riberalta, the plane on which we were to fly was grounded at another airport. The airlines refunded enough money for Faith and me to take a taxi to Guayeramerin where we boarded a Fokker F-27 plane to La Paz.

Providentially, Mr. Asef, our next-door neighbor who operated a taxi, was at the airport and took us home. On the way he drove through two main parts of La Paz so that we could see the beautiful Christmas lights. We were glad to be home after a wonderful time with missionary friends.

Early in the new year, Faith and I prepared materials for a two-day retreat with our pastors and the first of ten Daily Vacation Bible Schools in El Alto and on the high plains. The children were free to attend because it was their summer vacation. They were always happy to make a calendar by pasting a picture from an old calendar onto a piece of colored poster paper and adding a date pad available in local markets. For many of them it was probably the only calendar the family had in their home. A number of children sought the Lord, and in one of the churches, a family was saved as the result of their daughter attending the DVBS.

In March 1998 God protected me from a possible robbery. I had cashed a check for $800.00 (U.S.) to pay a mechanic and another man who was painting the Toyota station wagon. From the *Sudamer*, a money exchange, I went to a photo shop and then to the post office. At the post office I found a notice that we had a package. As I was going to the package department, a man called to me, "Mother, were you just at *Sudamer?*"

I was surprised and asked him why he was asking me. He opened a small black case he was carrying and showed me photocopies of Bolivian money. He said, "At *Sudamer* they gave you from B series. You must go back and exchange them for C series."

The *Sudamer,* a place to exchange money

"I am going to get a package, and if it is not very heavy, I will return to *Sudamer*," I replied.

The man asked, "Shall I wait for you?"

I answered, "No, I will go by myself."

After I got my small package, I returned to *Sudamer* and went to the window where I had cashed my check. The lady who was working there was surprised to see me again. I told her my story, and she said, "He was a thief. Did you give him anything?"

"No," I replied, "I am wiser than that."

"You better go directly home," the lady advised. I left and walked to a bus stop, all the time on the lookout for the thief. I soon got on a bus and went home without completing my errands. I was very thankful for God's protection!

Political unrest in Bolivia caused President Manley to cancel his visit for Easter week. We were forced to cancel Good Friday and Easter services, postpone the pastors' retreat, and delay the start of Bible Institute classes. We left our house only when it was necessary.

During that time La Paz and El Alto were experiencing an outbreak of cholera. Faith and I always disinfected produce that would be eaten raw, and either boiled or filtered our water to kill the bacteria. With the outbreak of cholera, we were extremely cautious. God faithfully took care of us. Praise His name!

May was a month full of activity and ministry for me. In addition to my regular mission business and my housework, I shared in an anniversary service at our Santiago II church, helped in a pastors' quarterly retreat, started teaching my classes at our two Bible Institutes, and visited our churches in Ullachapi and Huarcamarca. Whenever Faith and I went to Ullachapi, our day began at 3:00 a.m. and did not end until 10:00 p.m. Those hours were occupied with traveling and participating in two services. To visit our church in Huarcamarca took three days—two for travel and one for services on Sunday.

The anniversary celebration of the Collana church was held the last weekend in May, and Faith and I preached for the revival services. On Saturday we returned to La Paz and took Arturo Chambilla and David

Arturo Chambilla interpreting for me in the
Collana church in El Alto

Mamani with us and left them at Grand Poder in El Alto. We were to stop for them on our return to Collana. With many things on our minds, we almost forgot about them. As we approached a railroad crossing in El Alto, we suddenly remembered our promise to Arturo and David. We stopped and were getting ready to turn around when we heard a train approaching. I looked in the rearview mirror and saw a vehicle coming rapidly. I quickly opened the window and waved my hand to signal for the driver to stop.

He got stopped by pulling off the road parallel to the tracks. If I had not motioned for him to stop, a terrible accident might have occurred.

Political unrest had subsided enough so that a TLC team could come from Hobe Sound, Florida. They arrived on June 16 and stayed for three weeks. Tanya Sickler, a student at Penn View Bible Institute, came the next day to do her six-week internship. Three days later we took the team and Tanya to an army base, a trip of almost three hours, to attend the discharge celebration of the platoon in which Grabiel Chino, a young man from our Quillcoma church, was a member. We were given the honor of being in the grandstand. Pedro and Vito, two of Grabiel's brothers who were pastors with EFM, were present. I had been asked by his family to be his *madrina* or sponsor for the occasion. It meant that they needed some financial help, and they wanted me to buy some clothing for him; I accepted that responsibility. Just a few months previously, Grabiel's father had been killed while standing beside a well-traveled interurban road in El Alto. He had been hit by a drunken policeman who was driving a police vehicle. The policeman's wife begged Pedro, the oldest son, to forgive her husband, and Pedro magnanimously forgave him.

On June 29 Faith received a phone call from the States informing her of her father's death. With President Manley's permission, she quickly made arrangements to fly home for three weeks. I continued working with the TLC team during the final two Daily Vacation Bible Schools.

We were on our way to the Gran Poder church in El Alto for the closing DVBS program when the clutch overheated on our faithful 1982 Land Cruiser. On our way home after the program, the clutch overheated again. After making a few phone calls, I gave instructions to Tanya and the team and sent them home to Bolognia by bus. One young man from the TLC team stayed with the Land Cruiser, and I hailed a taxi to take me to the police station. Two policemen and I crowded into their tow truck and went to our disabled vehicle. The policemen, the young man, and I proceeded on the one-hour trip to our home in Bolognia, towing the Land Cruiser. The next day a mechanic began the needed repairs.

One day after the team left, Tanya and I went to El Alto on an errand. Before we reached Villa Tunari, we noticed there was a demonstration ahead. I turned around and started for home, but a group of young people quickly gathered and sat on the road in front of our Land Cruiser, making it impossible for me to pass. The demonstrators were not violent, and soon a middle-aged man came and persuaded them to allow me to continue.

Before Faith went to the States, Ricardo, the twenty-one-year-old son of our next-door neighbors came and told her, "I've decided that I want to come to your church." He came to one of the services while the team was with us, but he did not give his heart to the Lord.

Soon after Faith returned to Bolivia from attending her father's funeral, she looked out our dining room window and saw an ambulance parked near our house. About that time our doorbell rang, and it was Mr. Asef in distress. He said to Faith, "Ricardo died. My wife needs you."

Ricardo had not been in good health for some time. That morning his father called him to go to university classes, and he replied, "Oh, Dad, I'm so tired. Please let me sleep a little longer." Later when his mother checked on him, she found him unconscious. He was taken by ambulance to a health center across the river. They attempted to revive him but were not successful, and his body was brought home.

The father had come to our house asking Faith to come to console his wife, Beatriz. I soon went to their house, and after learning that they had not eaten breakfast, I returned to our house and prepared food for them. The family held a vigil that evening, and we went to be with them. Before we left, Faith read some Scripture and had prayer.

My birthday came on a Sunday, and we were attending special weekend services at Saavedra. To honor me that afternoon, a musical group led by one of our pastors sang and played while most of the people present came forward to greet me and wish me a happy birthday.

In September we had our second camp meeting, and Glen and Helen Reiff came to be the workers. Both of them speak Spanish fluently, and their ministry was a blessing to everybody. Their first Sunday we went to Quillcoma in the countryside, and Glen dedicated their new church. In the afternoon service he ordained Lorenzo Salinas to the ministry.

The next day we began a week of camp meeting services in our Santiago II church in El Alto. Glen gave illustrated messages on sin, the carnal nature, and the divine remedy for the twofold nature of sin. On Saturday Helen gave a very helpful seminar on child evangelism.

For a little relaxation we took Glen and Helen to Lake Titicaca and enjoyed a meal of fresh trout in a simple country restaurant before returning to the city. Most of their second week was spent in

Cochabamba and the Chapare. Many people sought help from the Lord. The Reiffs returned to the States from the airport in Cochabamba.

In early February 1999 we received a call from the home office in Bedford, Indiana, telling us of Carrie Boyer's death. Faith and I discussed the situation, and we agreed that because she had worked so closely with Carrie, she should go to the States for the funeral. At the end of the month, she returned to Bolivia.

President Manley came for the Easter convention that year, which was held in our Jocopampa church. About thirty people came by chartered bus from our church in Chapare, Cochabamba. A few came from faraway Huarcamarca over roads made treacherous by a long rainy season. Many arrived from our other churches in the La Paz district. It was wonderful to hear some testify to their deliverance from idolatry, witchcraft, and similar sins. Several received spiritual help.

Later Faith and I accompanied two members of the executive committee to visit our church in Ullachapi. When we had been there the previous April, one of the village authorities came to the service intoxicated. Now he was sober. He went to the platform to greet us and said, "Last year I came here drunk." He listened to the Word, and when the invitation to seek the Lord was given, he came forward. He told me at the close of the service that he had given his heart to the Lord, and added that two of his daughters were attending our church. I encouraged him to serve the Lord sincerely.

The first Sunday of May, Faith and I were with our Villa Tunari congregation. I preached on "The Christian Family" and dedicated five children. Asencio, a middle-aged man, and his three daughters were in the service. He had come with the intention of becoming a part of the church. Following the baby dedication, the pastor invited him to come forward to seek the Lord. When he came, his daughters followed. After a good time of prayer, he testified that Jesus had forgiven his sins. Praise the Lord, another name was written down in heaven.

Gaynell Thacker came to Bolivia to help for one year. She was a widow with experience in office work and accounting. When I learned that she was coming, I again made plans to retire from foreign missionary work. Gaynell arrived on August 3, and I stayed two weeks to orient her to the office work before I left for the States.

At the same time Mark and Nancy Budensiek were making plans to come to Bolivia in October. They had worked with EFM in Ethiopia from 1960 to 1971.

I sensed that it was time for me to leave Bolivia but not EFM. I left Bolivia on August 18, 1999, concluding my labors as a resident missionary. During my years in Bolivia, I had been privileged to visit the South American countries of Argentina, Brazil, and Chile.

Chapter 15

Serving in the U.S.A.
1999-2009

Stateside Activities

After I arrived in the States, I spent a few days with my nephew Bill and his family in New Jersey before we went to Shamokin and celebrated my 75th birthday and the birthday of Bill's wife, Marylea. While we were celebrating, we received news of the birth of my great-great-niece Katie in California.

I flew to Louisville, Kentucky, a few weeks later, and Howard and Jean Ayars took me to Corydon, Indiana, where they pastored the Wesleyan Holiness Church. I participated in a weekend convention there and then went with the Manleys to Bedford for a week. In the prayer

President Manley giving me a plaque for 50 years of service with EFM

meeting at the Faith Mission Church in Bedford, President Manley presented me with a plaque in recognition of my 50 years of service with EFM. What a surprise!

The following week I went by bus to Cincinnati and spent several pleasant days visiting friends and attending a missionary convention at GBS. That weekend I participated in another convention at the Wesleyan Evangelistic Church in Dayton, Ohio, where Mike Wetherald pastored. Monday I flew to Allentown. Doris, Harry, Eva, and I went to a restaurant owned by my nephew Randy. He was also the chef and prepared the meals in a kitchen located in the dining area where the customers could watch. After the meal Doris and I returned to Shamokin.

I was busy throughout October speaking in deputation services in eastern Pennsylvania. The last service of the month was a special one for me because it was at the Friendly Holiness Church in Helfenstein where in 1946 I first testified to my call to missionary service.

The Mission sent me by plane to Oklahoma City in December to work with Don and Devona Moore in a convention sponsored by two churches where Dale and LyNan Redman and Kenneth and Elizabeth Coker, parents of LyNan, were the pastors. It was a unique opportunity to share with three couples who had worked with EFM in Central America.

In January my brother Charles became seriously ill and passed away six days later. During the few days of his illness, I helped my sister-in-law Dorothy in whatever way she needed. My 86-year-old sister Doris was well enough to go with me to the funeral. A week later, Doris became ill and was taken to the emergency room. An X-ray revealed that she had pneumonia. I was excused from a couple deputation services to take care of her.

Later that month I was to participate in a one-day convention at the Thompson Bible Institute in Bellevue, Ohio. I was not eager to drive that far alone, so I called Anita Brechbill and asked if she could accompany me. She

In a convention at Thompson Bible Institute in Bellevue, Ohio

agreed to go and did most of the driving. What a blessing she was! At the Bible school I met Lee and Sharen Rickenbach and their children for the first time.

The Wesleyan Holiness Bible College in Point Pleasant, West Virginia, was my base while I was holding missionary services in that area the latter part of April and all of May. One day I was surprised to meet Gaynell Thacker who recently returned from Bolivia. She had stopped to visit with Glenda Kempa, a student in the college.

I attended the graduation some days later. Glenda was one of the graduates, and within a year she went to Bolivia under EFM. I was glad to meet members of her family whom I had known in the 1940s in New Jersey.

When I returned to Shamokin on June 1, Doris was in poor health. She had never recovered from her earlier bout with pneumonia. I asked to be relieved of most of my services, starting in July so that I could care for her. Faith was in the States, and she and Glenda took most of my scheduled services.

Doris attended church regularly, but was not born again. In my letters to her while I was overseas, I exhorted her to give her heart to the Lord. While I was Doris' primary caregiver during the last months of her life, I spoke several times with her about her spiritual condition. One day when I entered her bedroom, she said, "Irene, I have been confessing my sins." I asked her if God had forgiven her, and in her weakness she replied, "Yes." She passed away peacefully on August 20 after which I resumed my travels for EFM.

God made it possible for me to attend the centennial celebration of GBS, my alma mater. Then I went to Corydon to help in another convention, and from there I drove to Bedford to spend a few days with Faith before she returned to Bolivia.

From Bedford I traveled to Glouster, Ohio, for a missionary service at Number 10 Mission during their revival. After I spoke, a spirit of giving came upon the congregation, and as they gave, they rejoiced in the Lord and sang praises to Him. After some special times of prayer, the evangelist stood to preach at 8:45. The congregation urged him to give what God had laid on his heart as we all sensed the wonderful presence of the Lord. The service ended at 9:50.

My services for the remainder of 2000 were in Indiana, Ohio, and Pennsylvania. Immediately after Thanksgiving, Eva and I went to

Wesley Village, a Christian community near Brooksville, Florida. She was planning to sell their mobile home there but changed her mind at the urging of her children and friends. We then visited a friend from college days, Paul Light, and his wife, Lucy, and our brother Earl and his wife, Marie, and some of their family. That was my last time to see Lucy, Earl, and Marie. Earl died in March 2001, Lucy in December 2006, and Marie on my birthday in 2007. Shortly after Eva and I returned to Allentown, she fell and broke her right hip.

On Christmas Day I attended my home church in Lavelle, Pennsylvania, where William Peters, Sr., has been pastoring since 1983, and spent the remainder of the day with Bill and Marylea. The next day I visited Eva in the hospital in Allentown.

In the spring of 2001, Doris' children put her house up for sale, and I needed to move. My nephew Bill and I located a mobile home near Allentown that he and his siblings were planning to purchase for me. Before the sale was completed, Faith became ill in Bolivia.

When it appeared that she would need to return to the States, President Manley asked me if I would be willing to come to Bedford to help Faith until she was better. I agreed to come as soon as possible.

Glenda Kempa, who was then working in Bolivia with EFM, accompanied Faith to the Indianapolis airport on May 21. The Manleys took Faith to Bedford, and she stayed with them until I arrived a few days later. Glenda's unexpected trip brought her home in time to be present for her parents' 25th wedding anniversary in Colorado Springs. Before she returned to Bolivia on June 12 via Indianapolis, she attended the Illiana camp meeting in Indiana where she visited with her maternal grandparents.

Faith and I lived in the house located on the mission property. On June 9 God gave her a physical touch in answer to the prayers of God's people. However, the EFM Board agreed that it was best for Faith not to return to Bolivia for an extended stay. At the same time it was decided that I would move my belongings to Bedford, and Faith and I would continue living together in the mission house indefinitely. My nephew then cancelled the purchasing of the mobile home near Allentown.

By September Faith was strong enough so that I could go to Shamokin, sort and pack my belongings, and dispose of my furniture. Later the Manleys were in Pennsylvania for a missionary convention, and they helped me pack my things into a small U-Haul truck. President

Manley drove the truck to Bedford, followed by his wife in the mission vehicle. I stayed in Shamokin almost a month and held a few missionary services before returning to Bedford. The following weeks I was busy unpacking items that I would need and going with Faith to represent the Mission in services in Indiana.

I went to Colorado Springs in November to help my sister Helen and stayed until February. Her husband, Lester, was in an advanced stage of Alzheimer's disease and required much care. While I was in Colorado, Faith stayed in Muncie, Indiana, with Esther Norton, a friend and former missionary with EFM.

Members of Lester and Helen's family came from Nebraska for Thanksgiving. On Thanksgiving Day we enjoyed dinner at a Golden Corral restaurant after which we returned to Helen's home and looked at slides. Later that day we had a surprise birthday celebration for their son Joseph.

From my bedroom I watched fireworks on Pikes Peak at midnight of New Year's Eve. The cog railway and the road were closed because of snow, so people hiked to the top to make a display that lasted only a few minutes. Another exciting experience at that time was going to see a moose that had strayed into the city. Helen scared me as she kept running closer to take photos. I tried to stay at a safe distance and yet not lose sight of her.

Faith returned to Bedford a few days before I did. The day after my return on February 21, 2002, both of us went with the Manleys to Michigan to help Gertrude Campbell celebrate her 80th birthday. President Manley and Faith spoke at the event about Gertrude's wholehearted contribution to missions. The Mission had made arrangements to purchase a minivan while we were in Michigan, and after the weekend stay in Gertrude's home, Faith and I took one of the vehicles back to Bedford on Monday.

In early March Faith and I conducted a three-day seminar for the college students at the Wesleyan Holiness Bible College in Point Pleasant, West Virginia. We each presented six topics and took turns preaching in the evening services where everyone was welcome. After Faith spoke the last night, 20 young people dedicated their lives to God.

Before the end of the month, Faith and I went to Pennsylvania to attend the funeral of Hilda Straub, the wife of the late Marlin Straub, my pastor during my early twenties. Across the years Hilda had made many dresses and a few dress suits for me. After the funeral we visited some of my family and Pauline Stuck, a faithful supporter of EFM who was in a nursing home.

On Easter morning Faith and I spoke in my home church in Lavelle and in a nearby church that evening. The following weekend we shared a missionary convention with the Manleys at the Wesleyan Holiness Church in Portage, Pennsylvania. We then returned to Bedford and had services in Ohio and Indiana during the rest of April and the month of May.

God was present in a special way in our service in Bremen, Ohio. Three times during the service we had prayer around the altar. One was for people with serious physical problems, another time was for a young married woman who wanted to get back to the Lord, and then for her father-in-law who came to present himself to the Lord for His service. God's presence was so real that no one was in a hurry to leave the sanctuary.

During the middle of July, Faith and I were the missionary speakers at the Candy Run Youth Camp near Portsmouth, Ohio, where Thelma Bloomfield is the director. We spoke each morning in the missions hour. In the final morning session, most of the young people dedicated their lives to God for Christian service. Various pastors preached evangelistic messages in the evening services. One evening God came in a special way with some young people shouting while others sought God for help.

Participating in the Candy Run Youth Camp near Portsmouth, Ohio

Throughout the next month we traveled in Ohio, Indiana, and Kentucky to represent EFM. In a DVBS in Hamilton, Ohio, Faith and I were in charge of the missions class. What a joy to work with the children and the youth. Quite a few of the children, including several from unchurched homes, asked Jesus to come into their hearts.

Later that month my great-niece Eunice Bump and her fiancé, Scott Knight, were married in Colorado. They had a wedding reception there and then traveled to Scott's home area in Ohio where there was a second reception in September. I enjoyed attending the reception in Ohio.

With winter approaching, the Mission scheduled all our November services in churches in Indiana. On the second Sunday, tornado activity forced us to postpone an evening service at Terre Haute. We conducted that service two weeks later, and while we visited with the pastor and his wife, they told us that one of their sons and his wife had hydroplaned on I-70 two weeks previously, crossed the median strip, and stopped on the opposite side of I-70. Thankfully they did not hit another vehicle, and no one in the car was injured. When we heard that report, we were glad that our service had been postponed.

Whenever Faith and I were not in missionary services, we attended the Faith Mission Church in Bedford. During the Christmas season that year, our church had three programs that we enjoyed. We spent Christmas Eve with Esther Norton in Muncie and Christmas Day with Faith's family in the same area. Five inches of newly fallen snow made it a beautiful Christmas.

Visiting Bolivia in 2003

It was April 7, the day Faith and I had been anticipating for some time. We had been invited to go to Bolivia to speak in the pastors' retreat and in the Easter convention. J. Stevan and Helen Manley took us to the Indianapolis airport where we ate lunch before Faith and I went to our departure gate to board our flight to Chicago. It was a cold snowy day, and our plane was de-iced before leaving Chicago for Miami. On the flight we encountered some turbulence but arrived safely. About midnight we boarded a plane to La Paz, arriving at 6:00 the following morning. We were conscious of God's protection and thanked Him for His care.

Mark and Nancy Budensiek, five of the six pastors on the field executive committee, and Celia Ormachea of our Bolognia congregation with her two daughters and a granddaughter met us. The committee members presented two lovely baskets of fresh flowers to Faith and me, others gave us roses, and two of Faith's godchildren gave her little baskets of flowers. What a joy it was to see those dear workers and friends! We ate breakfast and enjoyed a time of fellowship before going our separate ways.

The Budensieks took Faith and me to the mission house in Bolognia. As we wound down the mountains, we were thrilled to see Mount Illimani with its permanently snowcapped peaks. By the time we reached Bolognia, we had been traveling about twenty-two hours and were tired, so we were happy to get a short rest before the afternoon meal. Because of the high altitude of Bolognia, I used oxygen briefly from the portable tank the Mission kept on hand. I had a head cold when I left Bedford, and that added to my discomfort.

The weekly Bible study was held in our Bolognia church that evening, and we attended. A former pastor gave Faith and me two roses each. Then the current pastor asked us to come up front for the people to welcome us with their traditional embraces.

Two evenings later the church gave us a reception tea at the mission house. Faith and I were the speakers for the revival services that began that evening and continued through Palm Sunday. Thank the Lord that there were seekers in every service. Several testified to receiving definite help.

Before the revival started, Faith and I were given a schedule of the classes we were to teach during the pastors' retreat the following week. We were surprised to find that we were to teach classes on sanctification, prophecy, homiletics, hermeneutics, theology, and Christian life. Word had not reached us regarding those subjects before we left the States. Our time for study was limited because of the weekend revival and the need to make several trips to the government offices in La Paz concerning the visas for Budensieks and me. Thankfully, we located some resource materials and, by rising early and staying up late, we were able to prepare lessons on the requested subjects except for hermeneutics.

Following Palm Sunday we went to our Villa Tunari church in El Alto for the retreat. The pastors and Mark spent the meal times of Monday and Tuesday in fasting and prayer. Nancy, Faith, and I spent part of the day with them on those days. During the week Faith and I taught the assigned subjects. Friday morning the pastors had a brief annual conference session, and we learned that in the past few years the Mission

Pastors' retreat in our Villa Tunari church

had opened works in three more villages. In the afternoon Mark gave a wonderful message concerning the shed blood of Christ for our redemption. It was followed by a sacred time of communion. Praise to the Lamb of God who gave Himself for us! It was wonderful to minister to and fellowship with our pastors during the retreat.

Faith and I took turns preaching in the evangelistic services on Wednesday, Thursday, and Friday evenings. People came from most of our churches located in El Alto, and several prayed at the close of the messages. Saturday the pastors returned to their homes to make preparations for bringing their people to the Easter services.

The field executive committee earlier had made arrangements to have a march in El Alto on Easter morning beginning at 5:00. About five hundred people from our churches participated in the march. Mark led the group, driving the mission Land Cruiser. As they passed through the neighborhoods, it was a wonderful testimony that Jesus lives and that He gives eternal life to those who surrender their lives to Him.

In the Easter morning service, people from our various churches sang special songs, bands from three of our churches played, and a sister sang, accompanied by a group who played stringed instruments. At the conclusion of the morning message given by Faith, many came to pray, and some found victory.

During our last week there, we had dinner or tea in various homes of our believers. We enjoyed the Bolivian food, especially *sajta de pollo*, a special chicken entrée.

On Thursday evening we went to El Alto to the home of Lorenzo Salinas, the conference president, where members of the field executive committee gave us soft drinks, tea, and bread. They presented to us pewter plates with their names engraved on them. One of the families gave each of us a small souvenir llama and a plaque showing various musical instruments used in Bolivia.

The Bolognia congregation requested that we share a time of fellowship with them on Friday evening. They joined us in the mission house where they presented Faith and me each a pewter plate on which was engraved the names of those who regularly attended the Bolognia church.

On Sunday morning we visited our 25 de Julio church. The building was completed and beautiful. Their band played several numbers in the street to welcome us. They also played a special during the service. In the morning worship hour, the people presented to Faith and me each a *chuspa*, a lovely woolen bag with a strap that is used to carry a Bible and a song book.

The 25 de Julio church band playing at an Easter convention in the Villa Tunari church

Chuspas given to us by Lorenzo and Jesusa Salinas from the
25 de Julio congregation

After that service we had dinner in the home of Patricio and Agustina, the parents of Freddy, my eleven-year-old godchild. In the afternoon we went to our Bautista Saavedra church. When we arrived, the band from the 25 de Julio church again played for us.

During our short visit to Bolivia, we certainly felt the warmth of the people's love for us. We rejoiced as they also expressed their love for their resident missionaries, Mark and Nancy Budensiek.

In the Homeland

After Faith and I returned to the States on April 29, we resumed deputation services. One of the highlights that spring was holding a children's revival in Hamilton, Ohio. Many of the children gave their hearts to the Lord. We continued to travel throughout the summer and fall. Our final service for the year was in November. We counted it a privilege to have ministered in that capacity for EFM and the Lord.

Faith and I were with her brother, John, and his family in Indiana for Christmas. The next day I received word that Harry, Eva's husband, had passed away. I attended the funeral on December 31 near Allentown.

The cry of my heart for the New Year was expressed in the following poem:

My New Year's Prayer

Dear Master, for this coming year
Just one request I bring.
I do not pray for happiness
Or any earthly thing.
I do not ask to understand
The way Thou leadest me.
But this I ask, "Teach me to do
The thing that pleaseth Thee."

I want to know Thy guiding voice,
To walk with thee each day.
Dear Master, make me swift to hear
And ready to obey.
And thus the year I now begin
A happy year will be,
If I am seeking just to do
"The thing that pleaseth Thee."
—Author unknown

I was scheduled to fly from Allentown to Philadelphia and then to Indianapolis on January 5. The plane was late reaching Allentown and then mechanical problems were found, so the flight was delayed again. Some of the passengers were rerouted, but I was not. However, as time passed, I became anxious about making connections in Philadelphia. After my third inquiry the clerk booked me through Pittsburgh instead of Philadelphia. Eva called me the next morning and told me that two terrorist suspects had been found at the Philadelphia airport the previous evening, and the airport had been closed. Had I gone to Philadelphia on schedule, most likely I would have been stranded. God used the events in Allentown to keep me away from the Philadelphia airport for which I thanked Him.

In March I flew to Colorado to attend the funeral of my brother-in-law Lester Bump. During the service I read Helen's memories of her husband. Steven Hight, vice-president of EFM, and Kathy, his wife, were able to attend the funeral because they were in the area participating in a missionary convention at the Immanuel Missionary Church. Helen and I attended some of those convention services.

Faith and I had a Sunday morning service at the Covenant Church in Clarksburg, Indiana, in April. We were scheduled to have an evening service at the Wesleyan Holiness Church in Dayton. On our way we had a flat tire on a narrow road. A young couple and another man in separate vehicles stopped to help us. Someone moved the mission van to a side road and then they changed the tire.

I called a friend in Dayton to tell her we might be late for our service, and she informed me of the tragic accident that John Brewer, his wife, and three children had that afternoon while on their way to the service where we were to speak. The older daughter, Hannah, called to be a missionary and engaged to be married in June, was killed; the mother was taken to the ICU at a hospital in Columbus, Ohio; the father and younger daughter, Bethany, were hospitalized; and Matthew, the only son, was treated and released.

Although we were a few minutes late for our evening service, God gave us help. That week we stayed with our friend Norma Rawlings and enjoyed attending the IHC together. On our return to Bedford on Saturday, we attended Hannah's funeral at Lynn, Indiana.

On May 29 Guy and Dana Troyer, Eugene and Fern Tierney, Ronald and Margaret Robbins, Ruth (Franklin) Gordon, and I, all former missionaries to Egypt with EFM, were present at the graduation exercises of GBS when they granted Saied Ibrahim, chairman of Faith Church of

EFM Egyptian missionaries with Saied and his wife

Egypt, the Doctor of Divinity degree. J. Stevan Manley and Steven E. Hight, our mission directors, and their wives were also present.

I was surprised and impressed to hear about the number of books Saied had written in Arabic, including *Commentary on the Book of Daniel, The Second Coming of Christ, The Deity of Christ,* and *Holiness.* In a special room in the school dining hall, we had dinner with Saied and his wife, Fawzia, Dr. Michael Avery, president of GBS, and his wife, and other friends of Saied to celebrate that special event.

Our late spring and summer services took us to several states, and we were conscious of God's protection while we traveled. On our way to a camp meeting in Bruceton Mills, West Virginia, we experienced delays on I-79 because of accidents. I was sitting too long, and it caused problems for my arthritic right knee, and I was unable to walk on my own that night. Faith was not feeling well either. However, by our scheduled speaking times the next day, we were much better. It was Faith's birthday, and at the close of the evening service, everyone sang "Happy Birthday" to her, and those staying on the grounds were invited to the dining room for ice cream and cake.

To help me celebrate my 80th birthday, which was August 23, Faith arranged a surprise at the August meeting of the Bedford chapter of Women of Worth. Two large decorated cakes and homemade ice cream were served in my honor. That evening I received several gifts and 42 cards. I appreciated Faith's thoughtfulness and the kindness of the 50 ladies who were present.

Doris' children sent money to the mission office for a birthday celebration for me. Because Juddie Peyton's 80th birthday was the day before mine, the Mission decided to help with the cost for a special meal to celebrate our birthdays. The Peytons, EFM office staff, three former EFM couples, Faith, and I were present. The meal was

With Juddie Peyton celebrating our 80th birthdays in 2004

Unwinding 80 one-dollar bills

delicious and included two beautifully decorated cakes. The Mission gave Juddie and me each 80 one-dollar bills that were taped together and rolled up, and we each pulled them out of a small box. I received a total of 116 cards that year.

Bolivia in 2004

Faith and I were asked to go to Bolivia so that we would be present to welcome the Elmer Sánchez family, who was coming from Guatemala to be the missionaries in Bolivia. Faith was to acquaint Elmer with the work and the pastors. We arrived in La Paz on Wednesday morning, November 17. Lorenzo and three other executive committee members and their wives were at the airport to meet us. After Lorenzo drove us to the mission house and unloaded our baggage, he took us to another part of the city to a money exchange and to a large grocery store where we bought necessary food items. We found a Burger King nearby and had lunch together. When we returned to the house, Lorenzo gave us the mission Mitsubishi station wagon to use during our time in Bolivia, and he went to his home an hour away by public transportation.

On Saturday afternoon I returned to the weekly market in Bolognia to buy something that we had forgotten in the morning. When I was leaving, a lady approached me and said, "Senorita Irene Maurer." It was Cici. While riding in a bus, she saw me, got off at the next corner, and returned to find me. I invited her home with me for a short visit. Because it was close to her birthday, we each signed a card and enclosed a little money, gave her a small gift, and sang "Happy Birthday" to her. Tears filled her eyes. It certainly was a delight to see her again because she had been our maid for 18 years.

Faith and I spoke in the local church on Sunday, the week of Thanksgiving. That week we were busy with housecleaning, washing windows and curtains, and preparing for the arrival of the Elmer Sánchez family. Rebecca, our maid during our visit, was a big help with that cleaning project. On Thanksgiving Day Rebecca, Faith, and I had a special Thanksgiving dinner.

The field executive committee members met at the mission house in Bolognia early in December for their monthly meeting. They invited us to join them while they dealt with a number of important issues and prepared a schedule for us to visit as many of our churches as possible. The next day our pastors gathered in Bolognia for their monthly prayer and fast service. It was thoughtful of them to choose Bolognia because it enabled us to attend the meeting.

One evening a few weeks after our arrival, we were caught in traffic congestion in El Alto. Vehicles of all description packed the streets, and sometimes there were six lanes of traffic on a highway made for four. People were walking between the vehicles, some of them with babies and little children, others carrying heavy loads on their backs. People were everywhere, and it was nerve-racking for Faith who was driving.

Gregorio and Elena lived in the neighborhood where Lorenzo and his family lived. At times when Gregorio drank, he would beat his wife. She tired of it and left him and their small children. The children cried for their mother and wanted her to come back home. Gregorio came to Lorenzo with his problem and prayed. Several days later while we were visiting Lorenzo and his family, Gregorio and Elena came for spiritual help. We spoke with them and had prayer. It was precious when the couple asked forgiveness of each other and were reconciled.

Faith worked with the children in the Bolognia congregation and prepared an inspiring Christmas program, which was given on the evening of December 23. It was a special time not only for the children but also for all who attended.

The day after Christmas, Mariano and Juana, his wife, joined us for a visit to our Cosmos '79 and Villa Adela churches. Faith preached and the pastor gave the children treats supplied by the local church. After the service we shared our food in the churchyard. When we got ready to leave, Faith asked Mariano to drive to our Villa Adela church. From there he drove to Lorenzo's house in Villa Tunari. No one was at home, so we proceeded toward Mariano and Juana's home in the 25 de Julio zone. When we approached the main intersection of Villa Tunari, our traffic light was green, but a minibus driver who had a red light did not stop. He hit us, and the impact was so loud that I thought an explosion had occurred nearby. Mariano, Faith, and I were lifted off our seats and hit the roof of the Toyota; we realized it later when we found glass underneath us on the seat and had sore spots on our heads. Juana's face was injured, but an X-ray the next day showed that no bones were broken. At first I did not think I had been hurt, but both my legs had minor abrasions that later became badly infected. They eventually healed by using antibiotics.

Elmer Sánchez and his wife, Onelia, with their children, Armenia and Aner, arrived on January 17, 2005. Elmer came to serve as an advisor to the field executive committee, to teach in the Bible Institute, and to minister in the churches.

Elmer Sánchez in back with the field executive committee

For several days Elmer was busy going to various government offices to transact business for his stay in Bolivia. An air force colonel who attended our Bolognia church befriended him and helped with some of his paperwork. Faith and I also took him to a special meeting with our pastors and explained his role among them.

A few weeks later Faith and I went with the field committee to Sacaba in the Cochabamba area to see about a property problem. From there we went to F. Tropical to visit our church. After the service a young man came to Faith and me to greet us. I said, "I think that in the past I dedicated someone from your family."

"Yes," he said, "it was I." It gave me joy to see him and to know that he was walking with the Lord and keeping active in the church.

After a three-month stay in Bolivia, Faith and I returned to the States on February 22. On our way home, I had the opportunity to witness to a young man assigned to our row of seats on our flight to Miami. From our conversation I learned that he was searching for something to meet his spiritual need. I also witnessed to another man on our flight to Indianapolis. The Manleys met us at the Indianapolis airport and brought us to Bedford.

Golden Years

The day Faith and I left Bolivia, my sister Eva underwent major surgery in Allentown. Various complications followed and she required emergency surgery in April. When she was discharged after the second surgery, she needed much help in her home. A couple from our church in Bedford made it financially possible for Faith and me to go to Allentown the latter part of May and help her for three weeks. During that time she regained a good measure of strength. The last two Sundays we were there, we spoke in two deputation services each Sunday and received good offerings for EFM.

Faith and I left Eva's home in June, drove to Salem, Ohio, and spent a night with Faith Dell Ford for whom Faith was named. Although she was 96 years old, she had a clear mind. We then had a service at Union Tabernacle in Zanesville, Ohio. That church has helped to support Faith since she went to the mission field in 1961.

Because we were scheduled to hold a missionary service in northeastern Indiana, rather than go home to Bedford, we went from Zanesville to Dayton to be with our friend Norma. One day while we were there, we visited the Air Force Museum. I especially wanted to see the *Storch*, a plane that my cousin Lieutenant Colonel Perry Schreffler had helped to restore and donate to the museum. People at the information desk gave us clear directions to find it. While in the museum we learned that the pilot on its final flight was Brigadier General "Chuck"

Yeager. Then Norma informed us that her mother had been Chuck's chauffeur in WWII. What an interesting day that was!

It was a delight to attend EFM's centennial celebration held on June 25, 2005, at the Faith Mission Church in Bedford. About forty EFM missionaries, past and current, were present. Several Egyptian and Eritrean Christians spoke of how God used EFM to change their lives. Various missionaries recounted key events from the different fields. The centennial book, *We've a Story to Tell* prepared by Ronald and Anna Smith, was presented and made available for purchase.

Helen came from Colorado in August for a three-week visit with Faith and me. We took her to a few camp meeting services, which were a special delight to her. Helen had heard of Old Paths Tract Society and Singing Hill Camp, both in the area of Shoals, Indiana, and wished to see them, so we accommodated her wishes. Another time we took her and Isabelle (LaRoche) Henry to the famous Black Buggy restaurant in Washington, Indiana. Helen had heard of Isabelle but had never met her.

On my birthday Faith arranged for the ladies Tuesday prayer group of the Faith Mission Church to meet at our house. After prayer, Faith and Helen served tea and cake. We took the remainder of the cake to the mission office for the staff to enjoy.

Faith and I spent Christmas Day, which came on Sunday, with her family in Winchester, Indiana. In the morning we were advised that everyone should bring a candle for the evening candlelight service. That evening each person went forward, one at a time, carrying a candle, and the pastor or one of his young sons lit the candle. Then each individual was to give an account of how the Lord helped him to let his light shine in this world. It was an uplifting service.

In early spring the Manleys, the Hights, Faith and I shared in a missionary convention at the Crystal Park Wesleyan Church in Canton, Ohio. We had four wonderful services with a great sense of God's presence and help. On our return to Bedford after the Sunday evening service, we came close to having a serious accident. Just as Steven Hight, who was driving the mission van west on I-70, began to overtake a tractor trailer, it moved across the white line into our lane. Steven swerved to avoid being hit. The van rocked a bit, but the Lord helped him to keep the vehicle under control. We thanked the Lord for taking care of us.

We enjoyed three special events that summer. First, we attended the wedding of the son of Russtom and Selas Ghebremichael, one of our

Eritrean families living in Indianapolis. The second event was a reunion of EFM missionaries held in the Faith Mission Church in Bedford. The Saturday morning service was followed by a meal and a time of fellowship in the activity center of the school operated by the church. The third event was the wedding of EFM missionaries James Rickenbach and Rachel Arndt in Frankfort, Indiana. James and Rachel were under appointment to Guatemala.

The remainder of the summer was filled with missionary services and visiting family and friends. It was especially good to attend the camp meeting in Clinton, Pennsylvania, because it had been years since neither Faith nor I was privileged to be there.

That fall Faith and I conducted a revival at the Wesleyan Church in Holton, Indiana, with missions being the focus of the Sunday morning service. Various individuals received help from the Lord, for which we gave Him thanks.

As the new year approached, my thoughts went to the first verse of the song "O God, Our Help in Ages Past" by Isaac Watts. That verse reads:

O God, our Help in ages past,
Our Hope for years to come,
Our Shelter from the stormy blast,
And our eternal Home!

Faith and I were scheduled to speak at the missions seminar at the Wesleyan Holiness Bible College in Point Pleasant in March 2007. We were each to give five lessons during the three days and speak in the evening missionary services. However, I was sick most of February with bronchitis and heart flutters and could not go, so David Middleton went in my place. I shared with him what material I had prepared, and he used it for some of his lessons. Helen Manley went with Faith to help with the driving and to keep her company.

In March and early April, Faith and I were to help in three missionary conventions in Pennsylvania. Due to my continued physical difficulties, I was unable to go. After Faith returned from Pennsylvania, I was strong enough to go with her to a convention at the Wesleyan Holiness Church in Corydon, Indiana. We also attended the IHC in Dayton.

By May I was physically able to attend a missionary convention at the Wesleyan Holiness Church in Indianapolis. The Manleys, the Hights, the Adamses, and Faith were also present for all or part of the convention. Faith and I then went to Cincinnati for part of the GBS camp meeting and the graduation service. We were surprised to find that one of the graduates was Brooke Robbins, a daughter of Dennis Robbins. He is the son of Ronald and Margaret Robbins with whom I had worked in Egypt and Ethiopia. We accepted Dennis' invitation to have dinner with them in their home to honor Brooke.

I also helped Faith at the Candy Run Youth Camp in Ohio and in camp meeting services in various states throughout the summer. Between services we visited Eva and other members of my family in Allentown.

Events for that fall included going to Tennessee for a convention, attending the revival in our local church, working with Ronald and Anna Smith on this book, enjoying homecoming activities at GBS, and entertaining guests in our home.

My nephew Daniel Bump with his daughter Sharon and grandson Joshua came to Bedford for three days during the Christmas holiday. It was the first time since 2001 that I was with some of my family for Christmas. Faith's brother, John, came and took her so that she could spend Christmas Day with him and his family.

The Scripture that came to me for the new year is found in Psalm 103:1-4: "Bless the LORD, O my soul: and all that is within me, bless his holy name. Bless the LORD, O my soul, and forget not all his benefits: Who forgiveth all thine iniquities; who healeth all thy diseases; Who redeemeth thy life from destruction; who crowneth thee with lovingkindness and tender mercies;" and also verse 11: "For as the heaven is high above the earth, so great is his mercy toward them that fear him."

In May 2008 I had the special privilege of attending the graduation of my great-nephew Stephen Bump from the United States Air Force Academy in Colorado Springs. His class of 1,200 cadets, including a number of women, was the 50th class to graduate from the Academy. President George W. Bush was the guest speaker. It was special to see the President walk alone to his place on the platform and hear the Air Force band play the national anthem. As each cadet came to the platform to receive his diploma, President Bush saluted and shook hands with the cadet before he returned to his seat. While the Thunderbirds flew overhead, the cadets followed the tradition of tossing their hats into the air.

Any child between the ages of seven and ten who caught a hat was allowed to keep it.

In the afternoon the Bump family sponsored a picnic in honor of Stephen and his sister, Sharon, who has been hearing impaired from birth and recently graduated with a master's degree in social work. Stephen's cake was decorated with a replica of the Air Force Academy Chapel. Sharon's cake decorations included yellow roses and a statement congratulating her as the first in her family to earn a master's degree. Three days later Stephen and his fiancée, Caitlin Burns, were married in the Air Force Academy Chapel. Caitlin had just completed her nurse's training a few days prior to Stephen's graduation. Sunday evening I spoke in a missionary service at a local church before returning to Bedford.

Workers together for the kingdom

Shortly after I returned from Colorado, Faith and I attended the 50th wedding anniversary celebration of Leroy and Myrtle Adams in Indianapolis. Donna DeArmond, our friend, entertained us in her comfortable home and attended the celebration with us. That weekend we also spoke at the West Broad Missionary Chapel in Columbus, Ohio, where Esther Hershey was our thoughtful hostess. After the service on Sunday evening, we visited with Tekie and Elsabet, an Eritrean couple living in Columbus.

Faith and I were once again the missionary speakers at the Candy Run Youth Camp. That was our fourth time to be there. Each time we sensed the Holy Spirit dealing with the children and the youth. Thelma Bloomfield, the director, estimated that 90 per cent of those who came to the camp that year left rejoicing in the Lord for the spiritual help they received.

The Mission has its annual board meeting in August. Whenever Faith and I are in Bedford at the time of the board meeting, we are invited to join the Board, their wives, and the office staff for the noon meal. That

A beautiful cake to celebrate my
service with EFM

President Manley presenting me with a
plaque in recognition of my 60 years of
missionary service with EFM

year President Manley surprised me when he presented me with a plaque
commemorating my 60 years of working with EFM, and a decorated cake
was served for dessert.

As I end my story, I want to give honor to God for His saving grace,
His sanctifying power, and His faithfulness to me. He has given me a
long life and the privilege of serving Him for many years on three continents. I have had the privilege of training men and women for the
ministry in Egypt, Ethiopia, and Bolivia.

God has been with me in the good times and the bad, in times of
safety and danger, in joy and sorrow, and in triumphs and trials. He never
has failed me and never will. His promises are true. He has promised to be
with me to the end if I am faithful. The inspired Psalmist declared in
Psalm 23:6, "Surely goodness and mercy shall follow me all the days of
my life: and I will dwell in the house of the Lord forever."